What people are saying about …

REBORN TO BE WILD

"In *Reborn to Be Wild* Ed Underwood writes about the last great revival the church has seen, the Jesus Movement of the 1960s and 1970s. Ed writes with passion, recalling the days of the Jesus People, and he fervently calls the next generation to go for Christ and light the revival fires once again! I highly recommend this book."

Josh D. McDowell, author/speaker

"The Jesus Movement of the late '60s and '70s was the birthplace of many influential Bible teachers and musical evangelists, and I'm still a 'musicianary' to this day. The Jesus Movement is still moving, but this book is a wake-up call to those who were part of the Jesus Movement who have fallen asleep. It's time to hear the trumpet and join together to reach the world for Jesus."

Darrell Mansfield, musician, songwriter, and
Blues Hall of Fame ambassador to California

"My fear as I read Ed Underwood's important new book is that those who were not part of the Jesus Movement would pass on buying it. Don't! This is a book for every believer who longs for revival and knows that only a risky and revolutionary dependence on Christ will cause it to happen. Ed gets it, lives it, and shares it powerfully with his readers. Take a chance on this book. You won't be sorry."

Dave Burchett, Emmy Award–winning
TV sports director and author of
When Bad Christians Happen to Good People

"A radical believer, Ed Underwood is rooted in Christ and writes with a fierceness for Christ. His desire is for you to see and feel what revival looks like from the inside. Underwood has the extraordinary faith found in Hebrews 11:1 (NLT): 'Faith is the confidence that what we hope for will actually happen; it gives us assurance about things we cannot see.' His passion in life is to see revival one more time. *Reborn to Be Wild* takes you on a journey of how you, as a Christian, can be part of that revival."

Jon R. Wallace, president of Azusa Pacific University

"Ed's book is a wild, helter-skelter trip back to the crazy, hazy days of the '60s and '70s. It brings me back to the time when one day I would be appearing with The Righteous Brothers and Sonny and Cher on radical new TV shows like 'Shindig' and 'Shivaree' … and the next day I would appear with Hal Lindsey on the UCLA campus sharing the gospel with glassy-eyed, half-dressed hippies. *Reborn to Be Wild* captures these extremes and everything in between in a wild ride that concludes with the challenge to revive our radical pursuit of Jesus!"

Jerry McClain, Grammy-nominated performer,
songwriter of the theme from "Happy Days"

"Ed brilliantly captures in this book, as few have, the incredible experience of God's grace and power in the Jesus Movement. The three of us were there too, and Ed wonderfully paints it in all its profound impact. But then he challenges us beyond a mere memory and the cynicism that says such a time is not possible again. He asks, 'Are you willing to do it all over again?' And we discover that a casual 'Yes' response is not nearly enough."

John Lynch, Bill Thrall, Bruce McNicol,
best-selling coauthors of *Bo's Café, TrueFaced,*
Behind the Mask, and *The Ascent of a Leader*

"Ed Underwood is the real thing. I have learned to listen carefully to what he has to say, as his own suffering has given him a unique voice of insight and courage. *Reborn to Be Wild* comes deep from within the heart of a true radical, and I recommend it highly."

David A. Horner, associate professor of philosophy
and biblical studies, Biola University

"For the American church struggling to keep the main thing the main thing, this book is prophetic. For the individual Christian desperate for the freedom and joy Jesus promised, this book is a godsend. Ed's candid testimony and history of the Jesus Movement shows us what passion for Christ can look like, how it can devolve into conflict and competition, and how we can recapture it. This book *will* surprise you."

Ken Wytsma, lead pastor of
Antioch Church in Bend, Oregon

"Having become a believer during the Jesus Movement, I remember well the time period that Ed Underwood writes so accurately about in his book *Reborn to Be Wild*. Ed's description of the adverse condition of the church today is one that we should all think deeply about. Especially true when considering the Jesus Movement adopted a 'come as you are' philosophy to a generation that was hungry to find the truth. Ed's call to return to the times of being led by the Holy Spirit and to live once again in revival is one that I pray we would all yearn for."

Mike Mitchell, western sales director of AVIA Shoes

REBORN
TO BE WILD

REBØRN
TO BE WILD

Reviving Our Radical
Pursuit of Jesus

ED UNDERWOOD

David C Cook®

transforming lives together

REBORN TO BE WILD
Published by David C. Cook
4050 Lee Vance View
Colorado Springs, CO 80918 U.S.A.

David C. Cook Distribution Canada
55 Woodslee Avenue, Paris, Ontario, Canada N3L 3E5

David C. Cook U.K., Kingsway Communications
Eastbourne, East Sussex BN23 6NT, England

David C. Cook and the graphic circle C logo
are registered trademarks of Cook Communications Ministries.

The Web site addresses recommended throughout this book are offered as a
resource to you. These Web sites are not intended in any way to be or imply an
endorsement on the part of David C. Cook, nor do we vouch for their content.

Unless otherwise noted, all Scripture quotations are taken from the New King James Version.
Copyright © 1982 by Thomas Nelson, Inc. Used by permission. All rights reserved. Scripture
quotations marked NASB are taken from the *New American Standard Bible*, © Copyright
1960, 1995 by The Lockman Foundation. Used by permission; NIV are taken from the *Holy
Bible, New International Version®. NIV®.* © 1973, 1978, 1984 International Bible Society.
Used by permission of Zondervan. All rights reserved; MSG are taken from *THE MESSAGE*.
Copyright © by Eugene H. Peterson 1993, 1994, 1995, 1996, 2000, 2001, 2002. Used by
permission of NavPress Publishing Group; NET are taken from THE NET BIBLE®, New English
Translation © 1996 by Biblical Studies Press, LLC. Used by permission. All rights reserved.

Beach photo in middle of book is from iStockphoto. Other photos and signs were provided
by the author with help from Dave Hollandsworth at One-Way.org and Terry Behimer.

LCCN 2010923223
ISBN 978-1-4347-0017-9
eISBN 978-0-7814-0445-7

© 2010 Ed Underwood
Published in association with the literary agency of D.C. Jacobson
& Associates LLC, an Author Management Company.
www.dcjacobson.com

The Team: Don Pape, Alex Field, Sarah Schultz, Jaci Schneider, Karen Athen
Cover Design: Amy Kiechlin
Cover Photo: iStockphoto
Back Cover Author Photo: Michael and Emi Heddon, EvokePhotography.com

Printed in the United States of America
First Edition 2010

1 2 3 4 5 6 7 8 9 10

040110

Dedication

This book is for anyone whose redeemed heart cries for more, believing that God is still doing radical works through His people.

Most of all, I want to thank those who introduced me to the wild realities of the new birth. Their commitment, patience, and encouragement in the Way made every difference in my life. Bobby Rader, Phil Walker, Keith Osborn, and Ted and Jo Stone—thank you, my dear friends, for drawing near to me in the name of the Savior.

Acknowledgments

With every word, writing this book has become more about passion and friendship than manuscripts and publishing. My thanks to Don Pape, Terry Behimer, Alex Field, and the entire team at David C. Cook for their passion for this book. Don Jacobson's friendship has become the most pleasant surprise in this journey as an author. Thanks, Don, Jenni Burke, and all at D. C. Jacobson & Associates.

Thanks for Bob Deffinbaugh's excellent exegesis of Luke, especially chapter 12 on Bible.org, which provided invaluable insights: *Greed: The Affliction of the Affluent* (Luke 12:13–21)[1] and *A Disciple's Perspective on Possessions* (Luke 12:22–34).[2]

Contents

Foreword by Bodie Thoene   15

Preface   19

Part One: A Revolution Takes Off

1. Meeting Jesus on the Streets   25

2. Taking Jesus to the Streets   45

3. Rebels and Revolutionaries   67

Then Why?   87

Part Two: A Revolution Stalls

4. More Is Better   93

5. "Churchianity" Is Enough   111

6. Power Is Good   129

7. Bigger Is Better   143

8. Enemies All Around   159

9. It's All Mine   179

Then How?   197

Part Three: A Revolution Reborn

10. Our Only Hope, Our Only Hero   203
11. Our Only Goal, Our Only Gold   223
12. Our Only Treasure, Our Only Investment   245
13. Our Only Community, Our Only Care   263
14. Our Only Plan, Our Only Power   283

What If?   307
Could It Be?   313
An Invitation   315
Notes   317

Foreword by Bodie Thoene

When he first heard about Jesus of Nazareth, Nathanael asked his brother, "Can anything good come out of Nazareth?"

The Holy Spirit often surprises the world as God chooses the most unlikely people and unexpected places to turn the world upside down for the kingdom of God.

Reborn to Be Wild is an eyewitness account of the Jesus Movement of the 1960s and '70s. What God did in our generation ranks among the great spiritual revivals since the day of Pentecost, when Peter stood up and shouted to the religious establishment: "Men of Jerusalem! This Jesus whom you crucified is alive!"

Personally meeting the risen Jesus changes *everything*. It happened to our generation in a movement so powerful and unique that it will be mentioned in church history along with the revivals of Wesley, Moody, and Billy Graham.

But somehow the Jesus Generation got derailed.

We first heard our dear friend Ed Underwood talk about the importance of being *reborn to be wild* in June 2007, at a forty-year reunion with dear friends in Bakersfield, California. Most of us who gathered in the summer heat of our old hometown were among those who experienced the wildfire of the Jesus Movement as it swept through our community in 1967. We were rebels. We were outsiders. We were high school friends who met the living Christ one after the other, falling before the Holy Spirit like dominos.

We heard the message of God's grace and mercy, and fell in love with Jesus. Many of us were baptized on the same night. Within *weeks* after meeting Jesus, students like Eddie Underwood and I and many others became Young Life leaders, heading up high school Bible studies.

Back in 1967, in the midst of a violent countercultural revolution in many parts of America, a Holy Spirit conflagration sparked in our hometown.

No doubt the question in 1967 reflected that of the first century: "Can anything good come out of … *Bakersfield?*" But what came out of that unlikely beginning for us was a spiritual firestorm that emboldened our lives, changed our community, impacted our nation, and influenced the world.

Many of us went on to serve Christ in ministries all around the globe, as pastors, missionaries, artists, and writers.

But something happened in the years *since* 1967. Something quenched the flames and stifled the fervor.

Like the Lord of Creation said to the Ephesians in Revelation chapter 2, "I have this against you: You have lost your first love."

Where did we lose our way?

Reborn to Be Wild responds to that question, and many more, including, "Why and how did the Jesus Generation become lukewarm?"

More importantly, this book lays out a plan to answer the *big* question— *How can the spark of true spiritual revival once again ignite within the souls of a new generation?*

Since the first moment tongues of Holy Spirit fire rested on the heads of those who watched and prayed and waited, the Lord has longed to send revival to every generation.

It happened to us. We were there when the revolutionary message of God's grace blazed up in our hearts. And *Reborn to Be Wild* sends a clear message to this generation: "Spiritual revival can happen again, here and now!"

Read it to be convicted.

Read it to be challenged.

Read it to be part of the next Great Revival.

Preface

Do you believe God has the ability to stop you in the middle of a sentence with a thought so powerful and a question so profound that you have to write a book?

I do because it happened to me.

I was agreeing with another theologically trained church leader about the excesses and dangers of the "emergent" church when God's Spirit broke in with this rebuking thought, *You sound just like the church leaders who shamed and discouraged you back then!*

Back then, when I was part of an extreme movement of younger Christians.

Back then, when our hearts were full of unusual ideas about Jesus and His church.

Back then, when we were the ones church people talked about in sentences full of mistrust and shame.

Back then, when a generation bent on rebellion and destruction found peace and a reason for living in the teachings of a carpenter.

Back then, when we were the revolutionaries God's Spirit called to a radical commitment to Jesus Christ.

Instantly my heart felt disgusted by so much of what we had become. A question screamed from my soul about the Jesus Movement of the 1960s and 1970s.

God was asking me to answer the question, first for me, then for all of us, especially those of us who were there:

How did spiritual revolutionaries become tame evangelicals?

The answer to that question is in the pages of this book. This book investigates how the generation that refused to accept the conclusions of the comfortable, institutionalized church has morphed into a hipper and wealthier expression of those who stood against the revival of their youth. Whatever happened to the Jesus Movement?

We had a front-row seat to the raw power of God—true revival on a scale that has not occurred since in America, but we settled for the safety of the tame Christianity of the suburbs. We were convinced that we, unlike all others, were *reborn to be wild,* but we're anything but wild today. Somewhere along the way, we got sidetracked.

In the pages ahead you will feel as if you were there in the 1960s when everyone talked about Jesus, and the Spirit set hearts on fire for Christ. I want you to know what revival looks and feels like from the inside. When you're a part of a revival, you know it.

Revival is a powerful movement of God sweeping through a culture, accompanied by spontaneous spiritual joy and deep awareness that your life counts for Christ. By counts, I mean fulfilling what Christ asks of us—making disciples by introducing unbelievers to Him and encouraging believers to follow Him. We knew little but believed much, and God used us mightily.

Then you will wonder with me why the Jesus Movement *quit moving.* You will marvel at the parallel between our revival of the 1960s and the revival in Asia Minor recorded in the New Testament. Satan neutralized the boomer generation of believers by applying the same tactics he used in the first century. Six lies sidetracked us, and if you also believe these lies, they will distract you from the central truths of Christianity and the mission of the twenty-first-century church.

By learning from mistakes of the first-century church and our failure to heed the warnings of Christ and His apostles, you will know that there is a way to see this revival through—to finish well, to get moving again, to get back on track, to reenergize the wild heart of sold-out believers. The truth is, God wants every generation to risk revival. What is He asking you to risk?

Everything. That's right, everything. That's the cost of revival, the cost of discipleship—*everything*. But you will not miss any of it.

I want to help you become the type of devoted disciple the Lord uses in a revival. I'm asking God to use this book to show those of us from the Jesus Movement generation how to finish what we started. But more than that, I'm begging Him to call Christians of every generation to the radical commitment that fuels revival.

This is a book for those who want to live expectantly and wake up every morning thinking about Jesus and what we can do for Him, and go to heaven with stories of what He did in our lives that we will be talking about forever!

If words like *radical, revolutionary*, and *revival* scare you or make you uncomfortable, put this book down. Give it back to the person who gave it to you. Or take it back to the place where you bought it and ask for your money back.

But if these words spark something in your heart that you always knew was there—something wild and exhilarating; if you know that these ideas have always been just under the surface of your thoughts about Jesus and you have been praying for the freedom to think and talk about them; if the possibility of living a revival now rather than reading about one back then speaks to the core of who you are on the inside in Christ since the day you believed, and who you want to be for Him on the outside more than anything else, then—

God stopped me in the middle of a sentence with a thought so powerful and a question so profound that I had to write this book … just for you.

Part One

A Revolution Takes Off

Why Did the Jesus Movement Move?

Chapter 1

Meeting Jesus on the Streets

I don't have to wonder what it would be like to be a part of a genuine revival. I lived through one in the late 1960s and 1970s. I was there. I didn't meet Jesus in a church—I met Him on the streets of Bakersfield, California.

If you knew me in those days before I met Jesus, you would never have thought that I would be writing about revival forty years later. Especially if you knew and thought what religious people knew and thought back then.

There was no way the people who knew and believed that stuff would have chosen me to be on their team. I was the guy who didn't even know that the Bible had books, the one who went to church only because it was Mother's Day, or because my grandmother's church had some type of pack-a-pew-for-Jesus event and my grandmother, Sister Patrick to her friends, was part of it. You didn't have to worry about me coming to your church, because I didn't want to be there in the first place. I was the guy telling dirty jokes in class and buying beer for my friends, the one who loved it that the teachers couldn't figure out, "What has happened to Eddie? He used to be such a good boy."

Well, I wasn't a good boy anymore and I liked it that way. I hated just about everything having to do with authority, and if you had anything to do with God, you had a lot to do with authority. So I didn't want to be on your sorry team.

No, if you had anything to do with religion or church or God, you wouldn't have chosen me to be on your team. You wouldn't have picked any of my friends either. In your most undisciplined theological imagination, you would never have dreamed that my friends and I had anything to offer "God's Team."

Fortunately for me, and for them, God doesn't let religious people choose who gets to be on His team.

I became part of a very special team chosen by God, a handpicked army of revolutionaries who took our culture by storm—thousands of us at the center of the last great revival of American history, *the Jesus Movement*.

But to understand our revival, you have to know more about us, my generation. I graduated from high school in 1968.

1968

I like Tom Brokaw a lot. His books and documentaries move me because he is more than accurate; he is passionate and honest. When he told the stories of the men who went to war with my dad and the women they left behind, I felt like he was letting others know what I already understood about those boys who gathered into bands of brothers and stared down Hitler,

Mussolini, Tojo, and Stalin. They were the *greatest generation* because they saved our skins and didn't brag about it.

He also wrote about my generation in his book *Boom! Voices of the Sixties.* When I read and listen to him it's like hearing the slightly older brother or very young uncle I never had but always wished for explain what happened to us—to me. How we could be so noble and so screwed up at the same time. So open to ideas, but so unbending in our convictions. So full of advice, but so unwilling to listen. So bent on changing the wide, wide world, but so incapable of changing the little worlds around us: our marriages, our families, and our neighborhoods. So full of hope for the future, but so full of anger about the past.

His documentary *1968 with Tom Brokaw* takes us through what historians tell us is one of the most tumultuous and decisive years in American history. For twelve months America stood at the crossroads of who we always were and who we might become. The anger fueling the debates over politics, civil rights, feminism, music, and recreational drugs turned to rage in 1968.

In a single summer, terrorists shot and silenced two of the most powerful voices for change when a homegrown bigot gunned down Martin Luther King Jr. for "his people," and an angry Palestinian from Jerusalem placed a small-caliber pistol to the back of Bobby Kennedy's head and pulled the trigger "for his country."

Riots broke out; we burned our own neighborhoods and beat our own people over the head with nightsticks. We watched a war on TV in all its gruesome reality and wondered why our boys couldn't stop the real enemy in their Tet Offensive and why they had to shoot women and children in a tiny hamlet named My Lai. Our brothers were dying in Vietnam and our sisters were burning their bras. Bob Dylan had warned us in 1964, "The times, they are a-changin'."

They weren't just a-changin'; they were a-fallin' apart!

We questioned everything, read the writings of revolutionaries, and decided to start one. Our motto was simple, "Don't trust anyone over thirty!" Ours was a revolution of the people, and it happened on the streets of our campuses and cities.

Brokaw brilliantly depicts the political and cultural aspects of the revolution using images and firsthand accounts. Everything he says about the 1960s is true, but there was more—a revolution he never mentions, a revolution that maybe he didn't see, a revolution that hardly ever made the nightly news on earth but a revolution that was big news in heaven.

It was a revolution of the Spirit of God.

Toward the end of the documentary, Bruce Springsteen says, "The 1960s made room for outsiders and their ideas."

I was one of those outsiders for whom the *spiritual* revolution of the sixties made room, and the ideas erupting from our redeemed hearts hit the streets of the campuses and cities of America with the freshest expression of the good news modern man had ever heard.

The Outsiders

It intrigues me that Springsteen used the same word the apostle Paul used to describe those who now find room for their ideas in a revolution—*outsiders*.

Paul used the Greek term three times to remind Christians of their responsibility to live in a way that "outsiders" (NIV, NASB) or "those who are outside" (NKJV) would want to know more about Jesus (1 Cor. 5:12; Col. 4:5; 1 Thess. 4:12). *Outsider* is his technical theological description of people who live outside of God's mercy and grace. Outsiders were those living in the domain of darkness, outside the borders of the kingdom of the Son of His love (Col. 1:13).

Even if I didn't know what the Bible called it, I couldn't think of a better title for the place we lived before God's love brought us inside— *darkness*. The revolution reached into the darkness outside, where we lived:

- Tough, hip neighborhoods where God was for dorky church kids and the only thing we liked about Jesus was that He wore long hair and sandals.
- Busy, preoccupied homes that didn't have time for the silly charades of religious folk.
- A culture in which grace was when a well-starched family took the booth next to yours in a restaurant, bowed their heads, and folded their hands in a way that made everyone around them feel weird.
- Neighborhoods where loyal, lifelong friendships seemed to be unraveling from the pressures of growing up, where mercy was what you called for just before blacking out when the big neighbor kid caught you in his famous "sleeper hold."

Oh, it was darkness all right. But it didn't seem dark to us then, before we saw the light. It was just life, our reality, our dark reality. From the core of our blackened souls to the gloomy, immoral rhythms of our everyday lives, to the sinister generational evil we were trying to ignore, we were incapable of knowing anything but darkness.

I think our hopelessness had a lot to do with our revolution that became a revival. From the darkness of our lives, we couldn't see the light, had never seen it before. We didn't entertain ideas about how much the light might need us or how it could improve our lives in ways that would enhance our career or get us to heaven when we were through doing what we wanted to do down here. We were blinded by the light.

Before we met Jesus, we were outsiders and we knew it. After we took Him at His word, we were insiders, and we knew that, too. And we knew how we got on the inside. Jesus rescued us from darkness. We couldn't quote it from memory because we probably didn't know where to find it in our crisp new American Standard New Testaments, but when we read His words, we knew Peter was talking about us when he said:

> But you are a chosen generation, a royal priesthood, a holy
> nation, His own special people, that you may proclaim the
> praises of Him who called you out of darkness into His
> marvelous light; who once were not a people but are now
> the people of God, who had not obtained mercy but now
> have obtained mercy. (1 Peter 2:9–10)

If you're going to have a revolution, you need to have new ideas. If
you're going to find new ideas, they will never come from those who are
comfortably inside. They come from the outside, from outsiders. Even
though we were now inside the borders of the kingdom of the Son of God's
love, the old insiders never did embrace us. To them we would always be
outsiders.

It didn't bother us much. Actually, it didn't bother us at all. To be totally
honest, we dug it. Our hearts were on fire with the love of Christ and we
didn't really trust them with the fire anyway. All they wanted to do was
douse it, control it, or worse, take credit for it.

And so we did what outsiders often do, we started a revolution fueled
by a passion insiders can't know … unless they reach out to us. And like
revolutions everywhere, our fresh expressions of truth didn't move along
the protected stained-glass corridors of the institutional church. Our revival
happened in the very places that had been deserted by most religious insiders as they watched in horror, threw up their hands, and screamed bloody
murder from inside their cloistered fortresses of irrelevance. It happened on
the street.

Street Scenes

When I hear most other Christians talk about their spiritual journeys,
I'm reminded of how different our stories are. They talk about hearing a

powerful sermon and deciding to do this or being at a Christian retreat and realizing that, or the way a Sunday school teacher or youth pastor told them what they needed to hear. The story usually starts at church or some religious event surrounded by Christians.

I didn't know any people who were Christians, but a lot of the people I did know were becoming Christians. None of it happened at church.

The very first conversation I remember ever having about God was with an old drinking buddy and fellow degenerate. It was during homeroom at South High. Mike, Jim, and I always sat together near the back. That way Miss Beane couldn't tell that we weren't discussing our assignments. I can't remember what we were talking about but I'm sure it had something to do with girls or beer or sports. I'm also sure it had a lot to do with the fact that everyone else around us was stupid. Mike, Jim, and I were smarter than most of our peers and we knew it. We thought we were cooler than everyone else too, but we probably weren't.

One of us brought up the subject of Bobby. Bobby used to do everything with us. He was our contact at the local grocery store where he stocked shelves. We would give Bobby the money to pay for the massive amounts of beer we needed for the weekend, and he would put the money in the cash register before sneaking cases of Coors in bottles out the back door in big toilet paper boxes. We didn't want to steal.

"So what do you think? Is Bobby a Jesus freak? I heard that he's not going to get us beer anymore."

Somehow the next comment turned the conversation in a way that amazes me today. I know it happened because I was a part of the discussion, I just can't believe that we were talking about it.

"Hey, how does this work anyway? If there is a God, then He has to know everything, doesn't He?"

"Yeah, seems like He should."

"Okay, if He knows everything, then He must cause everything. Right?"

"Wait a minute. Slow down, what are you getting at?"

"Well, if I'm supposed to somehow accept Jesus, but God already knows what I'm going to decide, because He's controlling me, then how can He send me to hell if I don't do it?

"Do what?"

"Accept Him, or Jesus, or whatever it is we're supposed to do."

"How can He send anyone to hell? It's all His fault, isn't it?"

Mike broke in. "I asked Bobby about that. He said he didn't know, but he would ask someone. He said the important thing is that we should know that God loves us and that He wants to have a relationship with us."

Jim and I immediately reacted. "What? Have you been talking to Bobby about this (let me use a better word than we used on that day) … *stuff?*"

That's how the revival started, how it began moving. People like Bobby were everywhere. On every football team, in every car club, every drinking buddies club, every neighborhood, every dorm, every locker room, every Spanish, history, and physics class, every cheerleading camp, cruising every strip, sitting in every McDonald's, every group waiting to catch the next wave at Huntington Beach, every work crew improving trails in the High Sierras, at every family reunion, every wedding, every party, every spirit rally and dance in the school gym. At every event that gathered high school and college students together—there was a Bobby. There was someone who had just discovered the grace and mercy of God and who simply refused to stop talking about Jesus.

The penetration was that broad and that deep. When I think of it now, it absolutely blows me away. We were three pagan kids sitting in our little corner of the universe debating the sovereignty of God and the free will of man!

The critical time in each of our lives was when God came onto our scene, to our street, our homeroom, our team, our dorm. He did this by sending a Bobby. The scenes of my life shifted dramatically as God brought my Bobby to my street.

Scene 1, Home Phone

"Hey Eddie, this is Bobby. I'm on my way out to Phil's new ranch. He needs me to watch the ranch house for him tonight. He has to work. You want to come with me? I'll cook you some steaks from the steer we butchered last week."

Before I said yes, I thought it through. I had heard about this so-called ranch. Phil was the first one to fall for Bobby's Jesus message, and he was all in. I never saw him in the old places anymore. His girlfriend told people that he broke up with her because he didn't think that their relationship was "pleasing to God." Since I knew what they were up to (the same things we were all up to), I had to agree with him on that point. If there was a God, He probably didn't like the things we were doing with our girlfriends. Phil and a couple of his new Jesus friends had actually rented a ranch outside of town. How they did it, I didn't know. *How do three guys our age rent a whole ranch?*

Word on the street was that they got together out there and had Jesus meetings. They would all work together to care for the stock and keep the place up. Guys, girls, all together feeding cows, cleaning stalls, brushing horses, watering crops, washing walls, painting the barn, cooking meals, and doing dishes. In the evening, they would all get around a campfire and someone who knew something about Jesus would teach stuff from the Bible and they would all sing "Kumbaya" and then pray and hug each other.

Anyway, that was what someone told us.

It sounded boring compared to our Friday nights of cruising the strip, getting drunk, and picking up some girls if we got lucky, or getting in a fight with guys from North High if our luck ran out.

But I did hear that some of the best-looking girls in Kern County were there. And Bobby was my friend. I calculated.

What do I have to lose? What could happen on a Tuesday night anyway? Besides, I could use some steak and nobody else will be there. It was a good excuse to get out of the house.

"Okay, Bob. Come on by. But I don't want to talk about Jesus all the time."

"I promise, Eddie."

Scene 2, The Ranch

"Great steak, Bobby. But I sure could use a beer."

"Sorry, no beer out here. What do you think of the place?"

"Pretty nice. Feels good to be out here. You come here a lot?"

"Most nights after work at the market. I like getting away. We really have a lot of fun out here, Eddie."

"You mean at your 'Jesus parties'?"

"That's not what we call them. We're just a bunch of Christians getting together. I'm no different from you, Eddie. Only forgiven …"

"Bobby, you promised," I stopped him.

"You're right. Sorry. Oh, I forgot to tell you. Mo's coming by tonight on his way down to LA. He's just crashing here for the night."

"No problem. Just don't wake me up when he gets here."

I had heard about Mo. His real name was Craig and he was Phil's old friend who used to live in Bakersfield but now lived up north. He went to Chico State and all the Jesus people talked about him like he was the coolest thing since whipped butter. Long hair parted down the middle, drove an MG, talked a lot about philosophy and religion, understood some things about the Bible, and lived in some type of Jesus commune or something. He was a student leader of this "club." They called it Young Life.

I didn't want to talk to that character, so I made sure they thought I was asleep when he showed up around midnight. But I listened to this guy and my friend Bobby talk late into the morning. I heard every word. I still tear up today as I write these words telling you what their sentences awakened in my heart that night: a spiritual desire for Jesus more powerful than any sensual desire I had ever experienced.

They were talking about Jesus like they were talking about a friend, only different. They not only admired Jesus, it seemed like Jesus was really a part of their lives. I began to wonder if maybe they had something, if maybe I was missing something, something big, something forever.

Then they began to talk to God about people, some of the people I knew. I guessed that this must be how they prayed. Didn't sound like any prayer I had ever heard at Grandma Sister Patrick's little country church. It was just conversation and they weren't telling God how bad these people were; they were asking Him to help them show these people how much He loved them. They asked God how they could help these people believe in Jesus, how they could tell them about what a difference Jesus was making in their lives.

And then they mentioned me. As far as I knew then, this was the first time anyone had ever talked to God about me in a way that wasn't bringing up all the stuff I hoped He hadn't noticed.

I stared at the wall, didn't move a muscle, and secretly hoped God was listening to them.

The next morning Bobby and I left before Mo stirred.

"You okay, Eddie? Pretty quiet. Did we wake you up last night? We tried not to be loud."

"No," I lied. "I'm just thinking about my day."

No I wasn't. I was thinking about my night, last night and the rest of my life and beyond. I was deciding that maybe I needed to ask Bobby more about Jesus, that maybe I wanted to meet this guy, Mo, or Craig, or whatever his name was. Maybe I wanted to be able to talk about God and to God in the same way they did.

But not right now, I told myself as we hit the first red light back into town. I needed time to think and room to breathe.

Scene 3, Kern County

I had plenty of time to think, but no room to breathe. I remember the months following the night Bobby and Mo prayed for me at Phil's ranch as the most miserable months of my life. The darkness was beginning to smother me.

- Larry got killed in Vietnam just a few months after I organized his going-away party, where we all got drunk and told him he was "too ornery to get killed." No, he wasn't; I helped carry his casket from the chapel to his grave. And then we all "remembered" his death by having another party in the same place with the same people. The only difference was that this time we all loaded up in my '69 GTO and a couple of other muscle cars and went out to Beach Park where the hippies and protestors hung out and beat a couple of them within an inch of their lives. We told ourselves that we did it for Larry and America, but we knew better. We knew we were just being mean because we didn't know what else to do with the pain.
- My girlfriend, the one I hoped God didn't know what I was doing with in the backseat of my GTO, met some guy at a ski resort in the Sierras and decided that she wanted to become an Olympic skier and that she needed some "space" to train. Right.
- I launched a very short and unsuccessful career as a petty thief. I felt horrible when we stole stuff from friend's garages, batteries from tourists' cars, and hard liquor from anywhere I happened to be when I noticed it on the shelves. I didn't even want the stuff, but it made me popular with my friends. I gained quite a rep as a reckless dude, until I got caught and spent the night in jail, scared spitless. My dad didn't say much on the drive home. He just kept looking at me with that "What happened to my

son?" look I was beginning to recognize. I had no answers to that question because I was asking it myself.

- And college? Forget that. All of my smart friends who had been with me in the smart kids' classes since first grade were off to places like UCLA, USC, and even the Air Force Academy. Me? I was flunking out of the local community college because I spent all my time at the lake waterskiing or at the pool hall, honing my "skills" in these two life-success-critical talents.

Kern County was my open-air playground—skiing on pristine lakes in the foothills on weekdays when we were the only boat in the water, hunting quail in the Sierras whenever I felt like it, skipping class and heading to the pool hall where an old guy sold us drinks as if he really believed we were twenty-one. We were living the 1960s dream expressed in the songs we listened to on the radio—we took "surfin' safaris" whenever we felt like it, drove "country roads" proving that we were "born to be wild," got lovin' "eight days a week," and "lived for today."

But the dream was turning into a nightmare for me. Especially when I was alone. When I was alone, the desperate lyric of the day seemed more appropriate—"Hello darkness, my old friend."

As the suffocating shadows closed in, proving that Simon and Garfunkel didn't know what they were talking about—that darkness was not my friend—another friend dropped by, a friend whose smile brought a glimmer of light to my dark existence.

Bobby.

Scene 4, Keith's House

The smell of the sizzling quail filled the house. Mom and Dad were gone somewhere and I was all set to watch something on TV when Bobby walked

in the way he used to when we were close. He never knocked, because he
didn't need to. My family loved him. He was the only one I ever knew who
did that; it was just his way.

He popped in to report that Billy Graham was going to be on TV later
and told me I should listen to him. Then, just as quickly as he had arrived,
Bobby left. On his way out he said this: "See you, Eddie. If you want to
talk, come on by."

I don't remember any of what Dr. Graham had to say, but it was enough
to get me to drive the few blocks to Bobby's house for the first time in over
a year.

"Bobby, I need to talk to you. I did watch Billy Graham; that's why I
came here tonight. I don't know what to do. I have to talk to someone."

Bobby smiled. "I know just how you feel, Eddie. I don't know a lot, but
I do know this …"

As my friend explained the core message of the good news that he and
my other "Jesus friends" had believed, I knew this was the best news I had
ever heard. Bobby quoted the first Bible verse my ears would ever *really*
hear:

> For God so loved the world that He gave His only begotten
> Son, that whoever believes in Him should not perish but
> have everlasting life. (John 3:16)

The questions poured from me. Bobby tried to keep up and then held
up his hand and said, "Let's go ask Keith."

I had never met Keith, but I knew he was talking about Keith Osborn.
Keith had quit his job teaching and coaching in a local high school to
become the Kern County Young Life leader. A few months prior, Keith had
been the last person I wanted to talk to; now I couldn't wait.

We drove the few blocks to Keith's house. His wife met us at the door.

"Keith's at a club meeting. He should be back soon. Come on in."

"No," I offered, "we'll just wait outside."

I didn't want to be rude, but I wanted to talk more with Bobby about God and Jesus. It didn't seem like we could do that in some stranger's living room.

Keith drove up in an old beat-up car. I picture him in my mind today and he looks tired, but I didn't even notice any of that; I just had to know more about God. Keith was easy to talk to. He smiled when he saw me and said he had been praying for me. I gave Bobby a look that said, "Have you been talking about me to all these Jesus guys?"

He winked and smiled.

Keith took a seat on the curb in front of his house, invited me to sit down next to him, and opened his Bible. I remember it didn't look like any Bible I had ever seen before—the huge ones on coffee tables in religious homes or the big black ones the people in Sister Patrick's church carried under their arms. Keith's Bible was ragged and used, he had scribbled notes all over the pages and underlined a bunch of sentences. *Wow, this guy actually reads this,* I thought.

Keith began talking about God and Jesus and truth and mercy and a word that I was especially attracted to: *grace.* He was so gentle, so real, and so different from anyone who had ever talked about God around me before. And it was on that curb in Bakersfield, California, on that summer night, that the Jesus Movement moved into my heart.

This man I had just met asked me to pray with him, and I did. In everyday sentences, I told God that I knew I was a sinner, that I believed Jesus died for my sins, and that I wanted to receive Christ as my Savior. Keith said "Amen," grabbed me in his arms, hugged me wildly, and read from his Bible how the angels were having a party right now because they were so excited that I had become a Christian.

That was the night the light dawned in my heart and the darkness lifted from my life. Like the thousands of others who were meeting Jesus through the Bobbies and Keiths in their lives, I knew I was different. Especially when the darkness tried to hang on while Jesus pulled me from its death grip.

Scene 5, Jeff's Car

We called it the "Hole." It was a huge depression in the desert floor outside of town, a perfect place to party. If you didn't know it was there, you couldn't find the source of the rock music blasting from the huge speakers someone wired to their eight-track tape player. If you knew the unmarked way, you would slow down just before you hit the edge of our four- or five-acre crater turned rock concert. As you dropped into a lower gear you would look for a place to park, pull out your drug of choice, depending on whether you were a "juicer" or a "head," and start partying. The cops couldn't find us so it got pretty wild.

My new Christian friends had warned me against hanging out with the guys from the neighborhood. They said something about not having "fellowship with darkness." I had already figured out that fellowship was Christian-talk for friendship, but I didn't see any harm in spending a Friday night with my old buddies at the Hole.

Jeff promised he wouldn't tell Bobby I was going out there with him. I was already learning how to be a hypocrite. And besides, what would a few beers and some laughs with my buddies hurt? I never wanted to become some holy nutcase.

I tried to have fun like before, but it just didn't take. I had another beer and danced with some pretty girls to see if that would help. It just got worse.

I walked over to Jeff's Malibu, sat on the hood, and talked about Jesus with a guy I had only met a few times. I remember thinking as I talked about Christ that I was becoming a Bobby. I also remember deciding that I didn't care.

My most distinct memory from that night was leaving the Hole riding shotgun in Jeff's car with a buzz on from the alcohol and hearing God say plainly, *You don't belong here anymore. This is not your life; there's nothing here for you. Your future is with me.*

I never looked back.

I made mistakes and still committed a lot of sins, including many of the same sins I was committing before I met Jesus. But I always knew that it wasn't the real me, or the new me, doing these things. That was just the old me messing up on the way to my real future, the one I really wanted, my future with Jesus.

You Say You Want a Revolution

We said we wanted revolution and that we wanted to change the world. John Lennon sang about it. We immortalized it.

Tom Brokaw tells us now that some things changed for good and some things changed for worse. As I said earlier, I think he's correct in everything he says, but he missed the most significant world change, the most lasting revolution of the 1960s.

It didn't start in Berkeley or at Woodstock. It began in Southern California with the Bobbies of Santa Ana, Huntington Beach, Venice, and Westwood. It spilled over the mountains, as the Bobbies came home to places like Bakersfield, Santa Barbara, and Chico. It was a revolution that happened on the streets, but it was a revolution of the heart.

We called it the Jesus Movement, and it consumed us. Only one word accurately describes what it was—*revival*. If you're a Christian, you're already thinking about what you hope is coming next. There is a question in your heart that you hope I'm going to answer. You want to know if there was a pattern, a path to follow toward revival.

For years my answer to that was always, "No, it just happened. God just did it." My wife, Judy, changed my mind when she said, "Honey, when I read 2 Corinthians 4:15, it makes me think of when we came to Christ in Bakersfield."

> For all things *are* for your sakes, that grace, having spread through the many, may cause thanksgiving to abound to the glory of God. (2 Cor. 4:15)

Have you ever had one of those moments when you suddenly understood something so perfectly that you were able to say what you felt so intensely with absolute clarity? Something you always had to get out of your soul but you just couldn't find the words, and then it unfolds and the words just flow from your lips, and as you hear yourself, you're thinking, *That's it!*

I had one of those moments in our living room that day just before breakfast when Judy read 2 Corinthians 4:15. The apostle Paul had condensed everything that happened to us in the Jesus Movement into one sentence: "The grace God planted in our hearts spread through the many and caused thanksgiving to abound to the glory of God."

That's it. That's the path to revival.

When I checked 2 Corinthians 4:15 in my favorite paraphrase, *The Message*, I was really fired up because it divided the path to revival into three progressive steps:

> We're not keeping this quiet, not on your life. Just like the psalmist who wrote, "I believed it, so I said it," we say what we believe. And what we believe is that the One who raised up the Master Jesus will just as certainly raise us up with you, alive. Every detail works to your advantage and to God's glory: more and more grace, more and more people, more and more praise! (2 Cor. 4:13–15 MSG)

There it is, the path to revival: more and more grace, more and more people, more and more praise! Grace, People, Praise.

If you want to change the world for Christ, if you want to start a spiritual revolution, it all begins with *grace,* and lots of it.

More and More Grace

The only starting point is grace, pure and free. If you want revival, you must embrace grace, or it's not Christianity. Grace sets Christianity apart from all other religions. It's what makes our message good news.

Years ago a group of British thinkers on comparative religion furiously debated whether one belief set Christianity apart from other world religions. C. S. Lewis wandered in late, took a seat, and asked, "What's the rumpus about?" When they told him they were trying to determine Christianity's unique contribution among world religions. Without hesitation he replied, "Oh, that's easy. It's grace."[3]

It's grace. Would you say that? Without hesitation? If not, you're not ready for revival. Whether you met Jesus in the Jesus Movement like me or you're an emergent Christian or you're a believer anywhere in between who's asking God to use you to make a revival-difference in this world, you have to get this straight.

Only those who are willing to join God in risking grace by extending it to sinners without hesitation or compromise will know the spontaneous spiritual joy that sparks spiritual revolution.

Undeserved, unending, unearned, unconditional, uncontrollable, unblinking, unbound, undefiled, undeniable, unequivocal, unfaltering, unhinging, unlimited, unmistakable, unprecedented, unsettling—grace—God's gift of life to all who believe in His Son, unheard of anywhere else but in Christ.

To us, grace was so much more than a theological doctrine. It was the air we breathed and the new reality of our existence. We never thought for one minute that we were walking a path of measuring up to God. We knew we were walking a path of trusting God. Those two paths never lead in the same direction. One leads to a world of failure, defeat, and misery; the other leads to a world of strength, victory, and joy.

The ones on the path of measuring up never invited us along. Even if they did, we would have told them what they could do with their religious selves. The ones on the path of trusting couldn't contain the message of grace or the joy in their hearts. And so, like my friend Bobby, they invited us to trust God with them ... and we did.

If you were there, you remember when your Bobby came to your street and the moment the light of Christ began to shine in the darkness. But that's not all you remember. You remember how it felt, the adventure of living on the edge of a powerful movement of God. And you know that you want to feel that way again.

If you're a Christian but you weren't there and the institutional church has yet to anesthetize your heart, perhaps you're reading about something you would love to experience. Maybe you never even thought of yourself as someone who could be part of a revival.

By the time you finish reading this book, you will know that it can happen again. You will understand that in order to get a clear picture of revival you don't need to strategize, analyze, contextualize, or market Jesus the way some leaders are telling you today. For revival, you simply need to get back on the path of grace, the path wild revolutionaries walk, the path of trusting God. Then, you will look at the streets of your life and imagine what would happen if you decided to be a Bobby.

That's what we did. As soon as we met Jesus on the streets by hearing His message of grace, we couldn't keep it quiet—more and more grace. Every detail worked to God's glory as more and more people praised God as we took Jesus to the streets.

Chapter 2

Taking Jesus to the Streets

It's amazing the things God did not use to move this revival forward.

No books on "how we grew our church with this grand scheme or that newest insight."

No deep-pocketed donors got behind a vision for "reaching the world for Christ."

No study revealing statistics and insights that rocked the evangelical world.

No "new paradigm" for church leadership that would make pastors and their churches suddenly relevant.

God grew an army of Bobbies, and His Spirit focused us on one simple marching order. It has been the same since His Son taught the first revivalists. The church talks about it mostly in theory, while mostly ignoring it in practice. It is Christ's number-one priority, His main concern, His Great Commission:

> And Jesus came and spoke to them, saying, "All authority
> has been given to Me in heaven and on earth. Go therefore
> and make disciples of all the nations, baptizing them in the
> name of the Father and of the Son and of the Holy Spirit,
> teaching them to observe all things that I have commanded
> you; and lo, I am with you always, even to the end of the
> age." (Matt. 28:18–20)

We were refreshingly naive, didn't know any better, never thought of explaining this command away with *evangotalk* models of why this didn't mean *us*. We just took Jesus at His word—He had the power and did what He said. We told people about Him and trained them to tell others.

It happened much faster than you would expect if you have read any books about evangelism and discipleship that tell you that most Christians aren't capable of telling people about Jesus until they have memorized *their* stuff or been to *their* seminars or learned how to be more churchlike.

But if you've read the story of the early church in Acts, perhaps you've tried to picture that revival in your mind. If so, maybe you already know that this is how it always happens: People who barely know Jesus make some of the best introductions to Jesus. The part of that first revival that reminds me the most of ours was what God did in Ephesus.

Picturing Revival

One sentence inside the story of Paul's work in Ephesus describes its impact in words I would use to tell people what happened in the Jesus Movement:

"And this continued for two years, so that all who dwelt in Asia heard the word of the Lord Jesus" (Acts 19:10).

Nowhere in the entire Bible is there another report of the love and knowledge of Christ growing so quickly and deeply into a culture. In only two years *everyone* living in the Roman province of Asia—today's Turkey—*had heard* the word of the Lord Jesus. It's amazing to me that most of the people who speak in order to help us understand God's Word try to explain it away.

In one of my "only for preachers and other smart religious people who know Greek" books about Acts 19:10, the author drones on about how the time reference is obviously hyperbole because it really isn't possible for God to do something that big that fast. He concludes that Paul must have meant to say "a lot of people" instead of "all." In bold red ink, I wrote in the margins: "That's because you've never seen revival."

I have. And it moves just that fast. And it penetrates just that deep.

But it's not only the scope and depth of the Asian revival that reminds me of the Jesus Movement; it's also the *way* it happened. Reporting the result of Paul's work in Ephesus, Luke tells us, "And this continued for two years" (Acts 19:10).

The *this* that had continued for two years was the daily class on the Way of Christ that Paul taught to a handful of outsiders in Ephesus. We only know that there were *about twelve* of them (Acts 19:7), and that the religious insiders kicked them out when they refused to compromise on Jesus' claims about the kingdom of God. Rather than trying to measure up to the religious status quo, Paul relocated his headquarters to a secular school and they followed.

You don't need my help picturing the main events of the Asian revival. On his third missionary journey in AD 52–55, Paul devoted over two years to an Asian ministry headquartered in Ephesus. He mentored a group of disciples to Christ, who then took the word of Christ throughout the province. They were so effective that everyone heard (Acts 19:1–10). Who am I to try to improve on Luke's inspired history?

I may be able to help you connect the revival dots and color in the revival lines if you will take a seat with me in Paul's class in the School of Tyrannus. You and I are only important because of what we are observing and reporting about Paul's relationship with the "Phil Walker" (Phil was the guy who discipled a lot of us in Bakersfield) of the class, one of his star pupils—*Epaphras*.

Epaphras doesn't usually come up in books or conversations about the world-changers of the New Testament. But just as Jesus Movement leaders like Keith and Ted noticed guys like my friends Bobby and Phil, Paul noticed Epaphras. There was something about this young man that set him apart in Paul's mind as a follower of Christ and a potential catalyst for revival.

We know that Epaphras met Christ through Paul's ministry in Ephesus and that he carried the word of Christ to his home one hundred miles to the east in the Lycus Valley (Col. 4:12–13; Philem. 23). He probably either started or helped start three churches in the valley of his birth in the cities of Colossae, Hierapolis, and Laodicea. In AD 61, Epaphras traveled to Rome to ask for Paul's help. Epaphras was Paul's devoted fellow servant who had taught his hometown friends the grace of God in truth and reported their great love for one another (Col. 1:6–8). He poured his life into these new disciples of Christ and poured out his heart for them in prayer (Col. 4:12–13).

Now on to Paul's class in the School of Tyrannus. We've never heard anyone teach like this man who openly admits that he was Christ's enemy before he met Him on a road. His words set our hearts on fire. He talks about Jesus and the world to come. He tells us that we're not alone, that we're not outsiders any more. He assures us of God's love by teaching us a new vocabulary—words like *grace, mercy,* and *pressing on* find their way into our sentences. He tells stories about Jesus that he heard from the ones who walked with Him before He was crucified. Then he opens his scrolls and shows us how the Hebrew Scriptures promised that Jesus would bring a new way of life to the world. He never fails to talk about all of this in ways that make us know that we are part of the story, that God wants us in His family and expects us to live for His Son, Jesus.

The magnitude of that privilege overwhelms us, and we never miss an opportunity to talk with Paul about *the Way*. We wonder what God wants us to do, but not Epaphras. He's sure of what all this means to him—it means going home.

Epaphras couldn't get enough. He was the one who stood in line after every class to ask Paul to clarify or explain further. His face lit up when he talked about taking the message of Christ home to the Lycus Valley. Some of the students seemed a little jealous of Epaphras. Others thought he was just a dreamer. *Sure, this guy is going to be the one who tells a whole valley about Jesus*, they probably thought.

When you see the tears running down his face when Paul brings up the subject of how desperate and hopeless life is apart from Christ, you know it's real. You've even heard Paul try to calm him down, make him wait.

"Paul, I need to get back home," Epaphras might have said. "My family, my friends, they've never heard about Jesus. If I wouldn't have been outside the synagogue the day you and your disciples were kicked out and the Jews were telling everyone you were evil and dangerous, I wonder if I would have ever heard. I can't put it off any longer. I know enough to tell them about Jesus' offer of eternal life. I'm leaving first thing tomorrow, before it's too late. They're all going to end up in hell if I don't."

You see the disappointment in his eyes as the apostle patiently reminds him of God's ability to get things done, and of his personal need to become more proficient as a follower of Christ before taking on such a huge assignment. And you feel the aged disciple's excitement in his assurances to the young man with a fire in his heart. "Epaphras, when the time comes you will know. Nothing will stop you then because God will be with you. Never think that when I say 'wait' that I mean 'don't go.' I believe God has chosen you to take the gospel to the Lycus Valley."

Over time everyone begins to view Epaphras differently. It's obvious that God is going to use him mightily. His interaction with Paul moves from the questions of a curious student of the war for souls to those of a soon-to-be comrade in arms. No more theory, only the things that will really matter if you're going to take Jesus' teaching seriously.

Then the day comes when Paul introduces Epaphras as your teacher for the day. Paul sits in the back and his face beams as Epaphras stumbles through the lesson. You wonder why Paul is wasting everyone's time by having this novice teach the stuff that he could explain so eloquently. But you have to admit, Epaphras seems to know what he is talking about. The next time Epaphras teaches, Paul isn't even there and the class is great. Epaphras brings up points you've never considered and he answers most of the questions with ease.

Over the next few months, you find yourself seeking out Epaphras, and you're not alone. One night you ask him to help you think about the village you came from, how you could "do something for Jesus" there, and he stays up all night listening to your thoughts, offering insights, and encouraging you.

Finally, the day comes, and Epaphras says good-bye. Paul says a few words about his burden for those who have never heard about Jesus and how wonderful it is when the Spirit shares the heavy weight of this burden with others. He calls Epaphras forward and lays his hands on him, commending him to take the gospel to his people back home in the Lycus Valley.

You wipe away tears as you try to let Epaphras know how much he means to you personally, and that you're going to pray for him. And then he says something that you will never forget.

"When are you going to take the gospel to your people? Paul tells me that you're really growing in your love for Christ and your understanding of the Scriptures. If I can do it, so can you. I appreciate your prayers, but I want to pray for you, for your ministry, for your people. I can't wait to hear about what you're doing for Christ someday."

Then he grabs your shoulders, looks you in the eye, and says, "Promise me you won't forget the things we talked about that night you told me about your burden, your love for the people from your neighborhood. Jesus wants you to go tell them about Him."

If you feel a lump in your throat because you're imagining what it would be like to be the one Epaphras is talking to, then you are beginning to form an accurate picture of revival.

That's how it happens—how the revival fires move from one heart to another. In the same way God burdened a first-century outsider to carry the gospel to his hometown, He also burdened my generation.

If the lump in your throat is your response to personal memories of events and conversations just like these forty years ago, or just a few months ago, then you will be thinking of your own revival scenes as I describe some of mine.

Revival Scenes

Revolutionaries tell others. Sometimes they go because of the momentum of the revolution, sometimes because they volunteer. When the revolution is spiritual and its leader is Jesus, they always feel they should. These three—the push, the would, and the should—explain the revival fires that blow across history and continents, but the flash points are local and surprising. Christians don't get up early one morning and say, "Let's start a revival." The revival just shows up one day and in ways that seem so ordinary. Until you look back on those days and say, "Wow, did we really do that?"

The "we" in that question is critical. Many Christians remember how they could not contain their excitement over Jesus after first hearing about His grace. That's not a revival memory, that's a personal evangelism memory. Revival memories connect people through momentous pivot points that gather them into mighty groups that influence eternity!

When my revival showed up, I signed up in the only way you can. I joined the spiritual guerilla warriors on the street. The battle was real, and the memories sacred.

Scene 1, Bakersfield High Club

"Now read verse fourteen."

Scanning down the page of the first chapter of John's gospel, I tried my very best, "And the Word became flesh and dwelt among us, and we beheld His glory, the glory as of the only begotten of the Father, full of grace and truth." I kept my finger on the page and tried to think of something holy to say just in case someone asked me what I thought. I remembered why I was so nervous:

It was my very first Bible study.

Bill was our leader. Keith Osborn, the Young Life guy in Kern County who introduced me to Christ, told me that as a college student I should get involved with the Young Life Club at Bakersfield High. The next two Tuesday nights I drove to some rich guy's house in the country club and sat down on the floor to take it all in. I remember thinking that it was a good thing that I wasn't doing this at South High because I didn't know a lot of these Bakersfield High guys. I hoped the ones I had met wouldn't connect my face with the night we squared off outside of Pizzaville and the cops told us we could either quit fighting or go to jail. I asked God to please stop the girl in the corner from remembering what we did last year on the night I met her at a party. Never thought I'd see her at a religious event.

Bill led some songs with his guitar. They were songs about Jesus that I had never heard before, but the tunes were straight from the street. I especially liked that song "Amazing Grace." The words fit perfectly with the bluesy melodies of Eric Burdon's "House of the Rising Sun." He put down his guitar and picked up his Bible. For a moment, I was afraid for Bill. *I'd hate to have to talk to this crowd about Jesus.*

As far as I can remember, that was the first time I told God I'd hate to do something just before He told me I had to. Back to verse fourteen.

Bill explained to us why the "Word" in verse fourteen was capitalized. "It goes back to verse 1. This is telling us that Jesus was God in the flesh. Never think of Jesus only as a man. He was the God-man." By now, I knew why I shouldn't have been afraid for Bill. When he opened his Bible and talked to a group of high school kids, he was deep, so deep that even college guys like me were impressed. Bill played football for Bakersfield College and was studying to be a doctor. Big, athletic, smart, and popular, he seemed to really know his Bible. *Good thing God found him,* I estimated. *Regular guys like me could never pull this off, especially if they've done the things I have.*

After he prayed, Bill told us that now that football season was over he was transferring to San Diego State. "Who's going to lead club?"

"Keith and I think Ed should."

I spun.

"Me? What do I know about leading club? I've only been a Christian a few weeks. I'm just here to learn, to help out. No way."

Bill's voice was strong and confident, with a slight edge of impatience. "You have the Bible and the Spirit. What else do you need? That's more than the apostles had. Besides, if you don't do it, we'll have to cancel club. Think of all the people at Bakersfield High who need Christ. If you don't tell them, nobody will."

If I'm all God has, then He's in a lot of trouble, I thought. And then another voice, from above, or maybe inside.

I thought you were serious about following Me.

I knew it was Jesus. The next Tuesday I stood in front of 120 high school students in a living room in Bakersfield Country Club hearing Bill introduce me to the "gang" as their new "leader." And then I told them everything I knew about Jesus in four or five minutes.

On the six days between club meetings for the next two years, I did anything and everything I could to find out more about Jesus so I could tell people. I read books, begged people to tell me what they thought, listened to Bible teachers, and even tried going to church. The church part took some time because even then I knew that most of what was going on there had nothing to do with the kids I stood in front of on Tuesday evenings.

And so it began. I probably taught about three heresies per week. I probably did a lot of things that made Keith wonder why he ever asked me to lead Bakersfield High's Young Life Club, and I distinctly remember that I still sinned a lot. But I never doubted that I was following Jesus and doing what He asked. And I agreed with everyone who told me that Bakersfield High School was my personal assignment from God.

I just assumed this was the way it happened for everyone—you get saved, spend a few weeks learning about Jesus, then start doing something important for Him. I didn't know I was in the middle of a revival.

Scene 2, Hume Lake

I don't belong here, and I'm not kidding this time, God.

It had been a long night. A growing realization of all that I didn't know about the Bible and Christianity had almost convinced me to tell Keith I was quitting. I decided to make this trip to my first Christian camp the deciding factor. If God wanted me to stay on as the Young Life leader for Bakersfield High, He would let me know.

He couldn't have been more clear.

In spite of my personal doubts, I had to admit that I loved it. I felt like God was actually using me on the bus ride up the valley and the western slope of the Sierras. I helped one little freshman find John 3:16 in his Bible and told him that I wanted to talk more about it in the mountains. A girl from Bakersfield High cried when I asked her how it was going with her boyfriend, so I took her to one of the female leaders and we prayed with her. I've always been a leader, so it just seemed right that I would take over when the buses pulled into Hume Lake Christian Camp.

"Everyone go get your luggage, then come see me. I have your cabin assignments. Throw your stuff on your bunk and meet me over there at the dining room. Dinner is in fifteen minutes."

Keith taught us that the most important time at camp was at night, in the cabin. "That's when they really open up. So be ready to stay up late."

I shared my cabin with seven church kids. They came to club every Tuesday, but they had grown up in church. One of them asked, "Ed, where is that verse that tells us to be careful not to get too close to the world?"

"Ah, I don't know off the top of my head."

See God, see what I'm facing here? I can't do this. I don't know anything.

"I think that's in Hezekiah," the church kid who dressed like a surfer said.

"Yeah, Hezekiah. Now I remember," I lied, "Hezekiah. Let's turn to Hezekiah, anyone remember the exact verse? I'm having a little trouble recalling that one."

I pretended I was turning the pages of my Bible past the table of contents, paused, and desperately looked for Hezekiah. *Must be in the Old Testament. Sounds like an Old Testament guy,* I thought to myself.

Muffled laughter.

Come on God, Hezekiah. *Help me here. How hard can it be to find Hezekiah?*

One of the kids jumped down from the top bunk. On the bus ride up, this particular boy had let me know what a waste of time all of this was to him. He was a really important leader in his youth group at church and didn't like being around young Christians. "I'm into theology. I like the deep stuff." He put the roaring laughter coming from the sleeping bags in perspective for me.

"Ed, Hezekiah didn't write a book of the Bible. He was a king of Israel. Everyone knows that. I can't believe this."

He walked out the door, turned left, and screamed to the kids hanging outside the cabins, "Hey, get this. Our leader doesn't even know the books of the Bible!"

I followed him out the door, turned right, and walked into the night.

That night I slept in the snow on some pine needles. For the first time church people had cruelly affirmed my own suspicion that I just didn't fit into Christianity. It wouldn't be the last time, but it was the most painful.

I cried some, prayed a lot, and decided to quit.

****

"Sit down, Ed." Keith and I left the trail and found a nice rock overlooking the high country.

"Do you think you're the only one who ever felt like this? How do you think Paul felt when religious people kicked him out of their meetings and told lies about him?

"How do you think I feel when pastors call me up and tell me that they're not going to allow their students to come to club because we use guitars and ask me who I think I am telling people about Jesus when I haven't even been to Bible college?

"This is something you have to determine right now, here on this rock and for the rest of your life. Are you going to quit when it's hard? Then quit right now, and never look back. But you need to decide who you are going to try to please: Christians or Jesus Christ?"

I decided to please Christ; I also decided that Keith Osborn was my hero.

I walked back to the cabin, gathered the guys together, and gave one of the most theologically concise sermons of my life.

"If you guys think that what you did last night was funny, you're wrong. If you think that you're going to get me to quit, you're wrong. If you think that knowing about the Bible is important, you're right. But if you think that knowing about the Bible is more important than knowing Jesus, you're wrong. I'm going to reach Bakersfield High School for Jesus Christ. If you want to join me, great. If not, screw you and the holy huddle you rode up here with."

Sometimes when you're taking Jesus to the street, a little street talk is just what you need to separate the religious from the revolutionaries.

Scene 3, Fruitvale

The pastor stood up to speak. He was trimmer than any preacher I had ever seen and he had sideburns. *Maybe this won't be as bad as I thought.*

I thought it would be like the other three or four times somebody talked me into going to their church. "Come on, Ed. The Lord says you should. Come to church with me. You'll love it." About five minutes into the service and I felt like asking them, *What do you think I love the best about this? The lady who told me to get a haircut? The girl I knew in sixth grade who asked me, "What are you doing here, Eddie?" The organist who plays songs I've never heard before so that they all look at me like I'm an idiot for not knowing the words? The guy up there talking about things I don't care about? Or when the pastor stands in the center aisle forever begging someone to come forward to accept Jesus? I'm having a hard time choosing a favorite. Help me here!*

Phil told me about this church out in the country where a lot of our friends from Young Life and Campus Crusade for Christ went. He said it didn't feel like church at all and promised me that the guy didn't preach, he just taught the Bible. "Kind of like we do in club, except he really knows more than us. He even writes Greek and Hebrew words on an overhead projector, like in math class. I've never heard anyone teach the Bible like him. He's cool."

Phil had really helped me since I became a Christian. He had become a serious student of the Word of God and served in a college ministry across the street from Bakersfield College that they called the College Life House. I trusted Phil, so I thought I might give church one more try.

"Oh, yeah. And you can just wear your Levis."

That did it. I had to see this church out in the country they simply called Fruitvale Community Church.

"If you have your Bible with you today, open to the book of First Corinthians."

For the next thirty or forty minutes, the pastor just went right through about three or four paragraphs of Paul's first letter to the Corinthian church. I felt like he was talking only to me as he explained what some of the words meant in the original Greek, brought in background information about the city of Corinth, and told stories about how he tried to do what the verses said. I took furious notes because it never occurred to me that I could come back next week! *So this is where guys like Keith get all the stuff they write in the margins of their Bibles.*

Then he said something I couldn't believe. "Last week I really blew it with my wife. I lost my temper and said some things that sure didn't fit with what these verses teach. I had to ask her forgiveness and then ask God to forgive me before I could stand up here today and teach His Word."

What? A preacher who admitted mistakes? I gotta meet this guy. I loved it that they didn't call him reverend or pastor. He was just Ted.

"Hey, Ted," Phil said. "This is my friend Eddie. The one I told you about."

"So good to finally meet you, Eddie. I've heard a lot of good things about what's going on at Bakersfield High School. Good for you. If you need any help, any help at all, you let me know. Here's my card. Call me next week. Promise?"

Ted had taken my right hand in both of his and was shaking it with strength and warmth. I smiled and promised to call him. At that first moment, I knew I was looking into the face of the man God would use to change my life.

The change occurred at a table in a restaurant, in someone's living room, and in Ted's office talking about God, the Bible, Jesus, and people. I didn't have a name for it yet because I hadn't learned to talk Christian. I know now that it was discipleship and that Ted Stone was simply doing what his Savior told him to do. He was making a disciple of Jesus Christ—*me*. The most dramatic meeting of all was the one that helped me see my life from God's perspective.

"Let's go to lunch somewhere near Bakersfield High School today, Eddie. You always come here to my place of ministry. I want to go see yours."

Wow. Ted thinks I'm in the ministry, just like him. Never thought of it that way. On the way to the burger joint, Ted wheeled onto the campus of Bakersfield High School. He parked in front of the administration building.

"Eddie, what kind of people walk into that building, the administration offices?"

What does this have to do with ministry? "Well, there's the principal, some counselors, and … I don't know, educators?"

"Pretty important people?"

"Yeah, I guess. Sure, really important people. I mean the principal, he's powerful."

I had had some personal experiences with the principal at South High that I hoped Ted hadn't heard about. I remember being afraid that he was going to say, "Well, I just talked to the principal from South High and he told me that you …"

My mouth went dry because Ted might not want to meet with a sinner like me anymore. But he was going in the opposite direction. He didn't care about looking back; my pastor was looking forward in a way nobody in my life had ever done before.

"But who is the most important person to walk onto this campus every week?"

"I don't know. It must be the principal, unless the superintendent shows up."

"No, Eddie, the most important person to walk onto this campus every week is you. You are the one who comes here to tell people about Jesus and offer them life in His name. All these others can only tell them how to get by, you can tell them how to get to heaven. They can only tell them about success, you can tell them about significance." He opened his Bible and read these words:

> Now then, we are ambassadors for Christ, as though God were pleading through us: we implore you on Christ's behalf, be reconciled to God. (2 Cor. 5:20)

Ted's kind face begged me to believe what he was about to tell me, and I did.

"Eddie, if you follow Christ, everywhere you go you will be the most important person there. Right now, it's Bakersfield High School, but in the years ahead it will be other places. Never forget that you represent Christ, you are His ambassador."

Nothing scares the enemy more than a warrior recklessly committed to his leader. Ted's 2 Corinthians 5:20 commissioning made me dangerous to every enemy of Christ on that winter day.

Scene 4, Arrowhead Springs

Ted was the exception. Most church leaders didn't know what to do with us. After church, they would ask us if we were interested in their youth program or college ministry. Our common ground was that we didn't want to come to their traditional church events any more than they really wanted us there. Both sides politely nodded as we imagined insane pictures of a group of long-haired, T-shirt-clad, huarache-sandaled guys demonstrating their Scripture-memory proficiency to a crowd of clean-cut, white-shirt-and-tie, loafered-up church kids and leaders. It never worked.

We were looking for places to gather, and a few visionaries said, "Gather here."

One of those was Dr. Bill Bright, founder of Campus Crusade for Christ. He bought the famed Arrowhead Springs and Spa, a two thousand-acre playground to the stars in the San Bernardino Mountains, and turned it into his world headquarters and conference center. He invited us to be trained to serve the Lord Jesus and we came, by the thousands. It became one of the epicenters of our revival, a place where outsiders fit in because what mattered most to us mattered most to Dr. Bright—*souls*.

We thought we came simply to be trained, but God had a lot more in mind. He knows that there is no such thing as a local revolution, a confined revival. Entrenched power knows what to do with small revolutions. They simply let the stallions run around the stable as they fortify the fences and move them in while no one is looking. It's when the stallions jump the fence and gather in the high country that they know they're in trouble. In the high country, the stallions congregate and discover that they are not alone.

Phil and I decided to go to one of Dr. Bright's weekend Student Mobilization Conferences. We grabbed a couple of guys to ride in the backseat and help pay for gas. We bunked with a couple dozen other Bakersfield guys. I can still remember some of the conversations we had almost word for word.

"We call it the JC Light and Power Company. It's a Bible school next to UCLA. Our teacher used to be a tugboat captain on the Mississippi. His name is Hal Lindsey and hundreds of kids come and listen to him. We meet in small groups all through the week. You should bring up a busload from Bakersfield."

"On New Year's Day we're all going to the Rose Parade to share our faith. You want to be a part of it?"

"You know how to surf? Cool. Our group holds meetings on the beach. We surf together and invite kids to our meeting while we're waiting for waves. Our Young Life leader sets up camp on the beach and starts cooking. You know how hungry you get surfing. He plays music real loud, not religious stuff, the kind of music everyone listens to—Beatles, Stones. Then, after their plates are full and they're sitting around, he turns off the music and tells them about Jesus. Here is where we'll be next week …"

"We're trying to get something started at UCSB. Where do you go to college now? Ever think about transferring to Santa Barbara to tell people about Jesus? Here's my card. I'm kind of heading this thing up."

Two days later, as we dropped down the Grapevine Pass from Tejon Summit into the fog-shrouded Central Valley, Phil and I knew that those borders would never again limit our world. Our days in the stable were over. We had to run with the stallions. We were *reborn to be wild*.

The Gathering Storm

Revolutions gain momentum under the radar. An irresistible idea or dream flares in the hearts of a few on the unthreatening edges of a kingdom, beyond the interest of the gatekeepers. Rumors of unrest trickle into centers of power, but no one is alarmed. The arrogance of power consistently underestimates the threat. By the time the king finally looks up, it's too late.

I don't know what preoccupied the mind of Satan just before our revival swept through his kingdom of darkness. Maybe he was too busy energizing anarchy to notice guys like Bobby speaking Christ's words into dissatisfied souls ripe for the heavenly harvest. Maybe, as his demon hordes exalted over the addictions enslaving the hippies, street people, and rock groups in places like Venice, Isla Vista, and Haight-Ashbury, they overlooked the Jesus rock streaming from small outposts of grace in places like the ranch in Bakersfield, JC Light and Power Company at UCLA, and Arrowhead Springs in the San Bernardino mountains. Maybe, while he and his wicked generals pored over strategies to unleash the anger festering in the hearts of bigots and their victims, rock stars and their fans, and dissenters and their admirers, he never noticed a couple of guys driving along Highway 99 talking about Jesus and their plans to change the world.

Had the devil known what God was up to, he would have marshaled his forces against us with murderous rage. Christians underestimate the power of grace, but Satan never does. He knows the danger. He saw it before when John the Baptizer pointed to Jesus of Nazareth, declaring, "Behold! The Lamb of God who takes away the sin of the world!" (John 1:29). Since then, he tried every malicious weapon and committed every wicked warrior to his defense against grace. Nothing works; grace is too powerful and pure.

God pumped *more and more grace* into the lives of a few of us and organized us into cells of grace-givers who were "not ashamed of the gospel of Christ" because we knew "it is the power of God to salvation for everyone who believes" (Rom. 1:16). Grace was so much more than a theological word; it was our delivering truth—our transforming experience. We had received the "fullness of Christ" and our lives were overflowing with ever-increasing experiences of grace—"grace for grace" (John 1:16).

C. S. Lewis observed, "God gives His gifts where He finds the vessel empty enough to receive them."[4] While the devil busied himself draining lives of all meaning and hope, God poured His amazing grace into the lives of more and more of us to the point of saturation. Conditions were right for the perfect storm of revival—hearts overflowed with grace, and friends with desperately empty souls surrounded us.

More and More People

I fell in love with my Jesus Movement sweetheart during those exciting revival days in Bakersfield. After we married, Judy and I left Kern County, but we will never forget those grace encounters.

I can still see Tom, a guy I played trumpet with in our high school band telling me about how he accepted Christ. "I was in the shower, thinking about what you told me about Jesus," he said. "It was the weirdest thing, I just knew God wanted me to accept Jesus, so I did."

Judy can still see the living room full of junior high girls to whom she taught the Bible every week. She remembers them staring up at her eagerly as she taught, the big high school cheerleader. Many prayed to receive Christ. I can still see the rock a jeepload of us stood on in the mountains claiming "Kern County for Christ," and how we really believed it would happen. I can still picture in my mind our Young Life leaders' meeting and the surprising reports of answers to that simple prayer.

I can still feel our innocent expectation that God would work mightily in His children, and the spontaneous spiritual joy of revival.

Oh, how I want to see and feel it again. I want the raw power of more and more grace spreading to more and more people.

You may think you want this too. But before you ask God to sign you up, you really need to think it through. Our revival never would have tipped toward the more and more praise of a mighty movement of God apart from the courageous guidance of a handful of spiritual leaders who saw what God was doing.

It only took a handful. A few people who believed in God's desire for a full-on revival. Not many mature Christians answered God's call to love, encourage, and train these ragamuffins.

We were an army of Epaphrases desperately needing our Pauls. A few brave leaders stepped forward. You've already met some of them. They paid a heavy price. The next chapter tells their story.

Chapter 3

Rebels and Revolutionaries

There's a big difference between a rebellion and a revolution.

Rebellions are short-lived outbreaks against authority that usually fail. Revolutions bring radical change. It doesn't take much to be a rebel—you just need to be angry and stand against something. But it takes a lot to be a revolutionary—you must be courageous and stand for something bigger than yourself.

At first, we were just a bunch of rebels, even after we became Christians. Without the revolutionaries who led us, there wouldn't have been a revival; it wouldn't have happened. God raised up leaders and had them in place before we rebels ever heard about His Son. The leaders of our revival brought radical change to our hearts, our families, and our lives. This chapter tells their story—the revolutionaries God used to turn a bunch of ragamuffin rebels into spiritual revolutionaries themselves. But as I would discover, we were still just rebels to those preserving the spiritual status quo.

I remember the night Keith asked a group of us from Young Life to tell our personal stories to some people in a church—how we met Jesus and the difference He had made in our lives. But the crowd seemed unresponsive and I couldn't understand why. Usually older people in the churches we talked to at least smiled when we talked about how we found Jesus. But this was like talking to a picture.

Some of us, me included, embellished our experience a little, hoping to generate some reaction. Keith gave us a look indicating that this wasn't really a good idea. We didn't have to exaggerate when describing our ministry.

I talked about the Bakersfield High Club and how it had grown to over two hundred kids coming every week, and the discipleship groups that were meeting in public parks near the campus at 6 a.m. to study the Bible and pray, and the many kids who had trusted Jesus on our recent trips to Hume Lake and Woodleaf Christian conference centers.

Jim, the leader at West High, described our weekly Friday evening visits to juvenile hall, how we brought a band to play before one of us presented the gospel, and that we then divided into small groups to interact more personally with these troubled kids. He reported the astounding number of decisions for Christ.

Bodie, the most polished speaker of our group, told stories of the South High girls in her Campaigner group ("Campaigner" is Young Life-talk for serious disciples of Christ) and the amazing things they were doing every week, not only at South High but also in the junior high schools that would feed into South.

Finally, Keith explained the simple formula Young Life used to reach kids for Christ—earn the right to be heard. He closed, asking them to please pray for him, the rest of us, and the youth of Kern County.

To me, this report was awesome. I was ready to applaud us myself, but I had learned enough about church to know that clapping was for some reason unspiritual. I expected some movement, maybe a couple of smiles from the sweet ladies in the front or one of those "amens" you hear when church people are happy.

Nothing, nada, zilch. The still picture of that audience remained.

The pastor thanked us awkwardly and invited us to the fellowship hall, whatever that was, so we filed out behind Keith and down a hallway.

My first impression of this place called a fellowship hall was, *Right on!* What a concept! Tables full of good things to eat—sandwiches, homemade pies and cookies, and salads, too, for the girls, I guessed. I changed my mind when a lady cornered me next to the blueberry pie for some "fellowship."

"Young man, where do you go to church?"

"Excuse me, ma'am?" I asked, swallowing a bite of pie that was way too big, gagging a little.

"I said, 'Where do you go to church?'" she repeated with a little attitude that put me on guard. I felt like I was back in the principal's office at South High after I jazzed up the call to the colors on my trumpet at our morning flag-raising ceremony.

"I go to Fruitvale Community Church, out on Rosedale Highway. My pastor's name is Ted Stone. He's discipling me and I …" I was trying to tell her anything I could think of that might impress a church lady. It didn't work. She took a step back, put her hands on her hips, and interrupted me midsentence.

"Fruitvale? That's just what I thought. All of you Jesus people go out there. Why are you all going there? There are plenty of churches around here. Why don't some of you come to our church? What's wrong with us?"

Only God's Spirit within me throttled the garbage mouth that was mine just a few short months ago. That and my loyalty to Keith kept me from saying what I was actually thinking. Instead, I answered politely.

"Well, you see, I didn't have a church before I got saved. A friend invited me to go to Fruitvale, so I went. It's not like I left a church to go there. That's just where the Lord led me."

"Well, just as I thought," she said. "A bunch of hellions all running out to the country trying to be different. I can tell you one thing, I'm not impressed. Not one bit!"

Suddenly, I lost my appetite for blueberry pie *and* fellowship, at least the kind they had in *this* hall.

It was my first run-in with the spiritual status quo, a small skirmish at the edge of a war that had been raging for years. It was a war the real heroes of the revival had protected us from as they fought vicious battles on our behalf.

As I look back on those years, I realize that we were not alone. The Lord Jesus had prepared a few hearts to lead us—those with the foresight to look past our rebellious culture and into our revival hearts.

The Template: Courageous Leadership

Nothing exposes the need for revival more than the criticisms thrown at its leaders. Entrenched ecclesiastical powers measure others by values and standards that long ago lost contact with earthly realities and heavenly concerns. They're irrelevant and don't know it, unscriptural and don't care. Blinded by religious categories, they miss what the Spirit is doing. Comfortable in their unchallenged conclusions, they ignore what God has said.

What sets the revolutionaries that lead spiritual revivals apart from political or cultural revolutionaries is a resource that forces every honest mind to evaluate his or her message and methods by the divine standard. We call it the Bible.

As the most effective Christian leader ever, Paul learned that he could never satisfy his critics. All it did was give them greater opportunity to find fault. Instead, he set the standard for authentic spiritual leadership—he defended himself *only* to the point that it mattered to his followers. He absolutely did not care what the antirevival spiritual power brokers of his day thought of him, but he cared deeply about the impact of their charges on the disciples of Christ.

His defense revolved around two irrefutable truths: (1) You know I loved you, even when it cost me dearly, and (2) you know God used me to change your life. The paragraph he devotes to reminding his friends in Thessalonica of the selfless ways his team served them is the template for New Testament leadership (1 Thess. 2:1–12).

After reminding the readers of their life change from idol worshippers to servants of Christ eagerly awaiting His return (1 Thess. 1:9–10), he explains how it happened. If I didn't know that these were Paul's words to the Thessalonians in the first century, I would think he was describing the ones who laid down their lives for us in the sixties and seventies.

Revolutionaries: Courage to Lead

The apostle Paul was one of the most revolutionary leaders in church history and a model to anyone called by God to lead His people in the revolutionary ways revival demands. Three characteristics will set these leaders apart from all others:

1. Courageously Teach Christ's Word

If you weren't there in the Jesus Movement, you might think this is a given, that the opinions offered to us about Christ came from the Bible. Actually, the use of Scripture set our leaders apart. Others were telling us what we should do and think and then attaching a verse to their message.

The ones we trusted started with the Bible, asked us if we understood, and relied on the Spirit's ability to sort it out—even when the plain meaning challenged strongly held convictions in the Christian community.

The Thessalonian Christians understood the cost of declaring the Word:

> For you yourselves know, brethren, that our coming to you was not in vain. But even after we had suffered before and were spitefully treated at Philippi, as you know, we were bold in our God to speak to you the gospel of God in much conflict. (1 Thess. 2:1–2)

Paul refused to let opposition keep him from his responsibility to boldly declare God's Word (*gospel of God, declaration*, v. 3; *speak the gospel*, v. 4; *word of God*, v. 13). He uses the evocative Greek term *hubrizo* ("spitefully treated") to characterize his suffering. "The word expresses insulting and outrageous treatment and especially treatment which is calculated to publicly insult and openly humiliate."[5]

At the time I remember being surprised that Ted wasn't bothered by my report of the church lady's attacks on him and his church. Now I understand why he shrugged off her cross-town verbal assault. Ted and Jo were engaged in desperate hand-to-hand combat with more dangerous foes. Some discontented leaders and troublemakers from their own church were reacting to the influx of Jesus people with mean and hurtful accusations:

- *Ted doesn't care about us anymore. He doesn't even visit us in the hospital.*
- *This music is from the devil and Ted's actually encouraging it. Guitars in church? I never.*
- *Instead of driving all over the county meeting with these new people, he should be teaching Bible studies here.*

- *Do you know where they're going on Sunday nights after church? They can't wait to get out of here. I heard …*

We never knew of the meetings late into the night or the extended telephone conversations. Over and over, again and again, our pastor patiently opened the Bible to text after text, sustaining his devotion to our revival and to us. A few objectors responded, but most finally moved on to churches ready to gossip about his weird ideas and many shortcomings.

As smoke follows fire, criticism follows revival. When God's grace touches lives, God's enemy stirs. And as the Thessalonians knew, entrenched ecclesiastical authority is always ready for the devil's lie that change is a four-letter word.

2. Selflessly Seek Christ's Approval

I'm an awkward pastor. Until I started writing this book I thought it was just me—that I didn't fit in with other pastors. Now I see that I don't fit in because the leaders who coached me through my formative years as a believer didn't fit in, though I have come to see that as a good thing. Paul certainly didn't fit the mold of spiritual authority in his day. He wasn't in it for himself:

> For our exhortation did not come from error or uncleanness, nor was it in deceit. But as we have been approved by God to be entrusted with the gospel, even so we speak, not as pleasing men, but God who tests our hearts. For neither at any time did we use flattering words, as you know, nor a cloak for covetousness—God is witness. Nor did we seek glory from men, either from you or from others, when we might have made demands as apostles of Christ. (1 Thess. 2:3–6)

Clearly, Paul could have pulled rank on those he led and made demands on them as an apostle. He didn't, and they knew it. His willingness, as shown in verse 6, to forgo personal glory for the sake of Christ marked his ministry. Because of this he had no need to deceive, to strive to please men, or use flattering words as he climbed over people. He wasn't trying to hide his greedy and competitive heart. Since his constant and only aim was to please God, he was free to speak His truth regardless of what people thought of him.

I remember classes in seminary where they talked about the need to be humble as a servant of God. My reaction was, *Yeah, so what else is new?* That was all I knew. Only when others began to tell stories of churches where it was all about the pastor and power and politics did I begin to appreciate men like Keith and Ted.

It was never about them. Young Life didn't exist to somehow validate Keith. Fruitvale Community Church wasn't Ted's church; rather it was God's church, our church.

No wonder I feel awkward when Christians reverently call me "Pastor" as they drop their eyes dutifully. I honestly don't know how to respond sometimes, but I can't help thinking, *Where does this come from? What long line of prima donna, power-hungry, threatened little men caused this type of behavior in these poor people trying to approach their shepherd?*

Ted learned well from his mentor, Ray Stedman. Ray pastored Peninsula Bible Church in Cupertino, California. He was a visionary man way ahead of his time and one of the critical thinkers who influenced the Jesus Movement. When Ted joined Ray's staff he asked him for a job description like his seminary professors told him he should. "Don't thwart the Holy Spirit's ministry in these people's lives," Ray answered. "Your job description is to follow the Spirit's leading in your life, and we are here to support you!"

You're going to read what I think of the corporate church later in this book, but I'll sum up my opinion now in two words: It's sick! If you're a person with any spiritual authority, the sentences you just read recounting Ray Stedman's job description for a New Testament leader are worth the price of this book. No agenda, no secrets, no need for credit; just someone the Spirit can lead to release His work in others.

Leaders whose only goal is to please Christ by trusting Him are free to tell people what Christ wants them to hear. They don't worry about reputation or power, because they had none when they started. Leaders looking to polish their reputation or gain power never get to be a part of a revival. God makes sure of that because He wants the revival to succeed.

3. Lovingly Parent Christ's People

Something wonderful happened to me the day my firstborn child, Aimee, came into the world. For the first time in my life, I had totally selfless thoughts. Suddenly, I was holding in my arms someone who meant more to me than, well … me. At that moment, I knew that no sacrifice would be too great for this little girl I had just met but instantly cherished. Before I could become too proud of how dear she had become to me, I placed her in the arms of her mother. From the moment Judy began to nurse our baby girl, I knew they were experiencing a bond I would never know, could never be a part of.

If you're thinking of the birth of your child and your love for him or her or your father and mother and their love for you, then you are picturing the role of an authentic spiritual leader—*a parent*. Paul reminds his readers of the selfless motives of the team he brought to Thessalonica by describing their role. They were parents to their disciples, as gentle as a nurturing mother and as firmly encouraging as a concerned father:

> But we were gentle among you, just as a nursing mother
> cherishes her own children. So, affectionately longing for

you, we were well pleased to impart to you not only the gospel of God, but also our own lives, because you had become dear to us. For you remember, brethren, our labor and toil; for laboring night and day, that we might not be a burden to any of you, we preached to you the gospel of God. You are witnesses, and God also, how devoutly and justly and blamelessly we behaved ourselves among you who believe; as you know how we exhorted, and comforted, and charged every one of you, as a father does his own children, that you would walk worthy of God who calls you into His own kingdom and glory. (1 Thess. 2:7–12)

I've had the privilege of interviewing many Jesus Movement Christians who have great influence for Christ. In most of their stories there is someone who *parented* them, a more mature Christian who tenderly and patiently imparted the gospel, and also gave of their own lives. These true revolutionaries invited them into their homes, fed them, stayed up late into the night with them talking about Jesus and answering their questions, and opened their door in the middle of the night when they broke up with their girlfriend or boyfriend or had a fight with their mom or dad.

My wife remembers the powerful attraction of Ted and Jo's home. Like most of us, Judy grew up in a non-Christian home. After her father died, her mother turned to alcohol and briefly abandoned the family. The authorities took the children to the same juvenile hall where she would later share Christ with young people. A brand-new Christian, she discovered Romans 8:28 all on her own in a desperate search to tell her little sister and brother how God would help them.

"Walking into Ted and Jo's house was like entering an oasis," she recalls. "Jo's smile, Ted's warm conversation. I just soaked it all in. I even loved it when they had family fights. I was learning how a Christian home operates, hanging on every word and noticing every relational nuance."

And while Judy and I and dozens just like us clamored for Ted and Jo's wisdom, affirmation, and attention, they were going about life. Raising their own children, serving meals, trying to make ends meet on a pastor's budget, going to their sons' wrestling matches, helping them and us with homework. It all happened with us underfoot. I look back on it now and wonder when they had time to sleep, or just have an adult conversation!

It's impossible to understand how revival happens without the personal view of those it happened to. Jesus expressed His love to us not only in the wonderful message of the gospel but also in the lives of the messengers. Like salvation, revival is costly. Jesus paid the full price of salvation, but His followers must pay the price for revival. Shepherds like Ted and Jo Stone, Keith Osborn, and hundreds just like them throughout Southern California who opened their lives and their homes to us.

God honored them by filling their homes and churches with thousands of rebels turned spiritual revolutionaries. We would have taken a bullet for them back then, and still would today. More than that, the grace they pumped into our lives erupted into worship experiences known only to those who have experienced revival.

Worship Scenes

The profound dedication of spiritual parenting bonded their spiritual children. Worship felt organic because it was family—living and interwoven. And anytime the family gathered, worship happened. In the beginning, these were small gatherings outside of the church. As our leaders united their families into clans, our gatherings grew. Some of them were huge and impressive—even to our detractors. But the energy came from thousands of smaller events where the only worship leader was God's Spirit, the only teacher was His Word, and the only congregation was a group of innocently expectant newborns praising God for the privilege of new birth.

That's what happens when leaders are courageous enough to risk grace. Grace unleashes God's creative power and worship erupts in new and fresh ways that thrill His heart.

Scene 1, Grape Soda and Oreos

The four girls at a Campus Crusade conference couldn't get enough of God that night in 1970, so Judy (when her name was still Judy Christman rather than Judy Underwood) and three of her friends were reading 1 Corinthians in their J. B. Phillips New Testaments. One of them said, "Guys, this just says that Jesus wants us to remember His death. There's nothing here about being in church. I want to remember Him right now, tonight."

"Me, too."

"But we don't have the stuff."

"What stuff?"

"You know, the crackers and the juice and those little cups."

"It doesn't say anything here about crackers, juice, and little cups. What do we have?"

"I just bought a grape soda. That's kind of like grape juice."

"Wait a minute. I think I have some Oreos in my suitcase. Yeah, here they are."

"Well, should we?"

"Sure, what does it matter to Jesus? We love Him and He loves us. We're thankful that He died for us and He wants to hear us say thanks. This is perfect."

Out into the cool mountain air of Arrowhead Springs, four high school girls reverently walked to the creek at the foot of the grounds. Kneeling beside the water, they remembered the death of their Savior who also made the moon and the stars above them. One passed an Oreo and said solemnly, "This is Christ's body." They prayed heartfelt prayers thanking Christ for every minute of His bodily agony they could remember from the Bible or imagine in their own minds. Another worshipper passed the grape soda, reminding the others, "This is Christ's blood."

Offerings of thanks for His blood exploded from hearts that knew the power of His redemption and the deliverance of His blood from the decadent culture of the sixties. Tears flowed as Judy and her friends sang the simple songs of the Jesus Movement.

"In the stars, His handiwork I see … He's everything to me."

"Amazing Grace" to the tune of "House of the Rising Sun."

They closed their creekside meeting by holding hands, staring into that brilliant California night, and singing, "We are one in the Spirit."

I am sure that on that same weekend, Christians gathered in great cathedrals, beautiful sanctuaries, and churches all over the world to celebrate Communion. I doubt that any meant more to the Lord Jesus than the remembrance offered by some of His newest followers that night. They were a group of naive girls on a moonlit night who didn't know any better than to remember Him in their simple way, through their simple elements, with their simple devotion.

Scene 2, The B.O. Trio

One of the biggest mistakes I ever made was learning to play the trumpet. I was really good, but what do you do with a trumpet?

"Hey guys, let's sing some songs around the campfire. Wait a minute, let me go back to my tent and pull out my trumpet. Okay, one, two, three, everybody together!"

I never regretted not learning to play the guitar more than when God asked me to lead a Young Life Club. Not only didn't I have a guitar, I didn't have a voice. I made up for it by being loud.

I could talk about Jesus and share from the few Bible passages I knew. That's how I got to be a part of the hottest act in the Jesus Movement in Bakersfield, the B.O. Trio. The first thing you need to know is that it was a "trio" of four. Jerry, the North High leader, and another guy could actually strum a guitar and carry a tune. Stan couldn't play or sing, but he had a star quality. He was the funniest person I ever met, in a Robin Williams way. Dressed like hillbillies, we would sing while Stan acted out our songs with outrageously hilarious and strange antics. Usually near the end of our gig, I would tell our spiritual stories in the context of a biblical truth and then give people an opportunity to receive Christ.

The forum didn't seem to matter. From the country club dining room helping Keith explain Young Life to potential supporters, to living rooms all over the city, to all-city Young Life events, there was never an empty chair when the B.O. Trio was on the bill. Short on talent but long on enthusiasm, we weren't very good. Really, we were lousy. So why did they come to hear us?

I can only think of one reason we played to "sold-out" audiences everywhere: *It was a revival.* God was doing a new thing and He could not be stopped. The stones weren't crying out. They didn't need to. Jesus was making a huge difference in so many lives that worship happened in the most unlikely places and ways. Even through a four-man trio, or should I say a four-boy trio, with no redeeming value except for redemption itself.

Scene 3, The Berkeley Critic

One evening I was leading club in a particular home for the first time when I noticed a girl about my age wearing a peasant dress. She sat in the kitchen and appeared to be scrutinizing my every word and move.

Minutes later, I knew she was trouble.

Finally she interrupted me with this question, "Before you start another song, can I ask you if you think people who have never heard what you're singing about will go to heaven?"

Oh crud, I thought, *I knew she didn't fit here. She's probably really smart.*

"Hi, I don't think I've seen you at club before or on campus," I stalled.

"No, I graduated three years ago. This is my house. I'm a student at Berkeley."

I knew she was smart. *Now I'm really in trouble. Lord, get me out of this,* I prayed under my breath.

I tried out all three defenses of Christianity that I kind of understood. She shot them all down in flames. Then she started talking about her religion—Buddhism—in eloquent and convincing sentences.

When I think about it now, I realize she manipulated the situation in an inappropriate way. Though it's sad that she didn't know Christ, coming to our Christian meeting with her Buddhist agenda made her an agent of the enemy. I couldn't articulate that back then, but intuitively I knew a lot was at stake.

I prayed again: *Come on Lord. This is turning into a disaster. I wouldn't blame any of these kids for telling me to shut up and asking her to go on. How am I going to explain to Keith and Ted how all the kids at Bakersfield High decided to become Buddhists in one night?*

As my credibility circled the drain, Jesse asked, "Hey lady, can I ask you something?"

Jesse may have been my last choice to speak up at that moment. Jesse had embarrassed himself and me numerous times when it didn't count. Overweight and unpopular, Jesse always hung around but never seemed to get it. He was truly a Christian; I had led him to Christ myself. But beyond that he just seemed hopeless, a constant distraction.

"I'd be most happy to entertain your question," the Berkeley critic said confidently in the way of debaters and lawyers.

Here we go. I better listen closely so I can jump in and rescue at least some of this mess.

"Who'd Buddha die for?" Jesse asked.

"What? Could you repeat the question, please?"

"Sure," Jesse said, looking her in the eye. "Who did Buddha die for?"

I smiled, the kids applauded. The Berkeley critic had met her match.

Jesse came from a broken home, had very few friends, and his only argument was the gospel of Jesus Christ. I'm sure that Jesus would have wanted us to be a lot more sensitive to this poor, lost victim of a cult. But you have to remember, we were pretty raw. From our perspective, all that mattered was that Jesus had carried the day through one of His least likely followers.

Oh, it was a worship service of the best kind. Planned by the Father, led by the Spirit, and made possible by the Son. The One who died for the world, even the fuzzy-haired-hippie-critic sitting in the kitchen in a peasant dress.

Incubating Revival

Paul told His spiritual children, "He who calls you is faithful, who also will do it" (1 Thess. 5:24). We're told that those who carefully perceive and courageously pursue Christ's leading experience His power. This is a revival promise with an implicit warning. It assures us that during times of daunting opportunity God is greater than our assignment. But it also reminds us of our personal limitations—without Him revival is ridiculous and impossible.

Where does revival begin? History teaches us to view revival as God's powerful response to the heartfelt prayers of His people. The Jesus Movement was God's answer to the mighty cry of visionary leaders whose hearts were breaking over what was happening to my generation. While others pointed out our evil, these visionary leaders begged God to deliver us from evil.

God didn't suddenly say, "Hey, must be time for revival. I haven't done that for a couple of centuries. Okay, angels, dive down there and start saving high school and college students in Southern California by the thousands. And then empower them to tell others. Huddle up. One, two, three … break."

Years before His Spirit brought born-again Bobby to my door and moved thousands of other "Bobbys" to the doors of their friends, the ones God would privilege to become our spiritual parents pleaded for our souls at His throne of grace.

When God moved three talented Christian couples to teach in different high schools in Bakersfield, Ted and Jo gathered them into their living room for prayer. Boldly, they divided the city into four areas and asked the Lord to give each couple the youth of one-quarter of the city for Christ!

The same Keith who sat on a curb and told me about Jesus was one of the men in that prayer group. I will never forget the first time Jo told me about that prayer meeting, years later when I was a student at Dallas Theological Seminary. As I bemoaned the sorry state of American culture with all my seminary logic and self-righteousness, she said, "Eddie, if you spent as much time praying for America as you do griping about it, maybe God would change something. How do you think you came to Christ? We prayed for the youth of Bakersfield for years before God began to move."

Revelation 5:8 describes the prayers of the saints as the incense of heaven. So before God unleashed His Spirit through thousands of lost souls like ours, the Teds and Jos of the sixties filled His golden bowls of incense with daring requests purified by selfless commitment to a lost generation.

And when our lost generation realized that we were found, His amazing grace spread through the many, causing thanksgiving to abound to His glory.

More and More Praise

Jesus told the first outsider He met about a time "when the true worshipers will worship the Father in spirit and truth; for the Father is seeking such to worship him" (John 4:23). He described something far beyond anything that promiscuous Samaritan woman could imagine.

With His sovereign eye, the Lord could see the great worship gatherings of the church age. He knew that the borders of Palestine could not contain His Father's glory. He knew that in just a few years He would die for the sin of the world and rise again. He knew that just before He ascended to His Father's right hand, He would promise power to His followers so that they would be His witnesses to the end of the earth (Acts 1:8).

He could see it all. Knowing His deep and personal love for every sinner, we can be sure that His heart thrilled at each picture of a new heart accepting His love—from every tribe, tongue, and nation. He could also see special times of widespread belief, when hearts caught fire and His kingdom spread rapidly. These would be the times that thrilled His heart most, times when His people took His Great Commission seriously, asked for His power openly, and trusted Him courageously.

His people would call these periods of history *revival*. But He has always known that this could be true of every generation. If only they would take Him at His word and risk all to follow Him.

The Jesus Movement became one of those times. We took Him at His word and risked all to follow Him. We came into the 1960s as rebels, rejecting all authority and every assumption of our parents. We were ready to stand against the world, insisting on our own way. Jesus stepped in, grabbed our hearts, and made us ready to embrace the world to show it His way.

More and more grace spread to more and more people, resulting in more and more praise.

My story began in Bakersfield, but similar stories began in cities and towns up and down the state of California. Hundreds of Keith Osborns told thousands of Ed Underwoods about the love of Jesus Christ. Hundreds of Teds and Jos parented thousands of Eds and Judys. And thousands of Eds and Judys decided to dedicate their lives to the Lord Jesus. Our faith in Him defined us; we would live for Him no matter the cost.

We left the 1960s as spiritual revolutionaries. God offered the world to us, and we wanted nothing more than to win it for Him. We would pollinate His churches with enthusiasm and faith, raise our families according to His truth, and have stories to tell our children about the power of the living God. We would never settle for anything less than eternal significance. The world would never be the same because we had believed; thousands, maybe millions, poised to change the world for Jesus Christ.

Then Why?

Those of you who weren't part of our revival must be wondering why there isn't more evidence of its impact today. You look around you at the irrelevant landscape of your region of Christianity and ask the same questions I've heard over the years:

- If, as you say, the 1960s ended with thousands, maybe millions, of excited, sold-out believers just beginning their adult lives, then why are there still so many unreached people in the world? You were on the road to revival, what happened? I would think that more of these Jesus Movement converts would have been so burdened by the gospel that they would have rushed to the mission field to tell others about Jesus.
- Like you, Ed, I didn't grow up in a Christian home. Your stories

of the people who spiritually parented you encourage me. And then I look around my church at those who may have been around in the 1960s—those in their fifties and early sixties. If so many of you were blessed by the open hearts and homes of your spiritual parents, then why can't I find anyone your age who will take an interest in me and my family?

- I've met a lot of Jesus Movement people. Seems to me like they're stuck in the 1960s. They're all about how great it was *then*—when they first believed. But when they talk about what they're energized over *today*, they seem more preoccupied with right-wing political and social issues—a road too narrow to bring revival. If they have been reading their Bibles for forty years, then why don't they also share Jesus' care for poor people, people dying from AIDS, oppressed people, hungry people, or at least starving babies?

- I came home from college stoked over the spiritual energy in the emerging church. When I tried to explain my excitement to our church leaders, some of the Jesus Movement people seemed to be the most threatened and resistant to new ideas. If reactionaries to the way the Spirit moved their generation toward revival hurt them, then why are they so closed to our ideas?

These are the same contradictions haunting many of us who were a part of the revival. There's no question that the impact of our revival on the church today was profound. Converts from the Jesus Movement flocked to Bible schools and seminaries in the 1970s and 1980s. We've launched or joined global missions and parachurch organizations, planted or served in leadership in churches around the world. We've built businesses dedicated to the Lord, and infused our trades and professions with Christian leaders and values. We're teaching in seminaries and Bible schools, writing books, teaching on Christian radio, leading Bible studies, and serving on boards of churches.

But now the Holy Spirit is stirring us and we're wondering why our revival didn't produce the massive global changes we had anticipated. Some of us are also asking why the passion of those revival years faded. Why did we settle for so much less?

In a sentence: If the Jesus Movement was a true revival, then why didn't it make a greater difference for Christ in the last forty years?

Why did the Jesus Movement quit moving?

My answer to those questions is in the next six chapters. I hope you'll read them, especially if you were a part of my revival, or you're a part of what may turn out to be the revival of that generation calling themselves the emerging church. For us, these chapters will be an opportunity for repentance—to turn back to Christ, away from the enemy's lies that sidetracked our revival. For you, the pages ahead will be a warning to keep you on track—you don't have to learn your lessons in the same hard way we did. You can learn from our mistakes.

While our revival was rocking and rolling, our enemy was plotting its demise. He didn't have to think of anything new. Satan simply rolled out the same old lies he has used to neutralize every revival since the first one exploded from the streets of Jerusalem to the end of the earth.

If we had read our New Testament more closely, we might have resisted his tactics. But like the Christians of the first century, we didn't heed the warnings of Christ and His apostles.

We lost the wildness of our new birth and got sidetracked by six destructive lies.

Part Two

A Revolution Stalls

Six Lies We Believed

Chapter 4

More Is Better

Have you ever—in reading your Bible alone or sitting on a rock above a mountain meadow or standing with your hands held high in worship—suddenly wanted more of God? You know that your existing depth of commitment will never again satisfy you or Him. It's a stirring moment of dedication. You tell Him there is nothing you wouldn't do for Him.

This is a decision Paul offers to every believer in his letter to the Romans. In light of God's mercies (chapters 1—11), give Him your life—dedicate your life to Him (Rom. 12:1–2). Don't hold anything back, make your life all about Christ! It's a resolution that sets the trajectory of our lives toward serving Him because we are grateful. It's a choice that directs us to a maturity that maximizes our experience of new life in Christ.

If you know that feeling, then you know how we felt when we stepped *out* of the 1960s and moved into the rest of our lives. We were Romans 12:1–2 believers who had put our lives on the line for Christ—our careers, our relationships, our future families, *everything*.

If you understand what we told God, then you might be wondering about something. What could possibly have sidetracked these Christians? They had opened their lives to all that the Lord had for them. What lie could possibly tame their wild hearts?

If you've made that decision yourself—that Romans 12:1–2 dedication to Christ in response to His mercies—you may be questioning whether we were as dedicated as I've described. *Surely,* you might think, *if these Jesus people were as authentic in their allegiance to Christ as I am, they would still be turning the world upside down for Jesus. The devil may have sidetracked them, but not me, not my friends. We're different. Our devotion is real.*

What if I were to tell you that Satan, in his evil subtlety, has devised a heresy tailor-made for Christians just like we were then and just like you are now? I'm here to tell you, my friend, that his infernal majesty has developed a strategy that is especially attractive to those he fears the most—the sold-out, give-me-everything-you-got-Lord-and-don't-hold-anything-back worshipper. His tactics are extremely effective because they appeal to what you were feeling when you surrendered Jesus your life in this way—*your desire for more.*

It's not the prospect of less that derails the dedicated; it's the yearning for more.

Our Notebook's Bigger Than Your Notebook

The first "more" I remember being offered was more Bible. Phil had met some Christians enamored with a pastor from Texas, a military man with a reputation for profound teaching. Phil had been listening to this man on reel-to-reel tapes.

"Guys, I've discovered more from these tapes in two months than most Christians learn in a lifetime," he said.

We all wanted more, so we encouraged him to go on.

Stacked in front of Phil on the table were four huge binders bulging with notes he had taken from these teaching tapes. He told us about this colonel everyone called a "pastor-teacher," and we had to admit that his resume was impressive. As far as we could tell from Phil's introduction, this pastor-teacher was the only one who knew Greek and Hebrew well enough to actually teach the stuff in Phil's notebook.

Phil opened one of his notebooks to a page with a lot of neat diagrams and what looked like Greek words and he asked us this question, "Why did God create man?"

We nervously looked at the intimidating stack of notebooks and thought together, *Crud, what do we know? We don't even have a notebook.* But we gave it our best shot.

"Because He loves us?"

Phil rolled his eyes and smiled. "No, you're not thinking big enough."

"To have fellowship with us?"

Phil looked at his notebook and sighed, "Does God need us? He's a perfect God. Why does a perfect God need fellowship? Try to think back in the Bible, way back, all the way to Genesis."

I remember my exact thought. *Genesis? Genesis? You mean the first book that I've never read? The book in the Old Testament that I hardly ever read? Man, this is really deep!*

Someone braver than I offered, "Maybe to reveal His glory?"

"No, no, no." Phil looked around the table, put his finger on a place in his notebook, and said, "God created man to solve the angelic conflict."

"Wow, I never heard that before," someone said for all of us.

As Phil read through his notes on the angels and creation and God, he connected verses from books of the Bible I hadn't ever opened. It was amazing, impressive, enticing.

Then he turned on his massive new reel-to-reel tape recorder and we heard this man say authoritatively in one of the deepest voices ever, and in his personal translation from the Greek text, "All Scripture is God-breathed and is profitable for doctrine, reproof, correction, for instruction in righteousness that the man of God may be perfect, thoroughly furnished unto all good works. Study to show thyself approved unto God, a workman that needeth not to be ashamed, rightly dividing the word of truth" (2 Tim. 2:15; 3:16–17).

Usually we didn't like the King James English, but this was different. This guy was deep.

I was hooked. And so were many others from our close group of Christian friends. We pooled our resources, bought a few expensive reel-to-reel tape recorders, got on this pastor-teacher's mailing list, and spent hours listening to his teaching, frantically filling up our own notebooks.

We learned the Greek alphabet so that we could write down Greek words in our notebooks. Some of us took Greek at our secular universities. We learned an entire new vocabulary that only "tapers" understood and felt sorry for our shallow friends who didn't care enough about Bible doctrine to fill their notebooks.

Studying God's written Word consumed us. What we failed to notice, as the devil smiled, was that we were ignoring the living Word, the One who washed us from our sin in His own blood, the One who made Moses, Isaiah, and Paul and inspired them to write down the words we were poring over.

His name is Jesus. Tragically, the more we directed our laser focus on His Word, the less we saw of Him.

We Don't More Than You Don't

One morning, at a weekly Bible study, one of the guys told the waitress, "No bacon for me. I'll just have eggs and toast." By the time she came around the table to me, there were only two of us asking for the usual version of pork we had been happily eating for months.

"What's the deal? You guys on a diet or something?"

Silence, the kind that's uncomfortable when you have to make eye contact.

"No, we've just decided not to eat anything the Bible calls unclean."

"You mean like in the Old Testament Law? Wasn't that only for the Jews? I've never heard of Christians not eating pork. Only Jews and Muslims. Or was it Mormons? No, I'm sure, it was Muslims. Next thing you know, you're going to start keeping the Sabbath!"

"We went to a Shabbat service last Friday. It started at eighteen minutes before sundown and we lit two candles, read the Old Testament, and medi- tated. We decided not to do any work until we saw three stars on Saturday evening. My dad was furious when I wouldn't mow the lawn. But you know my dad, he's not saved and doesn't understand."

I couldn't take it anymore. "Well, I don't understand either. What are you talking about? This is nuts. We're Christians, New Testament people. What else don't you do? Do you come to church anymore, or have you found a synagogue?"

It was the last time we met for that Bible study, but it wasn't the first time a group among us would define themselves by the rules they kept.

This group decided to follow the Old Testament Law to be holy and judged the rest of us who didn't. Another faction took another look at the Protestant rules we had rejected and liked what they saw. They stopped going to dances and told us it was wrong to listen to the Rolling Stones but that the Beach Boys were still okay.

Those of us filling up our notebooks quoted verses from Galatians and Romans to them and met together to gripe about these "legalists." They quoted verses from James and Hebrews back to us and told us they couldn't hang around with us anymore because we were too "worldly."

Defending our side preoccupied us. The devil winked at his demons and nodded approvingly as our community divided into warring factions of rule-keepers and grace-defenders. And a tear dropped down the cheek of the One who offered us grace and promised to come to rule and reign. The debate over rules was ignoring the ruler.

His name is Jesus. Tragically, the more we argued about His grace, the less we thought about the grace-giver.

We Got the Power

"I just believe what I read in the Bible, don't you?"

With that question, a friend home for Christmas from Chico State University in Northern California answered my challenge.

"People say that you're a Holy Roller now, that you're speaking in tongues and hearing God's voice out loud," I said.

The name-calling was just beginning to divide us between the haves and the have-nots, the yes-we-dos and the no-you-don'ts. Claims and counterclaims deepened the rift.

"We're Spirit-filled."

"Oh, and we don't have the Holy Spirit?"

"I go to a full-gospel church," he said.

"What kind of a church do you call mine, half-gospel church?" I replied. "Which half of the gospel do you think we're missing? Our leaders went to seminary and Bible school. They know Greek and theology. That's why they don't believe that these gifts you claim are still around today. Nobody who knows anything agrees with you, except Pentecostals from the Ozarks."

"We still believe in the power of God. Show me the verse that proves that tongues and healing and prophecy suddenly stopped. You can't find it, can you? That's because it's not there. You care more about what people think of you than you care about experiencing God's power. While you're studying your theology we're getting things done. All I know is what I've felt. It's real and you can't tell me it isn't."

We piled up books and collected teachers who agreed with our side and tried to persuade the other side. It became a litmus test for fellowship. "Do you believe in the gift of tongues? How about the filling of the Spirit? What does that mean to you?"

The answers to those questions determined if you were with us or against us. Most of the pro-tongues, pro-miracle crowd gravitated toward groups like Teen Challenge, a Jesus Movement outreach to the drug culture started by a young Pentecostal preacher named David Wilkerson, and became charismatic evangelicals. The anti-tongues contingent settled into churches and movements led by graduates of places like Moody Bible Institute, Dallas Theological Seminary, and Biola University, and we called ourselves conservative evangelicals.

Only in the last ten years have some of us from both sides repented of our divisive and narrow behaviors and conversations. The healing has begun, but it's been forty years! Four decades of allowing those on the fringe of both circles to define us by what we were against rather than what we were for.

Who could envision Jesus' precious promise of a Comforter becoming so divisive? Only the accuser of the brethren, the divider of God's people, saw it coming and licked his evil lips, anticipating and even plotting the fight. The holy lips of the One seated at the right hand of the Father quivered with grief. His people divided over their only source of strength and it broke His heart.

His name is Jesus. Tragically, our preoccupation with the limits of His Spirit's work among us caused us to ignore Him.

To Choose or Not to Choose

Something had changed in the way some of our Young Life leaders told people about Jesus, but I couldn't explain it. We had all worked together for over two years and were so familiar with one another's style that we could almost finish each other's sentences.

It was more than the words; it was the passion. Before the change, Paul's expression of his own style to the Corinthians described our delivery: "Now then, we are ambassadors for Christ, as though God were pleading through us: we implore you on Christ's behalf, be reconciled to God" (2 Cor. 5:20). Now some of us seemed to be merely mouthing the words. "Believe on the Lord Jesus Christ, and you will be saved" (Acts 16:31).

They quit using anecdotes from real life and seldom asked new Christians to tell their stories. Their delivery became monotonous, reading the good news about how to get to heaven as if they were reading the instructions on how to build a model airplane to hobbyists. Except with less enthusiasm!

It was a "take Jesus or leave Him, it's up to you" approach. Technically, they still said the words of Jesus' ambassadors, but there was no pleading, no imploring on His behalf to be reconciled to God.

By the time I caught on, about half of our team had embraced a theology that explained their robotic style—they had become Calvinists. Now that I understand Calvinism better, I realize that they really didn't understand Calvin's teaching at all. What they had actually become were spiritual determinists who thought that people were divided between the elect and the nonelect, and God would see to it that the elect would believe. There was no mystery to God anymore, no reason to exhort or implore, not even much reason to try to avoid sin. If God willed it, it would happen; if it happened, it was God's will.

As young and restless believers often do, they pushed it to the extreme. I asked one of them why he even told people about the Lord anymore and he said with a super-holy smile that made me crazy, "I just like to see the look on their face when they realize they're elect."

The war was on. We started throwing around words and theological terms we could barely pronounce, let alone explain.

"What you really mean is you're a Presbyterian. And I'm not a Calvinist. I'm a dispensationalist, like my pastor, Ted Stone, and J. Vernon McGee, and Hal Lindsey, and all the other teachers who went to Dallas Seminary!"

"You don't even know what you're saying. For hundreds of years there wasn't any such thing as a dispensationalist. That's all new, thought up by a guy named Darby. What you really are is a Plymouth Brethren."

"How can I be a Plymouth Brethren? I don't even know what that is. Besides, I don't care about church history. All I care about is the Bible."

"Oh yeah, you think I don't care about the Bible? Well, what about Luther and Calvin and a lot of other leaders of the church from way, way back? It's church history and it happened when people were reading their Bibles. You're an Arminian, that's what you are! You think people can lose their salvation."

"I do not. What did you call me?"

Our first lessons in theology showed how the edges of theological systems chafe at one another like seismic plates. Wicked waves of energy emanate from the epicenters of division in ways that exalt the arrogance of man and play right into the devil's "divide and conquer" strategy. And the One who warned His people that divided kingdoms cannot stand and commanded them to love one another drops His head in despair.

His name is Jesus. Tragically, in pushing forward our varied theologies, we pushed Jesus to the side.

The New More Is the Old Less

As I mentioned earlier, the New Testament Christians who remind me most of the Jesus Movement generation are the churches of the Lycus Valley. Like us, they were a product of revival—everyone in the Roman province of Asia had heard about Jesus (Acts 19:10). Paul honors these three congregations

(Colossae, Hierapolis, and Laodicea) by attributing to them his triad of success (faith, hope, and love) in the opening sentences of his letter to them (Col. 1:3–5). This means they had reached a level of maturity matched only by the church at Thessalonica (1 Thess. 1:3).

With a history like this, you would expect to see Satan's strategy to derail the dedicated by offering them more. Paul wrote to them because they were in danger of losing their momentum, stalling the revival, and becoming sidetracked. The devil had planted false teachers who claimed a superior spirituality and seemed to offer so much more. Combining elements of Jewish legalism and Greek mysticism, they were enticing the believers with promises of *more*.

It's not hard to reconstruct their self-important spiritual theories. Their arguments had great philosophical appeal (Col. 2:8), emphasizing "a higher knowledge" known only to the initiated. They encouraged new believers to seek help from angels and were more than willing to depict their personal dreams and visions (Col. 2:18). Boasting of their ability to keep religious rules and deny their physical appetites (Col. 2:20–23), they impressed some and intimidated others.

As easy as it is to reconstruct their lies, it's even easier to identify the danger. The *more* they were offering was a *more* no believer should desire. It is a *more* that takes you and me beyond the One who is our all in all—His name is Jesus. No book of the New Testament exalts the Son of God more than Colossians. He is the deliverer of His people (Col. 1:13–14), the Lord of Creation, and Lord of the Church (Col. 1:15–20). His presence in us is our only hope of glory (Col. 1:27), therefore we preach only Him (Col. 1:28), and strive to please only Him (Col. 1:29).

The heartbreak of the Colossian heresies is that they appeal only to those who want more. The masses of Christians mucking along in the mediocrity of settling for the "less" this world offers will never be taken in. It's all they can do to give up three Sundays a month and a twenty-dollar bill every once in a while for Jesus. The devil has already neutralized them by getting them into some secret sin pattern, or materialism, or a bowling league, or the jazz music subculture. Something, anything, is already more important to them than Jesus. They're not looking for more; they're looking for less.

But disciples of Christ with *revival* in their wild hearts are looking for more. And the devil is right there to offer us more—more Bible, more rules, more experiences, more theology, more of anything *except Jesus.*

As I read Colossians today, I only wish someone would have told me then what I'm telling you now: Friend, any *more* that takes you beyond Christ is taking you to a place you do not want to go. *More is not always better; Christ is enough!*

Here We Go Again

Every year I return to one of my favorite places to teach the Bible: Ecola Bible School in Cannon Beach, Oregon. Years ago the school's director, David Duff, and I agreed that I would dedicate my week with the students to the book of Colossians.

Why? Because the devil's still trafficking the same old lies. Ecola students remind me of us back then—young, eager, and sold-out for God. Like us, all they want to do is make a difference for Christ, to see their lives count eternally. They wouldn't be there dedicating a year of their lives to studying the Bible and growing spiritually if they weren't serious Christians.

Every year David tells me again how much this particular class needs the message of Colossians. They need to hear that *more* is not always better; *that Christ is enough.* Amazingly, for over fifteen years, I've discovered some version of the more-is-better lie circulating among the students:

- A student handed out books and tapes promising "more faith" as the secret to success in the Christian life. The faith, of course, is not in Christ, but in "faith." The class began to divide between those who loved the message and those who mistrusted it. By the end of my week, the "more faith" group reported to the staff that I was singling them out, though I hadn't mentioned their particular more-is-better lie, which says we need more of faith, but less of Jesus.

- One girl marched up to the podium after the warnings against legalism in our session on Colossians 2. "I don't think Dave should have told you about me. He had no right!" she said. I explained that I hadn't even seen Dave yet. After a few questions, I discovered that her boyfriend was part of a "messianic church" that believed in "following the Law and keeping the Sabbath." It upset her when I asked her how a church could be messianic when it was doing exactly what the Messiah and His apostles said we shouldn't do by following the Law to become righteous. "Wouldn't you have to agree that since you've become so preoccupied with following the Law, you have been thinking less and less of Jesus?" She didn't answer.

- The talented worship leader asked me if I thought he was into a more-is-better problem. "I feel like I can talk to you about it because you seem to get what emergent worship is all about." I assured him that I was probably too old to "get it." But, I said, my Jesus Movement memories taught me that when I hit my fifties, I had better be open to music and worship I didn't understand because that was probably where the Holy Spirit was moving. "But tell me," I asked him, "why do you think you have a problem? You seem genuinely worshipful and authentic in your words in the times I've seen you. It moved me deeply." Holding back the tears, he said, "Since I've gotten into emergent worship, it's all I think about. When you asked, 'What in your life right now, no matter how spiritual, no matter how important to your ministry, no matter how much other Christians are telling you how great this is, what is becoming more important than the Lord Jesus?' I knew exactly how the Lord answered that for me. We are getting way more into worship than we are into Jesus."

My subject matter hasn't changed for fifteen years—a little book in the New Testament that lifts up the Lord Jesus like no other. Neither has its effectiveness. The best way to expose the more-is-better lies some believe is to exalt Christ. That's what Paul does.

- He is the image of the invisible God. (Col. 1:15)
- For it pleased the Father that in Him all the fullness should dwell. (Col. 1:19)
- Christ in you, the hope of glory. (Col. 1:27)
- For in Him dwells all the fullness of the Godhead bodily; and you are complete in Him, who is the head of all principality and power. (Col. 2:9–10)

My passion for this little book grows stronger every year. When I look into the eager faces of these Ecola students so in love with the Lord Jesus and impatient to change their world for Him, I remember the faces of many of my friends, then think about their lives today and cry.

Living Less with More

He was one of our best teachers. Extremely original and entertaining, he captivated audiences large and small with incredible insights from God's Word. He talked about Jesus constantly and we all wanted to know what he thought about this biblical passage or that practical Christian life issue.

I especially remember his personal devotion to anyone interested in Christ. When I bought my *Scofield Reference Bible*—the study Bible of the Jesus Movement—he skipped classes all day to highlight the verses referred to by the study notes on every page because, "Sometimes it's hard to find the verses the notes go with," he said.

She would have won the "most enthusiastic for Jesus" trophy for our group. During a week at Woodleaf, she was so enamored with the hymn "Stand Up, Stand Up for Jesus" that the speaker couldn't state two sentences without prompting her to once again stand and begin singing, "Stand up, stand up for Jesus, ye soldiers of the cross," until everyone in the room stood with her. It was a little annoying about the hundredth time, but we tolerated it because we knew she meant it.

While they were falling in love, he started listening to the military pastor-teacher's tapes I described earlier. During their engagement, he ordered her to submit to his authority by listening to at least two hours of "Bible doctrine" every day. All they talked about was this colonel guy and his teaching and the need for more—more Bible, more doctrine, more teaching, *more, more, more*. After they married, they moved to Texas to be a part of this man's church.

But more of this man's teaching meant far less of Christ, and somewhere along the way, they fell out of love with Jesus and one another. He calls me every few years to tell me about the kids, and how in spite of the divorce and her multiple marriages, he still loves her. She runs a small business in a resort town, but we don't think she goes to church anymore.

Satan never said, "Hey, you two, I've got an idea. Why don't you get weird and become so devoted to a man's teaching of the Bible that you forget the most important person in the Bible and begin to ignore one another until, after a few years, you can get a divorce and ruin your family?"

The devil knew they would never say yes to that! So, he just offered them a little *more*.

He was our most gifted and dedicated leader. His ministry at one of our high schools was solid and Keith often asked him to take more responsibility than the rest of us. Successful on every level—studies, athletics, socially—we all knew that when he went away to college, he would make something of himself.

Attracted to his strength—spiritual, mental, emotional, and physical—she joined him in his campus ministry at college. A friend invited both of them to a meeting of Christians who were really into the Holy Spirit. They met believers unlike any they had ever known. There was no denying that these people had something they lacked.

As they wrapped up their undergrad courses and he moved toward graduate school, they couldn't get enough of these meetings led by men telling them they needed *more*—more of the Spirit, more power, more deliverance. Old friends from Bakersfield would return from visits disturbed by their bizarre behaviors. "He can't seem to connect two thoughts anymore. They go to a little church ruled by a man who's freaky weird. She's like a zombie—vacant eyes, no smile. They don't even seem like the same people."

More and more power meant less and less of Jesus. By the time he finished his training and returned to Bakersfield as a professional, the flame for Jesus had left their hearts. Or should I say "they flamed out"? I've seen him a few times since. My parents were his clients and he served them well. But he never talks about Jesus. I asked him once if he ever heard from Keith. "No," he said distractedly, "not for years." I told him I had stayed in touch with the man who had led us to Christ and trained us in His way, and asked him if he wanted Keith's phone number. He looked up briefly and said, "No, not really."

Satan never said, "I think you need to hear about a type of power that will wow you and cause you to think about nothing else. You're going to want this power so much that you'll lose contact with all of your Christian friends and join an obscure church run by a threatened little dictator.

Finally, you will just give up and decide to live your life on your own. You won't raise your children in the church, and decades from now, you won't even care about your spiritual mentor. How about that?"

The devil knew they were much too levelheaded to swallow that! So instead he just offered them a little *more*.

Sidetracked by More?

Wishing for less didn't sidetrack our hearts and stall our momentum. Rather, our failure to choose the God-given longing for more of Jesus over our flesh-driven desire for counterfeit *mores* tamed us. The more we reached for, the less we found.

I hope you're not underestimating the power of these more-is-better lies in your own life. In chapter 10, "Our Only Hope, Our Only Hero," we will take a more in-depth look at the early church's majestic exaltation of our Lord Jesus.

But I can't wait until then to ask you this question:

Are you distracted?

Before you assume that you don't have a more-is-better spiritual problem, ask God what He thinks. None of us are immune. I know. Over the years, God's Spirit has reprimanded me numerous times for pursuing a more-is-better lie.

How would you respond to the same challenge that brought repentance to the young worship leader's heart: *What in your life right now, no matter how spiritual, no matter how important to your ministry, no matter how much other Christians are telling you how great this is, what is becoming more important than the Lord Jesus?*

How did God answer you? Is it your family? Your ministry? His Spirit? His Bible? Your church? Your Christian friends? Your marriage? Your children? Your concern for the poor? Your concern for the planet? Your concern for the unborn? Your devotion to our country? Your diet? Your dedication to spiritual disciplines?

Whatever *it* is, you can start over with the same prayer of repentance I say when I know something is replacing Jesus as the object of my worship:

> Father, I come to You now in deep repentance. I can't believe that I let Satan draw me into this. But there's no denying it. This has become more important to me than Your Son, Jesus. I confess my sin; I have pursued more instead of pursuing more of Jesus. Thank You, Father, for this new beginning. Rekindle my love for Jesus and my devotion to Him. Keep exposing the danger of this lie as I tell You now, I'm walking away from that and toward Jesus. In His precious and majestic name, amen.

The more-is-better lies divided the Jesus Movement and neutralized some of our most gifted leaders. Many have never recovered; others continue to pursue the empty promises of the enemy.

Because of the dedicated leaders I introduced in chapter 3 and the layered discipleship that characterized our revival, most of us went on with our Christian lives. Our enthusiasm for Christ and commitment to His teachings made us want to go to church. When they invited us to join them and settle in, we had no idea what some of them were truly asking.

Chapter 5

"Churchianity" Is Enough

The entire history of God's people is a story of one failure after another. The "desire" was always there, at least a little, but the "ability" wasn't enough to sustain the good intentions of the best of followers, including Israel's most renowned leader, King David. When Israel's deliverer came, He began to hint of a new and different way. They rejected Him. But Israel's official denunciation of Messiah opened a new door of wonder to the majestic plan of God. He had always planned to bless the nations through a redeemed people in whom His Spirit would dwell. Nothing like this had ever existed before.

Suddenly, Christ's church was born in Jerusalem, and for the first time in history, God's people could glorify Him in ways Israel had never dreamed. Jesus and His apostles spoke of the church in amazing words and promises:

- "The mystery of Christ" making "the unsearchable riches of Christ" available to all peoples (Eph. 3:1–13).
- "The body of Christ" uniting God's people by His Spirit (Eph. 4:1–12) under His headship (Col. 1:18).
- Christ's bride, His "glorious church" whom He "nourishes and cherishes" (Eph. 5:24–33).

As all of this began to hit our newly transformed hearts, we marveled at the family to which God had called us. Our mentors pointed to verses in the New Testament and told us, "You need to become a part of a church."

They were correct in telling us this, but they also should have warned us. Most of the existing church cultures we walked into had reverted back to the "want to" hopelessness and irrelevancy of the Pharisees. As soon as we started talking in our "able to" sentences and radical acceptance of what the Bible taught about the church, they tried to capture our energy and use it for their own purposes.

Oh, they wanted us in their churches … if we would knuckle under and settle for their watered-down version of Christianity. It was like they had heard a call of God to shape us up, to make us more presentable, to housebreak us so we looked more starchy, snobby, and superfluous.

The Pastor's Chair and a Baby's Bite

For Judy and me, like most Jesus Movement converts, the single most disappointing and discouraging aspect of our maturing walk with Christ was trying to assimilate into the existing church culture. Deep down we knew that most churches and their leaders didn't want us. They only wanted to capture and control our energy and commitment to the Lord Jesus and use it to their own ends. We resisted their efforts to housebreak us—and the incarcerating pressure to become good little church members.

Life ripped us from the protective love of Ted and Jo Stone and the nurturing community of Fruitvale Community Church when we moved to Santa Barbara with our baby, Aimee, to attend the University of California at Santa Barbara. Initially the adventure of finding a new church home seemed exciting. We asked every Christian we met, "Tell me about your church."

What an education we received! A few minutes in the pew usually convinced us that this church just wasn't for us. If the church was somewhat alive and the people a little friendly, the pastor's sermon convinced us we couldn't go there. I remember thinking how weird it felt to go to church, listen to a sermon, and never open my Bible.

Finally, we settled on a newer church near the university campus. It had a more Midwesterny-religious-stiffness feel than we were used to, but the pastor taught from the Bible, and the people seemed involved. And Jesus did tell us to go to church.

One afternoon the pastor dropped by our home. He looked way out of place walking through the married-student housing complex of UC Santa Barbara in a suit and tie in 1974, but he seemed like a nice guy. We visited for a while and then I asked him, "Do you do discipleship?"

"What do you mean by 'discipleship'?" he replied.

"You know, getting together with younger Christians like me to teach us how to walk with Christ. Our pastor in Bakersfield met with a few of us every week. I was just wondering if I could get into one of your discipleship groups."

"We have Sunday evening services and a midweek prayer meeting. Those are the meetings for serious people," he said.

"Oh, I know. We went to Sunday evening services at our last church. I can't come Wednesday nights because I work."

It seemed odd that I would have to explain the concept of discipleship to a pastor who had been to seminary.

"I'm meeting with another young man from the church next Tuesday," the pastor said. "We're going to make some plans for the church. Would you like to join us? It would give you an opportunity to meet someone your age."

What I really wanted to do was meet with a shepherd and a few other guys to talk about our lives and how Jesus could make a difference in us, and then pray together. Judy and I were going through some huge changes— new baby, new city, new demands of trying to balance university studies and a full-time job. But at least it was a start.

On the day we met, I felt nervous. I still didn't know the Bible as well as most church people who grew up in Sunday school listening to sermons. I didn't want to hold the other guy back from whatever lifelong Christians do when they meet with their pastor. A few minutes into the meeting, though, and I knew I didn't have to worry about that.

Instead of a Bible, they were studying the phone book. "Hi Ed, come on in and take a seat. We're planning our day next week."

After I shook hands with the other guy, the pastor explained. "I need a chair for my office. Next week we'll meet early in the morning and drive around the area so I can test them out. I've circled the places in red that I'm interested in. If you could call these three and ask them …"

He proceeded with an in-depth narrative on the qualities he was looking for in a chair, his back problems and special needs, the type of leather he preferred, how it should tilt and twirl, the height of his desk, even different color options.

The more he talked, the less I listened. Scenes from Ted's office flashed through my mind and filled my heart with longing: I recalled Phil, Bobby, and me sitting around with Bibles open asking Ted what this word meant, why Paul said this, or why Jesus did that. And then Ted took us from the meaning of the text to its meaning for our lives.

"So, Ed, how do you think this should make a difference in the way you express your love to Judy? Do you feel you're doing this well? What could you do better? When you go home, ask her how she feels about this. Next week, we'll look at the next chapter and talk about the assignments I just gave you men. Now, how can I pray for you?"

To tell you the truth, I had never noticed Ted's chair.

The next Sunday Judy went to pick up Aimee in the nursery after church. On the drive home, I knew something was wrong. "What's the matter, honey? Did I do something?"

"No, it's just that …" She burst into tears. "I thought we were good parents. We're trying to raise a Christian family. I know she's not a perfect child, but you'd think they would consider how young she is. She's really only a baby."

When we got home and Judy calmed down, she explained that our Aimee had bitten one of the other children in the nursery. This particular child happened to belong to someone important. The pastor's wife scolded Judy in front of everyone, "You should teach your child better manners."

"Better manners?" I was incredulous. "She's only two. Two-year-olds bite. I mean, I want to know if she's biting, but this woman's acting like something's wrong with us, with our little girl." As Judy lay crying on the bed, the phone rang. It was the pastor's wife. "I want you to call the mother of the child your daughter bit and ask her to forgive you."

The contrast was just too great. Where was the equipping? Where was the love? The grace? We couldn't take it anymore. We never went back to church during our university years.

A lot of our friends from the Jesus Movement never returned. Stories just like ours met them over and over again. Finally, they just gave up.

If you're reading these paragraphs thinking that some of this had to do with our rebellious sixties mind-set, you're correct. If you're also thinking that our decisions to abandon church weren't biblical, you're right again.

I'll be honest about our attitude toward the problem: Our defiance intensified our reaction. But you have to admit to the problem: Our expectations weren't unrealistic, they were biblical!

Theophil–who?

Before you get all "you need to be more dedicated to the local church" on me, I'd like to make two points—the first is personal, the second is logical.

I don't think I could be more committed to the local church. For over two decades, the local church has been our life, and I now pastor one of the most historic churches in America. Some of the most influential pastors in modern history have led Church of the Open Door since its birth in 1915. Our missionaries have served around the world, and our partnership with Biola University has launched worldwide ministries. I know what it's like to try to do authentic New Testament ministry in spite of all the administrative necessities, expectations of Christians, and underappreciated demands on a church staff. Judy and I know that we live in the glass house, the perfect target for stone-throwers.

But our love for the local church and appreciation of Christ's love for His bride shouldn't lead us to blindly defend her as codependent guardians. Our passion for the beauty of His bride should cause us to ask hard questions. And the first I would like to ask is this: *What would Theophilus think if he showed up at your church?*

You probably don't know anyone named Theophilus, but Luke did. The book of Acts is the second of a two-volume history written to Theophilus (the book of Luke being the first), that he "may know the certainty of those things in which you were instructed" (Luke 1:4). All we know from this verse and Acts 1:1–3 is that Luke seemed to know the "most excellent" Theophilus, and there was a need to recount to him the history of the church up to that point.

I picture Luke's friend eagerly opening the scroll of his sequel to the life of Christ, and his eyes widening as he begins to grasp the magnitude of what his faith in Christ has made him a part of. The words blur the first time through as he pictures the scenes in his mind.

Standing to stretch, Theophilus pours a glass of wine, sits back down, and reads it again … slowly. As he reads, Theophilus thinks of his friend:

Luke wants to make sure that I understand the enormity of what the Lord is doing through His church. Nothing can stop the people of God. Against all odds, with every social, political, and military power in the world arrayed against her, the gospel will move forward through the apostles and their disciples. When Christ comes again to establish His kingdom, the church, redeemed people from every nation will inherit that kingdom with Him!

Let's get back to our mutual love for the bride of Christ. The question isn't what we think of our church. The question is, "What does Christ think of our church?" And one of the best ways I know to logically objectify that question is to picture Theophilus showing up and imagining what he would say.

I can tell you what he wouldn't say: "Oh, I can't wait to spend an entire day looking for the pastor's new chair, and I agree with this new policy: 'No biters allowed in our nursery!'"

Acts exalts God's glorious plan to populate His kingdom with believers from every tribe, tongue, and nation. With an assignment that big, we really don't have time for most or all of the other stuff. I believe Theophilus would stand up in a lot of our churches today and say, "What's going on here? This is the church of the living God, the bride of Christ! Don't settle for anything less than what my friend Luke wrote about in his book!"

Our revival-experienced and Spirit-led hearts refused to settle for less, and neither should yours. Too much is at stake.

- "No, our staff doesn't actually meet with people one-on-one or even in small groups to teach the Bible and how to walk with

Christ. We put together great programs that a lot of people come to. It may not be the type of mentoring you're used to, but it's effective. It's just our way of doing discipleship."

- "Why are you always asking about 'leading people to Christ'? If they're truly seeking God, He'll find a way to get the gospel to them. And if one of our members actually knew a non-Christian, they'd invite them to our classes on salvation. It's our way of doing evangelism."

- "We're not that interested in new believers actually coming to our church. They probably wouldn't understand a lot of what we do, and we don't feel like we should have to make a lot of changes just to make them happy. But once a year, we call in an evangelist. He's real fiery and that's when some of our members invite unsaved people to church. It goes on every night for a week and we put signs outside and everything. He always has an altar call at the end. Now that's a revival!"

No, it's not. Neither does a program equate to discipleship or a theological understanding of salvation count as evangelism.

And if you've ever experienced genuine New Testament revival, you already know this. But you might be afraid to say so. I used to have that problem, and it restrained my passion for revival again and again.

Respected church leaders and esteemed Bible teachers would tell me that my dissatisfaction with the status quo was wrong and that I expected too much. I knew I wanted to lead a church that looked more like what Luke described in Acts. That vision drove me! But in order to pursue that vision, I would have to stand against an entire culture of evangelical Christianity and some powerful leaders within my own church. That petrified me!

I'd tell myself they were right, that I should stop pushing for change. One of my seminary professors' sentences would come to mind, "Fly low, go slow, don't blow." And another week of mediocrity added up to another month, another year.

It took a bout with lymphoma to shake me awake and stir my wild soul!

As my revival heart woke up, I knew I wanted to feel the fresh wind of New Testament Christianity in my face again. I could almost hear the revival fires roaring all around me and taste the joy only those with a front-row seat to God's power know.

It was only then that I realized how dangerously near to being house-broken I really was.

Decently and in Order

Dysfunctional families are all about control—the type that ignores, denies, or hides family secrets. There may be an abusive authority figure, but every member decides that the only option is to keep the secret at all costs. Even when their heart cries out for what could be, fear forces them to settle.

Communication is coded because truth would expose the lie. "Daddy's not feeling too good this morning" means "Daddy has a hangover." Learning this code is required of all who want to enter the dysfunctional family by friendship or marriage. After a few generations, the codes become the "truth" that orders the relationships and expectations of the family.

Like new in-laws flooding into a family culture, the young adults of the Jesus Movement revival collided with the spiritual families of American churches. When our enthusiasm over the raw power of God and His great plan to reach the world threatened the generational lies of dysfunctional churches, they controlled us by speaking a most effective code handed down by ineffectual generations of churchgoers. It was a code based on carefully selected Scriptures.

One of the most effective was 1 Corinthians 14:40: "Let all things be done decently and in order."

One young Jesus Movement couple gave up a professional career to attend Bible school. After graduation, they took a position in a church that was part of a solid, Bible-believing denomination. The leaders told them they were looking for a "pastor who will preach the Word and bring a lot of people to Christ."

They immediately saw that the people of the church didn't know how to tell others about Jesus or how to explain the most basic spiritual truths. He taught through Ephesians to give the congregation an accurate, biblical view of the church, and she started a monthly women's Bible study. Both started spending time discipling new Christians who were coming to the church. The attendance increased dramatically.

Soon, they started meeting with these growing believers in groups that met in their home. Some of those who had been a part of the church before they arrived joined these small groups. Leadership couples surfaced and they encouraged them to lead a group in their own home. Most of the new growth was coming from these groups, but it was a parallel ministry and the pastor and his wife knew they couldn't keep it up.

He approached his board with the idea of making some room in the schedule. "Could we think differently about the meetings we have here at the church so people can put more energy into our new small-group ministry? I was thinking that one of you could lead the Wednesday evening prayer meeting. That would give our groups a night to meet and provide an opportunity for my wife and me to train and encourage new leaders in our home."

The cold silence in the room and awkward shifting in chairs made him think that his wife's fear that the leaders didn't like what they were doing was valid. Finally Joe, the man who had always seemed most defiant, answered his request with a jolting ultimatum.

"Young man, you might think you know a lot, but you don't. We've always had a Wednesday prayer meeting. Only liberals don't have prayer meetings. Are you a liberal? Next thing you know you're going to want to cancel Sunday evening church!"

Instead of answering, he thought to himself, *How could they think I'm a liberal after sitting under my teaching for over a year?* And, *How did they know that I really do think our Sunday evenings could be better spent?*

Joe hadn't given him time to reply anyway. "And, another thing: Many of us, a lot of us, aren't entirely comfortable with these small groups of yours. How do we know what's going on? Some of the leaders of these groups have only been members a few months. Why, when I was younger, it took me over three years before they let me drive the bus for our bus ministry. You're moving too fast."

And then, Joe dropped the code card on the table: "Let all things be done decently and in order."

The pastor knew what he was really saying. "A lot of us" meant "my close friends and I who are used to running this place." "Decently and in order" meant "how we have always done it here."

Another Jesus Movement convert married a girl from the youth group of a healthy church. God's strong call to serve Him cross-culturally burned in the couple's hearts so they went off to seminary. They had no doubt about their call to a specific people group. He organized a prayer group in the seminary for these people and spoke in chapel about his passion for them. She worked full time to put him through seminary and joined him in learning the language of the people God was teaching them to love.

Their pastor back home grieved with them when they called him from overseas. After only eighteen months, they were coming home to go to law school. The pastor's suspicions that they were the victims of an abusive spiritual atmosphere were confirmed as they explained their decision. Their discouragement began when the area supervisor told the husband this:

"You spend entirely too much time meeting with people. You're neglecting your organizational responsibilities. You're naive and dangerous. Your talk about how all we need to do is build relationships and lead people to Christ is making the other missionaries feel like they're doing something wrong. I've talked this over with the home office. We think it's best for your development that you devote a couple of years learning the business end of missions."

He ended the conversation by bludgeoning the young missionary couple's objections and questions with the sledgehammer of code: "Let all things be done decently and in order."

Bruised beyond recovery, they knew what he really meant. "Best for your development" meant "punishment for not knuckling under like the rest of the people on our team." "Decently and in order" meant "whatever I tell you to do."

A third Jesus Movement man's company transferred him to a new city. He and his wife finally found a younger pastor who taught the Bible. At first they thought they could learn to love the organ and hymns so foreign to their experience. He was a gifted musician and easily learned the familiar church songs. He even played the piano during worship.

The chairwoman of the music committee asked him to serve. He wasn't much for committees but the pastor encouraged him to join the music committee "for him." When the pastor asked him to lunch to talk about ways "to get more young families to stay," he promised to do whatever he could. He told the pastor about his background and how he had led worship at his large church full of younger couples back home. "But," he warned, "our music was different. The words were just Scripture and the arrangements more modern."

"No problem," the pastor assured him. "Put together something different and we'll start this Sunday evening."

He poured himself into it. After a few months, Sunday evenings were packed with new and younger worshippers. The children's Sunday evening program exploded, and they had to recruit new leaders to accommodate all the growth from young families.

It surprised him when the pastor showed up at the monthly music committee meeting. He felt sick when he saw his name as the only item on that night's agenda. The chairwoman took her seat and asked the pastor to open the meeting with prayer. During the prayer, the young musician wondered if the fact that the chairwoman was married to the wealthiest man in the church would make any difference. When she started in on him, he knew the answer.

"I've been coming to this church all my life," she began. "My parents brought me to the same nursery you bring your daughter to. Our family donated the organ over thirty years ago."

This can't be good, he thought to himself.

"In all those years, nobody has ever led worship from the piano."

He tried to explain. "That's where I feel most comfortable, and no one else knows the music I play on Sunday nights."

Her face pinched when she smiled one of those shut-up-and-listen smiles he remembered from his mean aunt.

"Well, if you would sing the songs of the church, we have two very good piano players."

"But ..." He looked at the pastor for help. The pastor dropped his eyes to the floor. "But, we, I thought you wanted to reach young families. Haven't you seen how many of them are coming? Their children are learning the Bible; our pastor is teaching them about the Christian life. Just last week, two new people received Christ after the meeting. All I do is play the piano and lead them from the microphone ..."

"You mean like in a bar?" she interrupted.

"No, not like a bar at all. I make sure that every song is doctrinally accurate. Most of the words come straight from the Bible. I simply put God's inspired Word to music."

She glared. "Inspired to be read, not to be sung while people move their bodies like they're on a dance floor. You've turned our Sunday worship service into a honky-tonk!"

She ranted on for a few minutes, collected herself, and calmly thrust the hot blade of code into his revival heart: "Let all things be done decently and in order."

Sickened by despair, as this ministry he loved slipped from his life, he knew what she meant. "Like in a bar" meant "anything and everything I fear and don't understand." "Decently and in order" meant "we own this church."

Incredibly, the dark enemies of revival have twisted 1 Corinthians 14:40 into a *code verse* to control and consolidate power. But this verse is actually teaching how God's Spirit releases and exhibits power through the decent and orderly exercise of spiritual gifts in a vibrant community of faith. It has nothing to do with a church calendar, a business approach to ministry, or musical preferences.

Do you need to start thinking for yourself and thinking biblically again? Do these stories remind you of your own experience? Do you feel God asking you to wake up and stop lying about the dysfunction of your spiritual family? If so, does it scare you to picture the consequences of refusing to speak code any longer?

Let me turn you to a little book in your New Testament written to break the codes and shackles of spiritual exploitation: Galatians.

Stand Fast; Hands Up

The Galatian Christians caved in to the domesticating pressures of the spiritual bullies of the first century. Satan had been perfecting his sidetracking strategy of legalism among these new believers. "The grace of God isn't enough," his false teachers barked, "you need some rules, a little Old Testament law. There should be some human effort here. You can't expect God to do this for you. That's it, nice Christian, settle down now, you're pushing this grace and freedom thing too far. We'll show you how to be more respectable, more normal, more religious … how to be just like us."

Paul refuted the devil's lies about the dangers of freedom in Christ with his most passionate letter. The six chapters of Galatians called believers back to the grace of God and wildly unleashed His grace in their lives. His case is simple and irrefutable: Grace isn't optional; it's necessary. Freedom isn't dangerous; it's glorious!

Like most of Paul's letters, a critical hinge verse drives the message deep into the lives of his readers with a "therefore" command. His shepherd's heart would not rest until his readers knew what his theology meant to them personally. After devoting four chapters to defending his apostleship and the doctrine of grace, his anticipated "therefore" introduces a military command: *Stand fast in freedom!* (Gal. 5:1).

When the situation is desperate and the line begins to buckle, the commander calls to his troops, *Stand fast!*

When the ranks begin to collapse and cowards turn and run, the bold and the brave look at one another and shout, *Stand fast!*

When the battle seems lost and the enemy smells victory, the only hope is obedience to that simple command not to break rank, *Stand fast!*

"It was for freedom that Christ set us free; therefore keep standing firm [*stand fast!*] and do not be subject again to a yoke of slavery" (Gal. 5:1 NASB).

All that comes after this command—the unexplainable power and joy of freedom in Christ (Gal. 5:2—6:18)—depends on our courage to stand fast in the freedom that has been ours since the day Christ liberated us from sin.

The choice is clear—bondage or freedom; impotent, housebroken Churchianity or vigorous, untamed Christianity.

This is where I wish I could look up from the page and ask you, "So what is the issue in your life right now that binds you? What are you doing to please other Christians that is keeping you from running free for the Lord Jesus?"

I would ask you about your church, your background, and try to help you identify your personal stand-fast issue. I would also ask God to help you see beyond your fear to the fruit of victory—freedom to serve and worship Christ with all your heart.

My most memorable stand-fast moment came at the closing of our services the Sunday I returned to the pulpit of Church of the Open Door in 2000. In the weeks of my absence due to illness, I had become a closet hands-up worshipper. Desperately dependent on Jesus, I would sit alone in my house, praising Him with my hands lifted to the air. I had wanted to for years, but my particular conservative culture viewed this with mistrust, as a sure sign that someone was "going charismatic." I remember thinking, "Who cares? I'm dying. What can they do to me now?"

But there's a huge difference between the pastor of one of the most historic conservative evangelical congregations in church history raising his hands in worship at home and that same pastor standing in the front row of that same church lifting his hands to the heavens during the closing song. Especially when it's his first day back, and his hands may be the only ones in the air!

I distinctly remember the Spirit reminding me of a verse I had memorized years before in the New American Standard Bible: "It was for freedom that Christ set us free; therefore keep standing firm [*stand fast!*] and do not be subject again to a yoke of slavery" (Gal. 5:1). The title of a sermon I had preached from that verse also came to mind: *Stand fast, Ed. Stand fast.*

I lifted my hands to Jesus, praising Him with all my heart. I could almost feel the gasp of the congregation, but I didn't care. This wasn't about me; this was about Jesus. I knew He was asking me to worship Him *freely.*

That was years ago. I haven't become a charismatic Christian. Though I love my charismatic brothers and sisters, I still disagree with them on their interpretation of critical passages on the ministry of the Holy Spirit. What I have become is a much more fulfilled and, I believe, pleasing worshipper of the Lord Jesus.

It was a step away from sidetracked, housebroken Christianity and a step toward wild freedom in Christ. It was also a step back in time, to the days of revival when we only asked, "What pleases Jesus?" and had never even thought of asking, "What pleases religious people?"

Do you long to taste the freedom that is yours in Christ? Are you tired of trying to please other Christians and living down to their expectations? Would you have to admit that your wild revival heart has been sidetracked, that you're housebroken?

Then what is your stand-fast issue? Tell God right now that you want your personal stand-fast moment. I invite you to rejoin the ranks of the liberated, the brave and the bold who refuse to break ranks and run against the incessant attack of the "conform to our ideas and do what you're told" crowd:

> Father, I hate to admit that I have cared more about the expectations of others and my religious reputation than I care about pleasing Your Son. I know what my stand-fast issue is. I have felt Your Spirit pulling me toward freedom, but I have been a coward. I invite You to give me my stand-fast moment. And when You do, I will break the bondage of this lie and live free to serve Christ with all the exuberant joy and reckless obedience His cross made possible. Please give me courage because I'm going to need it. In Jesus' name, amen.

Sitting behind the walls of the institutional church are thousands of Jesus Movement Christians and would-be revolutionaries chained to imposter systems of righteousness based on works and submission to the status quo. Their only way of escape is the message of Galatians—it was for freedom that Christ set you free. Their only hope is the courage to trust Jesus' love enough to break the shackles of spiritual bullies whose only agenda for our lives is conformity.

Our revival lived on in a remnant that survived the housebreaking lies of entrenched ecclesiastical power. We gasped for breath as God's Word helped us break Satan's chokehold. Freedom in Christ brought the "able to" back into our "want to" lives. But just as the Jesus Movement radicals began to take in the sweet, pure air of grace again, we realized that some powerful people were clamoring for our attention—*politicians*.

Chapter 6

Power Is Good

In 1968, I was a left-leaning student, pulled by the noble core of progressive thought—concern for the poor, care for the helpless, defending the powerless, and pursuing the hope of peace and justice. I felt sick the night Bobby Kennedy died and sat with a black friend defiantly in a pizza parlor that refused to serve him.

The presidency and passion of John F. Kennedy awakened something in my generation that desired more than the safe suburban lives of our parents. We wanted change, and the voices from the left—Bobby Kennedy, Martin Luther King, and César Chávez—spoke our language.

We didn't call ourselves Democrats, because most of us hated Lyndon Johnson. But we were radically committed to civil rights and opposed to the war in Vietnam. And we surprised everyone when we became a political force to be reckoned with. Ours was the first generation of youth in America who flexed our political muscle by taking to the streets, closing down campuses, and devoting ourselves fanatically to causes and political figures. When Johnson withdrew from reelection in March of '68, we felt empowered. Newscasters even gave us partial credit.

Power tasted good. The political science departments of America's universities and colleges filled to overflowing. You couldn't walk across campus without meeting someone "going to law school." Most of us really believed that we could use our power to bring a revolution to American society that would change the world.

And then we met Christ and began thinking about revolution in a different way. We would be *spiritual* revolutionaries.

I don't know how it happened or when, but it was like we went to bed one night a warmhearted, caring, radical community of people who found Christ, and woke up the next morning coldhearted, self-protective Christians who had become a voting bloc. Spiritual revolutionaries had become mere Republicans.

Political power already impressed us, so we were ripe for the lie that the vote would be our world-changing tool. Then when we got the power, we wielded it in the same way the powerful always have—to protect our turf.

The Good Side of Power

Jesus and His apostles regarded citizenship as an essential responsibility for His followers. "Render therefore to Caesar the things that are Caesar's, and to God the things that are God's" (Matt. 22:21).

Using the illustrations "salt and light," Jesus speaks of the influence His people should have on the world. As salt, we should retain our Christlike character to fulfill our purpose in the world to preserve society against evil as we make others thirsty for Him. As light, we should shine the way toward righteousness and become a light-radiating community whose good deeds bring praise to our heavenly Father (Matt. 5:13–16).

I want to spend a moment examining the Bible's teaching about our relationship to civil authority.

Like all authority in the universe, civil authority comes from God (Rom. 13:1–2) and Christians should render to their government "all their due" (Rom. 13:7). First, by praying for our government leaders in a specific way—that they would govern in such a way that we could "lead a quiet and peaceable life in all godliness and reverence" so that the gospel can move forward in the world (1 Tim. 2:1–4). But our prayers for our country should cause us to embrace our God-given responsibility to serve our civil leaders "by doing good," using our "liberty" as "bondservants of God" to "honor all people" and "love the brotherhood" (1 Peter 2:13–17).

The universal truth for all followers of Christ is clear: *Use your citizenship to glorify God by serving your leaders in a way that maximizes righteousness and opportunities for the gospel, and minimizes oppression and evil.* This is God's will for Christians through the ages and throughout the world—whether they live under the tyranny of a dictator or the freedom of a democracy.

Until I understood these passages, I thought being an American was all about me. If I could get out of paying taxes, I would. The police should concern themselves with other people and leave me alone. If I wanted to speed, so what? Military service was for others who didn't have much to do with their life. But Scripture convinced me that being an American is all about God.

- My Christian accountant knows that I don't want to pay any more taxes than necessary, but I do want to follow the tax laws as if they came from heaven, because, in a way, they do!

- As the officer walks to my car after pulling me over for speed-ing, I keep telling myself, *This is God's servant. He is only pulling me over because God made it this way.* I respect him as God's peace officer, because he or she is!
- Judy and I dedicated four years of our lives to military service after college, encouraged our son to go to West Point and said good-bye to him the two times he went to war, and celebrate our son-in-law's service as an FBI agent. Our family serves this country proudly as if we're serving God, because we are!

When a Christian lives in a republic like the United States, he or she accepts a critical duty in addition to the historic responsibilities to pray for leaders, obey laws, pay taxes, and serve in the military: *voting.*

Voting is a rare privilege for Christians and a sacred responsibility. Believers fortunate enough to live in a country that counts their vote should make their vote count—*for God!*

But making our vote count for God is easily confused with making our vote count for what we want. When we begin to notice the number of our votes there are to count, we're tempted to use our vote to gain personal power and position.

Power or Influence?

Every time Jesus' first disciples dreamed of position and power, He warned them that "serving" was His measure of greatness (Mark 9:33–37; 10:35–45). My generation of spiritual revolutionaries ignored His warning, and dreams of position and power sidetracked us.

Books and sermons on a Christian's relationship to government often fail to distinguish between political power and cultural influence. The pri-mary passages on this subject (Matt. 5:13–16; Rom. 13:1–7; 1 Tim. 2:1–4;

1 Peter 2:13–16) clearly teach us that our role is to use whatever position we have to *influence* society toward righteousness as we submit to governmental authority.

Biblically, influence and power are not the same. The influence is ours, but the power is God's. Historically, when Christians confuse the two, we lose both.

Confusing influence and power diverts our energies from the only true hope for any society: *the transforming power of new life in Christ.* The Bible says we're new creations in Christ (2 Cor. 5:17), endowed with power from on high (Acts 1:8) to live a life distinguished by God's presence in us (John 14:20).

Where we choose to invest our time and resources depends largely on where we think the solution is. As more and more of us decided that the solution was in political power, it changed our priorities.

We know Christ commands us to influence our culture. And we know that one of the primary ways we do this as Americans is by voting. But, these are the questions that bother me most when I think of all the time and energy Christians have poured into the pursuit of political power in the decades since the Jesus Movement revival:

America hasn't become more righteous; it's become more decadent. What would have happened if we had devoted more effort to equipping Christians to get out and tell others about Christ and less to equipping people to get out the vote?

Families aren't getting healthier; they're falling apart. How do you think the families of our country would be different if we had been more passionate about transforming families in the way Christ values—through the hard work of disciple-making in the context of authentic spiritual communities and less obsessive about entrenching the family-values message in Washington DC?

The church doesn't have more impact; its influence is almost negligible. What if Christians had spent more time studying their Bibles and praying for their neighborhoods, communities, states, and nation, and less time glued to conservative talk radio and cable news while worrying about exit polls and economic trends?

Confusing influence and power also deflects our focus from the final destination of human beings—either with Jesus forever in heaven or estranged from God forever in hell. The Bible says we're ambassadors of Christ (2 Cor. 5:20) representing Him as strangers and pilgrims (Heb. 11:13). Our earthly citizenship is only temporary because we're citizens of a better, heavenly country (Heb. 11:16). Our true identity is in Christ and our true citizenship is in heaven (Phil. 3:20).

We said we were standing for righteousness. And we made our stand through our vote. But these are some more questions that bother me when I think of the way Christians have viewed their world through the political prism since the Jesus Movement revival:

What happens when the judges have all been appointed and the lawsuits have ended? Only faith in Christ can change a life on the inside.

When the schools have all been reoriented and the curricula have been sensitized to God's eternal truth, what then? Classrooms will still be full of rebellious hearts. Only God's Spirit can internalize the Word of God.

What happens when the wars have been fought, the soldiers have come home, and the suffering is over? Jesus Himself told us that peace couldn't last. Only in His kingdom will the world know lasting peace.

When the votes have all been counted and even if our side wins, what then? Each and every man and woman, boy and girl who has lived in the most righteous nation in history yet has not heard and believed the gospel of Jesus Christ will, when they die, slip into the darkness of a godless eternity.

I agree with C. S. Lewis, who said, "A sick society must think much about politics, as a sick man must think much about his digestion."[6] And I agree with Christian leaders who tell Christians to think about politics in our sick society.

I just think we've been thinking about politics too much. It's time to think a little less about our power to make a difference in this world and a lot more about our influence to make a difference in the world to come.

While our confusion with influence and power dissipated our energy and focus, it also distilled our message. But not in a good way.

Mean Love

The television celebrity impressed me deeply. I couldn't help thinking that if he and I had grown up together or had served together in the military, we would have been good friends. I liked him in spite of all the rumors about his lifestyle. He joked about being a "backslidden" worshipper from his childhood church. God brought our lives together for one fascinating afternoon when he introduced me to his media world and I talked with him about the history of Church of the Open Door.

Just before our day ended, he looked off and asked of no one in particular, "When did the church become so mean?"

I said, "*We're* not mean, why don't you come here and give us a chance?"

He laughed uncomfortably and said, "I might just come and visit you some Sunday, Ed."

I prayed for him and we shook hands. As I watched him drive away with his cameraman, his question haunted me.

On the drive home that night, I turned my radio dial to Christian talk radio. Appalled by the snarling arrogance of the host, I prayed that the man I had met that day wasn't listening. Whether the radio host knew it or not, his "We'll show those sinners when this bill gets passed," and "Just wait until God deals with these idiots," sent a message to those outside of God's grace: *God's on our side and He hates you.*

The Bible teaches that God is on the side of the righteous and emphasizes that ultimately our side will win. But our victory will not come through favorable voting returns, but at the return of Jesus Christ to rule and reign on earth.

The Bible does not teach that God hates sinners. The New Testament says that the message of the church is that "[God] has reconciled us to

Himself through Jesus Christ, and has given us the ministry of reconciliation" (2 Cor. 5:18).

If God hated sinners, those who are not reconciled to Him, this verse tells us He would have to start with us. Instead, He loves sinners and sent His Son to die in order to reconcile sinners like us. To us, the reconciled sinners, He has given this ministry of reconciliation, "that is, that God was in Christ reconciling the world to Himself, not imputing their trespasses to them, and has committed to us the word of reconciliation" (2 Cor. 5:19).

We're not called to be bitter prophets shouting condemnation at the world. Those who teach with condemnation allow their confusion between influence and power to trap them in the hopelessness of the Old Testament. We're "ambassadors for Christ, as though God were pleading through us: we implore you on Christ's behalf, be reconciled to God. For He made Him who knew no sin to be sin for us, that we might become the righteousness of God in Him" (2 Cor. 5:20–21).

Every time we feel like demanding our "rights" as citizens in ways that might make Christ's love sound mean, we need to pause and remember that we're aliens and strangers in foreign territory. When we go to our Father's house and return with His Son to make this world our home, we will have all power because we will be ruling and reigning eternally with our king—*Jesus*. Until then, we are ambassadors whose primary influence comes through His eternally powerful message: *I love you. Be reconciled to God through Me.*

What we really want, if we're listening to Him, is to watch His grace rescue those we meet in this alien land. And since we want to see people like the television celebrity in heaven, we should think less about our rights here on earth and more about the right way to heaven.

The way for them is the same way we discovered—through Jesus' love. That's the message I want to proclaim, a message that would cause unbelievers to look off and ask, "Why are Christians so kind to people like me? How could it be that Jesus loves someone who lives the way I live?"

Once you understand how our unhealthy emphasis on power is affecting our message, you'll start to wonder why we are so hard on some sinners and so easy on others.

Selective Righteousness

I reentered mainstream American Christianity in the summer of 1980, after an extended European assignment in the army. My seminary studies thrust Judy and me into the Christian culture of the Bible Belt. If the Bible Belt has a buckle, it's Dallas, Texas. The Bible teaching at Dallas Seminary was great, the commitment to the Lord among the students deep, and the politics decidedly right-wing.

"Reagan for President" bumper stickers adorned most of the cars in the parking lot. I remember feeling pretty smug when I picked up my big blue "Reagan for President" button and smiling when another man commented at the tiny pile of little green buttons supporting President Carter, "Small president, small button," he said.

I also remember the day I took the Reagan button off my lapel and never wore it again. Dr. Tony Evans, the lone African-American professor, preached one of the most courageous sermons I have ever heard, called "God Ain't No Republican." Tony challenged our "pick and choose" causes of righteousness and exposed some of them as simply personal preferences. He asked us how we thought his community felt about a God and a church that cared so much about the rights of the unborn but so little for the rights of children born in poverty. He wondered if we had missed Jesus' interest in the poor, the downtrodden, the powerless, and the marginalized. He warned us to think of the impact of identifying Christ with a political party.

I thought about the Dallas slums surrounding our campus and tried to view my Reagan button from the perspective of the minimum-wage-earning single mother serving me an Egg McMuffin and coffee every morning before class. I thought about the sergeants and fellow officers in my unit in Germany. Some of the very best were men from the mean streets of the city or sons of first-generation Latino laborers. I remembered their devotion to President Carter and knew what they would think about Christ if most Christians they met were wearing Reagan buttons.

My vote still belonged to Reagan, but not my devotion to his party. It bothered me that people viewed evangelicals as people who hated abortionists and homosexuals but loved landlords and tycoons. It bothered me that our political opinions always seemed to align with our economic interests.

Today I see many of the leaders of what is popularly known as the emerging church making the same mistake we made, except *they're* selecting the issues of the left. I hear their passion and even agree with their positions. But it could be just as distracting for this generation to focus on environmental concerns, social justice, and world peace while seeming to ignore the rights of the unborn and sexual immorality.

Friend, this isn't my warning; it's the warning of history. If church history teaches us anything it's this: There is an inverse relationship between political power and spiritual influence.

Historical Myopia

The irony is that our passionate desire to change the world comes from God. Evil societies and cultures grieve God's heart, and His Spirit moves us to do something about the problem. Along the way, that "something" changes from the unfailing power of new life in Christ to the ineffective power of imposed righteousness.

People who cite Moses' call to the people of Israel as proof that spiritual leaders should become politically powerful should read on. After centuries of failure, the Jewish prophets began talking of a new day. They predicted a time when the Spirit would come to actually indwell believers with divine power. Acts 2 records that moment—the day of Pentecost.

The message was so powerful that the early church's enemies rightly charged that Christians had "upset the world" (Acts 17:5–6 NASB). Their simple message that you will be saved if you believe in Jesus Christ transformed personal lives, marriages, families, and entire cities. In an empire known for its cruelty, Christians built compassionate communities of faith. Slaves and masters worshipped together, women were viewed as spiritual equals, and followers of Christ were known by their care for one another and others. By the end of the first century, though still relatively small in numbers, the church of Jesus Christ had spread throughout the Mediterranean world and beyond.

A few centuries later, the growing political power of the church that had turned the world upside down for Christ had turned Christians right side up in the eyes of the world. State and church mingled together and the lines blurred. The children of the first generation of believers established privileged and powerful bishops to preserve orthodoxy. Over the centuries church leaders became less concerned with orthodoxy and more concerned with privilege and power.

The all-powerful hierarchy of the medieval church defined a Christian as someone who conformed his or her duties to their authority. The rules of the church replaced relationship with Christ as the preserving influence of God on earth. Individual church members lost contact with the Scriptures and depended on experts to tell them what was right and wrong. The vibrant church of the second century was dead by the dawn of the Reformation in 1500.

Those of us who came to Christ in the Jesus Movement crammed this story that took centuries to develop into three short decades. The revivalists of the '60s became the power-broking turf defenders of the '90s. Nothing demonstrated this sad reality more than the hysteria in the evangelical community over the so-called "Y2K crisis"—the predicted worldwide pandemonium that would ensue as computer clocks tried to transition from 1999 to 2000. Even if the sky-is-falling prophecies of the doom mongers of the Christian right had come true, the plans being made in the name of the Lord were appalling.

Leaders encouraged survivalist tactics. Talk radio and Internet "experts" in Southern California warned of freeways choked with frantic and desperate refugees and gangs roaming the streets. A massive power grid failure would cause the breakdown of order on a massive scale. The entire Los Angeles Basin would run out of food and water.

And what were we to do?

Use this as an opportunity to serve the suffering in the name of Christ?

Shine the light of hope in Christ to a desperate and fearful population?

Fall to our knees in prayer and beg God to preserve our city?

No, churches stockpiled food and water and actually strategized how to keep nonmembers from their cache! Entire families made plans to road march on back highways to remote areas of northeastern California and Nevada. A few people I know actually bought property!

Christians scared out of their wits approached me after services. "What are we doing to protect our people? When are we going to have a meeting like the church down the road? What is our plan?"

I wanted to scream, "What's wrong with the church today? Come on people, we're on the winning side. When was the last time you read your New Testament? I wish you distracted people could have been there back in the day—in the Jesus Movement. That's when we knew what we were about, when our priorities were biblical, and our faith courageous."

And then it hit me. *We* were now the ones in charge. Many of the national leaders and radio preachers of the Y2K silliness were Jesus Movement people. We were the ones preaching the sermons and training the pastors, and sitting on the church and parachurch boards!

I can't help thinking that some of our terror had to do with our disappointment in our real ability to influence the world through our vote.

"Our" candidates had lost two presidential elections in a row. "Our" call for impeachment of the current president after an appalling moral scandal only drove his approval rating to an unprecedented 73 percent. The same politicians we put in office ignored "our" issues.

Nothing But Corn!

In a scene from one of my favorite movies, *Secondhand Lions,* two eccentric old men are hoeing in their garden when their great-nephew notices that all the plants look the same. When Uncle Hub takes a closer look, he discovers that the smooth-talking salesman had sold them a bunch of pretty packets promising a wide variety of beautiful vegetables. But they all contained corn, "nothing but corn!"

It doesn't matter what pictures are on the outside of the packet, my friend. It's the seeds inside that count! Paul says, "Do not be deceived, God is not mocked; for whatever a man sows, that he will also reap" (Gal. 6:7).

It's time for us to look up from the garden we've been sweating over for thirty years. The image on the front of the seed packets we sowed titled "Political Power" pictured neighborhoods of righteous families living securely in a nation dedicated to godly values. But what have we reaped? We're reaping the same old corn of unrighteousness—neighborhoods full of hopeless families disintegrating from the pressures of life apart from God. *Nothing but corn.*

It's time for us to blow the dust off that old packet titled "Spiritual Power" we laid on the shelf too many years ago. The image on the front is simple—God hanging on a cross. But the seeds inside—the gospel of Christ and the Word of God—will never fail to "establish your hearts blameless in holiness before our God and Father at the coming of our Lord Jesus Christ with all His saints" (1 Thess. 3:13).

If this is the first time you've looked up from your misplaced loyalties and hopes, this is the perfect time to turn your heart back to the Lord Jesus:

> Father, my only desire is to see Your will done "on earth as it is in heaven." But I have to confess that this good desire has become a bad obsession. I still want to be a voice for righteousness in this land. But what I want more is to be a force for eternal good in this world. Please make me a part of this world's only true hope—a revival of hearts touched by the gospel of Jesus Christ. In Jesus' name, amen.

If you've just prayed for revival, then you're asking God for the only real solution to this world's problems. But you'll need to watch for one of the most alluring lies Satan whispers into the ears of those longing for revival—*bigger is better*.

Chapter 7

Bigger Is Better

And then it happened. When we realized too late that our churches looked just like our parents' churches, we overreacted. Thinking that we were throwing out everything we thought about church, we talked about paradigm shifts and global strategies. We built megachurches on a corporate model and traded impact for growth. As a result, a generation that drove Volkswagen Bugs to small-group Bible studies and prayer meetings in homes now drive their BMWs and Mercedes to sprawling campuses that look like amusement parks with a Christian fish at the gates. And we sadly wonder why our children don't share our passion for Jesus.

We know that Christ commands us to share His love with the world.

And we know He is pleased with every new person who receives eternal life and follows Him. So why is church growth a bad thing?

It's not; church growth is a *good* thing. The church began with explosive growth. When Peter preached the first sermon of the church age, three thousand devout Jews turned to Christ and joined the ranks of the disciples of Christ (Acts 2:40–41). The city of Jerusalem and the world would never be the same.

This is not a chapter that points fingers at gifted leaders like Bill Hybels and Rick Warren or their churches. I'm a fan of both, and though I know neither personally, everything I hear and read of them convinces me that they are following God's good and perfect will.

They follow God's will for *them,* but not for me … and not for most pastors and most churches.

There are many hazards to equating God's will for these great men and their churches with the will of God for all church leaders and all churches. The riptide of our current evangelical culture, and especially its leaders, makes it hard to swim back to the shores of biblical sanity. It's deemed "reactionary" to question the effectiveness of Starbucks-esque visions of church growth.

But I'm convinced that one of the greatest threats to church health today is this: *the lie that bigger is better.* It begins in the ambitious hearts of church leaders … like me.

Sixty or Six Thousand

I don't go to pastors' conferences. I tried one not long after I graduated from seminary, but the bigger-is-better lie that infected my heart so polluted the air that I couldn't breathe.

Every speaker told big stories about his big church. I looked around at the men sitting with me in the auditorium. They looked just like me—envious and shameful. I knew how they felt because I felt it too—competitive envy.

If I had a big church like that, maybe I would feel better about myself.

I wonder what it would be like to be that guy, the guy on the stage who just flew in from the exciting place he was yesterday.

Envy is a feeling that brings shame along with it.

I wonder why God is using him in such a powerful way? Everybody wants to come to his big church—especially impressive people. Nobody wants to come to my little church, except a bunch of losers.

Must be the way he preaches. He's so eloquent, so charming, so riveting, so pithy.

Or maybe it's his leadership. He's so smooth, so sure, so convincing, so corporate. He's like Ronald Reagan with a Bible degree. He's talking about stuff I never even think about.

Why did God let me be a pastor? Why did He even save me in the first place?

He's a winner; I'm a loser. A loser pastor with a loser church.

The worst part of it was what we did with our envy and shame. We looked for a bigger loser with a smaller church. Every personal encounter teetered on the edge of the *question*. Every new conversation began a few words away from the *question*. Every gathering, large or small, was seconds away from the *question*.

"So, Ed, how big is your church?"

The answer to the *question* immediately sized up each man and determined the pecking order for the rest of the conference, for the rest of our days in ministry, for the rest of our lives.

I hadn't experienced these intense feelings of shame and envy since I tried to walk into the showers my freshman year in high school and the coach said, "Leave the towel on the hanger, Underwood."

I felt so threatened and fed up with it that it unleashed the rebel within me. I talked Kevin Butcher, my best friend from seminary, into joining me in a little "sociological study."

"Okay, Kevin, this is what we'll do," I explained. "The next time somebody asks you how big your church is, you tell him, 'About sixty.' When they ask me how big my church is, I will tell them, 'About six thousand!'"

At the closing dinner, two days later, I looked like some Christian Socrates. About a dozen guys were clamoring for my attention, asking me a million questions, laughing at all my jokes, and hanging on my every word. "Oh, Ed, that's great. I gotta write this down!"

Kevin?

Not so much.

In his own words, "Ed, I could slash my wrists, fall to the floor in a growing pool of blood, and these guys would be stepping over me as they called out, 'Ed, Ed, oh Ed?'"

When Kevin and I think back on that weekend we lied about the size of our churches with the decades of perspective we share today, we're both embarrassed by his initial reaction to my planned charade and my response.

"Hey, why do you get the big church?"

"My idea!"

We know now what we couldn't admit then. We believed the very lie we mockingly exposed: Bigger is better. Only a loser would admit that his church was small.

The hard years we both would face after having our fun that week in Chicago in 1986 would teach us that the real losers are the leaders who buy the lie.

Megachurch, Country-Style

Let's be honest. Pastors aren't the only ones playing the "my church is bigger than your church" game. This isn't a book just for pastors. It's a book for Christians who long for revival, especially those who have tasted revival, want to taste it again, and are willing to admit the mistakes we made.

For every spiritual leader wanting to prove himself or herself a "winner" by the size of his or her church or ministry, there are hundreds or thousands wanting to prove themselves "winners" by following him or her. The air becomes toxic with ungodly ambition and it only takes a spark to ignite a bigger-is-better firestorm.

We love being a part of something impressive, something that sets us apart, something big, what's happening, what's hip, what's hot.

I was a megachurch pastor once. Judy and I moved to a small mountain town to pastor a small country church with a bad reputation in the community. A core group of deeply committed and greatly gifted leaders locked arms with us. God worked mightily and the church exploded into a country version of the biggest, hippest, hottest church around. It lasted a little over eight years.

We were the ones strategizing our success and trying to explain to ourselves why we were such winners. We felt sorry for the other churches in the area that struggled along, never growing, lacking money. We felt really misunderstood when other Christians questioned the genuineness of our hearts just because we were big. I chose to view us as winners surrounded by runners-up. I was pretty full of myself as a leader, and I suspect that many of those who followed me were too.

We talked about ourselves a lot and joked with each other about how we should take our sign down so that we would still have a place to sit on Sundays. Don't get me wrong, a lot of people met and followed Jesus through that wonderful work. By the grace of God lives were turned around—marriages were saved, families were put back together, and addicts got sober. We taught the Word of God carefully, mentored new believers, and gave people hope.

Almost every sidetracked revolutionary I know, leader or follower, has gone through some version of this. We were part of something big and loved it, so we talked about it … a lot … maybe too much. That's the first sign that something is wrong with our bigness: We talk about it more than we talk about the Lord; we think about our church, our ministry, more than we think about Jesus.

Does this scenario describe your experience? Does it make you think of yourself and your church? Does it explain some of what you're feeling dissatisfied with right now, perhaps the reason why you picked up this book in the first place?

I believe the Spirit of God wants to use your great enthusiasm for what the Lord is doing in a place or through a specific group of people to make you passionate about what *He* is doing in the world through that place and those people.

We achieved our self-important summit when we went on the radio and finished our third building program. Our campus was a showpiece, the largest buildings and best-kept grounds in the area. I can hardly stand to write down what I was thinking. In a world of winners and losers, we were big winners.

Unless of course you're talking about winners and losers in the way Jesus talked about them. The real winners are those who lose by putting others first, by laying down their lives for their friends (Mark 10:44–45). The real losers are those who never question the lie their ambitious hearts embrace as they jealously cling to the confusion and evil they never see coming (James 3:14–16).

I was a loser, until a real winner reminded me of the way it used to be.

Twelve or Thirteen

I met him at a retreat for pastors of country churches and their wives. Since my "country church" was so successful—exploding numbers, a regional radio program, and famous guest speakers—I was the guy onstage. By any bigger-is-better measurement, I was measuring up.

Judy and I shared dinner with him and his wife—an older couple with kind faces. I turned to the man, "So tell me about your church." I was careful not to ask the *question*. I didn't want to discourage them with a reminder that their work was so small.

"Well, we've been there for over forty years now. I say 'been there,' but we're really only *there* three days a week. We met at Bible college and took jobs in the city after graduation. She's a nurse and I'm the parts manager of a large car dealership."

Probably because he had told the story to speakers at conferences before, he paused to study my face. He seemed surprised by the eye contact that showed him I was still listening.

"Anyway, we're both on a four-day work week, Monday through Thursday. We drive the six hours to our little town every Friday morning. It's mostly cowboys and ranch families, really remote. She teaches a women's Bible study on Friday evenings and I use that time to visit folks. You know, sick people, hurting people, new people to the community. We have a men's breakfast on Saturday, then I meet with the leaders for what you would call a board meeting. The rest of Saturday, I get some time to study a little to brush up for Sunday's sermon."

He checked again to see if he had lost me. He hadn't, so he went on.

"Sundays are the best. We both teach Sunday school, and then comes our worship service. After church, all the families get together for a potluck. Kids, grandparents, friends from out of town, visitors, everyone is invited. You can't beat the food. Those ranch families can really cook. The church has a cozy little house for the pastor. It works out great."

With every word, my respect for this man grew. "You do this every weekend? For forty years?"

"Yep. Most Sundays we wrap by three or four so that the wife and I can get some sleep before we hit the road for work Monday morning."

He looked to the left and then said something I knew he wanted me to hear. I was around mountain men a lot during the years I worked for the U.S. Forest Service fighting fire in the Sierras. I'm familiar with their ways. When they're saying something they feel deeply, they look off like that.

"I love it. Can't think of a better way to spend my life. I've learned a lot about the Lord from these people, and I think He's used me a little in their lives too. Some years, we've had as many as twelve or thirteen adults at a Sunday meeting."

He didn't wait for me to ask the *question,* he volunteered the information. No envy, no shame. To him, it was just a number, a meaningless number. As he continued with impassioned stories of what God had done over the years in that little place, my mind refused to measure this man's value by the size of his church. I could care less if it was twelve or thirteen, six thousand or sixty, or six.

I just wanted to hear more. I didn't want to hear about his systems, strategies, or studies. I wanted to hear about the people and their pastor. I wanted to go there, to be a part of this mighty work of God.

Shoot, I wanted him to be my pastor!

The pictures forming in my mind drew memories from my soul that brought tears to my eyes—tears of longing. Feelings the bigger-is-better lie had suppressed for years erupted from the folds of my redeemed soul.

Radical feelings.

Revival feelings.

Like being a part of something so big to God in heaven you didn't care if anyone on earth noticed.

Like watching the Light of the World dawn in the eyes of one single new citizen of heaven and knowing that you just witnessed an event being celebrated in heaven.

Like walking into some huge and impressive religio-circus and feeling good about the fact that you got it that this stuff really didn't count for much.

How long has it been since you felt these radical revival feelings? Would you have to admit that the bigger-is-better lie turned your eyes away from what really matters to God?

If so, brace yourself. You're about to walk into God's bigger-is-not-necessarily-better workshop. You're about to become a big loser, but you won't care. You're about to realize that the only measure of your life that matters is the one that compares the work you're doing now to the work that God prepared for you before you were born.

The Measures of Grace and Faith

If you've been a Christian for any length of time, you've probably heard a lot about the apostle Paul—the powerful leader of the early church. You picture him sailing and hiking around the New Testament world from this exotic city to that strategic city, going to big, important meetings like the Jerusalem council, hanging out with significant people like Peter and Jesus' half brother James, and writing theologically precise letters like Romans.

It may surprise you to know that the bigger-is-better crowd of his day considered him a big loser. They accused him of heresy, mocked him because his letters were far more impressive than his sermons, expressed disgust about his appearance, and tried to undermine his message as soon as he left.

It probably doesn't surprise you that he didn't care. He only cared about God's measuring stick—the one marked by grace and faith.

When people first started comparing him to those who "seemed to be something" in the church, he said it made no difference to him because God doesn't play favorites (Gal. 2:6–7). He cited the support of the pillars of the church—James, Cephas (Peter), and John—not because he performed for them but because they saw the Spirit working powerfully through him as he fulfilled his unique assignment from God. He described this personal commission as "the grace that had been given to me" (Gal. 2:9).

When he had to tell dear friends in Ephesus that he was in prison, he reminded them of his great privilege to make known the mystery of

Christ to the Gentiles through the gospel, "according to the gift of the grace of God given to me by the effective working of His power" (Eph. 3:7). This "grace" or unique personal assignment was given to him in spite of his own estimation of himself as "less than the least of all the saints" (Eph. 3:8).

He told these same Ephesians that Christ Himself measured out the personal scope of these assignments of grace (Eph. 4:7), and warned the Romans to only measure their lives against the standard of their personal assignment from God—their unique "measure of faith" (Rom. 12:3).

Paul didn't see other Christians as his competition; he didn't envy the other apostles' status as "pillars" of the church (Gal. 2:9). He didn't feel shame when some of the Corinthians were more loyal to Apollos or Cephas (Peter), or pride when others voiced their devotion to him (1 Cor. 1:12). He only cared about what Christ thought and how he would measure up to Jesus' expectations (Phil. 4:13).

He viewed life on earth as his opportunity to do the good works God had in mind for him when He saved him by grace (Eph. 2:8–10). He used a distinctive word to describe this opportunity offered to every Christian: *predestination*. The Greek word *proorizo* means to mark out a boundary decided beforehand. In the same way God predestined Christ to be crucified (Acts 4:27–28), the church to unfold the glory of redemption (1 Cor. 1), and believers to be adopted into His family (Eph. 1:5) and to be like His Son (Rom. 8:28–30). He predestined believers to glorify Him through the good works He prepared for each one (Eph. 1:4–6; 2:8–10; 4:1).

This had a lot to do with the confident demeanor of the country preacher with a congregation of twelve or thirteen. He wasn't worried about the size of the boundaries God had marked off for others; he only cared about what happened between the lines of his personal playing field. And he made sure he left it all on the field for Jesus.

He knew what every revival-desiring heart eventually discovers. Bigger is not better; smaller is not better; God's best for you is the best of all. He knew that his part of revival was special to God, but not to men. He knew that God measures greatness by grace and faith, not by size and sizzle.

How do you measure greatness?

Take a minute to check your own gauge of who measures up and who doesn't, and your definition of winners and losers. It's so easy to be swept up in the bigger-is-better hysteria. Our prideful hearts are so vulnerable to the addictive powers of esteem and status.

"Hi, my name's Ed and I'm an approbationaholic."

The road to recovery usually begins with a crisis of integrity, especially if you have a heart for true revival. I know mine did.

One, Niner, Niner

In the summer of 1996, Judy and I moved to Southern California to lead the Church of the Open Door, one of the most significant churches in the history of Los Angeles. The trauma of a decade of troubles had reduced this great church to a shell of its former self, and we knew God had called us to this strategic church. We looked forward to reliving the explosive story of our country megachurch here in this sprawling and thriving metropolis.

A few months after we arrived, I realized that this wouldn't be as easy as we thought. We assumed that people would rush to our church. Wasn't that how it always was with us? I'd preach the Word, love the people, and lead with my usual military confidence and effectiveness.

It didn't happen. Not only did we fail to grow, the attendance dropped sharply. A lot of people who were just hanging around until the new pastor came on the scene decided they didn't like me. They had plenty of big-church options to consider, in this the epicenter of megachurch theory and practice. In a city where size and sizzle definitely matter, and image is everything, we were very unimpressive.

We couldn't seem to break the two-hundred barrier. Falling back on my

Army lingo, I shamed myself to my friends and family by calling out our attendance with military precision, "one, niner, niner." Judy would walk in every Sunday, survey the huge but empty auditorium, and ask me, "Where is everybody?"

"You got me," I usually replied with as confident a look as I could muster. I told everyone I didn't care, but that was a lie because I still believed that bigger was better. I spent many Saturdays alone on my knees before the altar of Church of the Open Door crying out to God to make us bigger.

When the money ran out, I became desperate. I took some of our leaders to a bigger-is-better seminar, bought a bunch of bigger-is-better books, and started planning how to get bigger, how to measure up, how to "grow this church."

The process gained momentum and consumed me. Until the day God told me to stop it. I didn't hear His audible voice, but I knew it was Him.

Ed, this isn't you; you will never be satisfied with this. This is not your assignment.

I remember that Thursday afternoon when I took a walk with God around our beautiful but empty campus over a decade ago as if it was last Thursday. I argued with Him, told Him He didn't understand, asked Him not to make me tell the elders what He had said, and finally agreed with Him through tears of repentance and joy.

Without telling anyone what I was going to do—not Judy, the chairman of the elder board who had become a close friend, or even some of my most valued and trusted brothers around the country—I walked into the board meeting and said, "Gentlemen, this just isn't me. I can't do this. I preach the Word, disciple men, and build community. That's what I was put on this earth to do. I can understand if you feel like you need a more skilled church-growth man to lead this church. But that won't be me. I feel like the guy who wrote these books is pastoring this church. It's just not my style, my passion, or my giftedness. I'm willing to go and I won't cause any trouble. But if I stay, I'm going to do what God tells me to do, even if that means we won't grow as quickly as we feel we need to grow."

For what seemed like forever, nobody said a word. Finally, the board chairman, a man I had already come to respect and trust, spoke. "Whew, we thought you wanted this. I've had these exact same feelings. We've never been about the numbers, but we wanted to follow you."

It was the beginning of the turnaround of Church of the Open Door. We're still not a big church, but we're a healthy church. We still need more money and more people to do what we feel the Lord has called us to do, but we're moving forward one transformed life at a time.

The same day that started the turnaround of Church of the Open Door marked a turning back of my heart to its revivalist roots.

I forgot how good it felt to leave the impossible to God as you trust Him for your possible every day.

I forgot the thrill of living a life that could only be explained by His power and presence.

I forgot that I really didn't care what people thought about me as long as I knew that Jesus was pleased with me.

I forgot that God measures success by grace and faith rather than by nickels and noses.

I forgot that God really didn't need me to get His work done, but He did want to bless me by letting me be a part of what He's doing—a very specific part set aside just for me.

I'm so happy to be set free from the burden of the lie that bigger is better.

Have you forgotten what it felt like to be about your Father's business and only His business?

Have you forgotten what it feels like to pursue true revival?

Do you need to take a walk with God and talk with Him about your addiction to pride, envy, and shame?

Do you want to be set free from the lie of bigger is better?

If so, then Jesus will teach you a liberating lesson—the same lesson He taught His two most ambitious disciples.

Godly Ambition

It was an ambitious and manipulative request; a bigger-is-better type of demand made by sons of Zebedee.

"Teacher, we want You to do for us whatever we ask" (Mark 10:35). "Jesus, before we even tell You what we want You to do, promise us You'll say yes!"

Jesus was on to them, of course, but He let them ask. *"What do you want Me to do for you?"* (Mark 10:36).

"Oh, not much, just promise us that You'll give us the most prominent positions in Your coming kingdom." *"Grant us that we may sit, one on Your right hand and the other on Your left, in Your glory"* (Mark 10:37).

The reaction of the other ten disciples betrays the competitive envy and shame of their hearts. "Hey, wait a minute here. I didn't know that we were asking for personal favors. If anyone is going to get the most prestigious assignments in Your kingdom, it ought to be me. Or at least we could draw straws or something. This isn't fair!" *"And when the ten heard it, they began to be greatly displeased with James and John"* (Mark 10:41).

Before you conclude that ambition is always bad, notice that Jesus never corrects their ultimate desire to be great in His kingdom. Jesus affirms their longing to be great in His kingdom, but makes certain that they know what they're asking for.

"Are you sure?" *"You do not know what you ask"* (Mark 10:38).

"Greatness in My kingdom always involves suffering." *"Are you able to drink the cup that I drink, and be baptized with the baptism that I am baptized with?"* (Mark 10:38).

Drinking the cup and being baptized refer to the suffering and death

Jesus had just predicted (Mark 10:32–34). They would have to be willing to endure suffering in His name.

"Greatness in My kingdom involves God's sovereignty."

"To sit on My right hand and on My left is not Mine to give, but it is for those for whom it is prepared" (Mark 10:40). They would have to consent to the specific assignment God had prepared for them.

"Greatness in My kingdom involves serving." *"Whoever desires to become great among you shall be your servant"* (Mark 10:43). They would have to accept the role of a servant in His name.

My life changed the day I realized that the bigger-is-better lie had sidetracked my revolutionary heart. I never stopped being ambitious for Christ's kingdom, but I did stop being ambitious for mine. That's what I had always wanted anyway, and what Jesus always wanted to give me. I think God wants to know if we really want to be great according to His measure of grace and faith, if our ambition is really godly.

So will you make the same commitment I did concerning true greatness? Will you commit to firmly and finally rebuking the lie that bigger is better?

God is calling you back to the vision that pulled your heart toward greatness, the vision He planted in your heart when you first believed. Picture what your life will look like after you break free of the envy and shame of pursuing other Christians' boundaries. You will see His mighty hand working in your life again. You will know the satisfaction He reserves for those who live only to hear *His* applause. You will see those you love— your spouse, your children, your family and friends—drawn to Christ by the great adventure of your life.

First, you must tell God that you are willing to live large according to His Son's teaching. You must be willing to suffer for Christ, without setting limits on what you will or will not endure for His sake. You must be willing to take the place He planned for you in Christ's work—regardless of how big or small that may seem to you and others. And you must be willing to serve Christ's people—even when they do not deserve or appreciate your service.

If this is what you want, tell Him now:

> Father, I want to be great in Your eyes. I hate it that I was deceived by the lie that bigger is better. I confess that the deception had more to do with my envious heart than anything else. I want to be free of the shame that comparing and competing bring to my heart. I'm willing to suffer for the greatness I'm asking for right now. I'm willing to do what You have planned for me to do, however small or large that may be. I'm willing to serve Your people. In Jesus' name, amen.

Satan designed the lie that bigger is better to get you to waste your time competing for other Christians' positions. He's designed the next lie to keep you in the huddle.

Chapter 8

Enemies All Around

To everyone's amazement, the young rebels of the sixties came to Christ. After our conversion, we wanted to live out the potential of our new life in Christ. Our pastors' offices filled with dreamy-eyed, first-generation believers wanting to establish Christian homes.

We understood that the Christian life was and is inseparable from family. Nobody had to convince us of the truth of Psalm 127:1: "Unless the LORD builds the house, they labor in vain who build it." God had rescued us from homes firmly entrenched in the kingdom of darkness. Our parents may have been the greatest generation, but even they couldn't build homes of true happiness without Christ.

Our homes would be different—Jesus would build them. We didn't have a clue as to how Jesus would build our homes and what they would look like when He was done.

On the way home from our first premarital counseling appointment with pastor Ted, Judy and I were incredulous. Judy expressed our shock first.

"I can't understand why Ted didn't believe us when we told him we don't argue!" she said.

"Yeah," I agreed, "we're not going to be like our parents. We're Christians, what do we have to quarrel about?"

Then I offered my soon-to-be-bride my first wise plan as her spiritual leader. "Here's what we'll do. If we ever disagree, we'll just pray about it."

My plan worked perfectly after our wedding … for about three hours. I got lost on our way to our honeymoon and we did *not* pray about our disagreement over whether I should stop for directions!

That laughable story may help you understand our innocent devotion to the idea that our faith must make a difference in our marriages and for our children. However, it isn't funny that our pursuit of a Christian home grew desperate.

In trying to protect our children from the world, the Jesus Movement generation actually lost them to the world. Bigoted and self-protective theories of separation cloistered our families into homeschools, church compounds, and Christian universities. We built a subculture whose only values seemed to be safety and sameness. And most of our kids decided that the real excitement, challenge, and significance could only be found outside the holy huddle.

In this chapter, we will explore how our failure to balance the passages warning believers against friendship with the evil of this world with those exhorting you to reach the people of this world sidetracked us. Two stories of sincere Jesus Movement families demonstrate the cost of our excessive separation anxiety.

Little Houses on the Prairie

The summer Judy and I moved to the mountains of southern Oregon, we found a surprising number of Jesus Movement believers living in our little community. We looked forward to working with these "like-minded" couples in this needy place.

A few months after we settled in, we had dinner in the home of one of these families. I presumed that they would share our vision for reaching out to the local culture. Wasn't that how we viewed life here on earth? We imagined passionate pleas to God and bold moves to touch the lives of these proud and rugged mountain people reeling from the collapse of the timber industry.

After only a few minutes with them, I knew that would never happen. The husband talked very little, and when he did it was about the sad state of the school system and their decision to homeschool their children. The wife went on and on about her dream that her kids would grow up in the innocence of the country, "just like in *Little House on the Prairie*." They wouldn't watch television or have any other unnecessary contact with the outside world. She even dressed her daughter in a Laura Ingalls–style wardrobe.

Like most of us, these two had grown up in an unholy mess. They were sure of what they didn't want for their children. They didn't want them to have to deal with the evil they had struggled with—the debilitating sin patterns of infidelity, alcoholism, drug abuse, and divorce.

And like too many of us, they falsely concluded that the only way to protect their children from the pain was to keep them away from the sin. They didn't move to Oregon to reach the world, they had moved to the mountains to get away from the world.

Maybe this is your strategy and you're committed to establishing a holy home by minimizing your family's exposure to the sinful world. You believe that it is possible to frame life in such a way that your children will not have to fight their personal battles with sin. But it seems fair to ask, "Lord

Marching Students
No wonder they called us "Jesus Freaks." A march for Jesus along a SoCal highway expressing the wild reborn hearts of new converts.

WANTED: JESUS CHRIST

Jeans for Jesus!
Karen Gifford and Cheryl Molinar from South Bakersfield High School represent for Jesus.

Smile
The well-worn cover of a Jesus Movement
disciple's Living Bible from back in the day.

The B.O. Trio
It didn't matter that there were sometimes four, sometimes five of us.
"Performing" at an all-city Young Life event and sharing the gospel with
hundreds of non-Christian students. I'm on the far left.

Young Life Leadership Team

This is the Young Life leadership team in Bakersfield, California, when I trusted Christ. Keith Osborn (far right) organized this team of college students who led seven different high school clubs and touched thousands of lives. Bobby Rader is top left, and Phil Walker is fourth from the left on the top row.

Sisters in Christ

Judy Christman Underwood's cheerleading friends who all came to Christ together (left to right): Ellen Elmore, Karen Gifford, Marlene Devries, and Judy. These are the four girls who celebrated Communion with Oreos and grape soda.

Leaders of Woodleaf Young Life Camp

I'm in the back. Craig (Mo) Smith, the cool dude from Chico, is front and center. This team, along with Keith, would take six busloads of students to Woodleaf every spring vacation.

Epicenter of the Jesus Movement
The SoCal beach today. Many came to Christ on these
beaches and were baptized in the Pacific Ocean.

Still Rockin'!
Me (right) with Jesus Movement rocker and blues legend
Darrell Mansfield. Darrell still looks hip. I just look old.

Jesus, do You expect this to work? Will removing our lives from the world guarantee holiness?"

The separatists of Jesus' day promoted a holiness based solely on separation. They framed countless petty regulations and social rules sincerely designed to promote a culture of purity and piety. Jesus openly disagreed with their teaching, saying that their zeal undermined God's commandments (Matt. 15:1–20).

Jesus taught His followers that true holiness comes from the inside. In that sense, the internal reality of transformed lives is where authentic holiness starts. It's the inescapable law of spiritual congruence: True obedience to the commands of God flows from a heart fully inclined toward Him.

Doesn't it trouble you that no outward system of holiness in history has been able to produce results? From the Pharisees of Jesus' day, to the legalistic cults throughout church history, trying to produce holiness by keeping sin out never works.

As a father and grandfather, I have mixed feelings on this problem. I hate the idea of my grandchildren's innocence being polluted by the decadence of our culture. I definitely wouldn't discourage parents from pursuing options that minimize that contamination. One of our children attended Christian schools during her adolescent years and two went to Christian universities. The Old Testament is full of examples of how sinful civilizations eroded the holiness of God's people. But the New Testament consistently warns against viewing disassociation from sinners as an effective and permanent step toward holiness.

Jesus specifically asked the Father not to take us out of the world while keeping us from evil (John 17:15). Paul warned the Corinthians against separating from the immoral people of this world, "since then you would need to go out of the world" (1 Cor. 5:10). New Testament righteousness is inner (Rom. 3:19–26; Col. 2:16–23), and the New Testament community is a go-to community, not a stay-away-from community (Heb. 13:10–13).

Jesus clearly taught that outward changes and appearances should never be confused with authentic godliness. Staying away from sin or just quitting it for a while isn't a reliable indicator of life change:

> Woe to you, experts in the law and you Pharisees, hypocrites! You clean the outside of the cup and the dish, but inside they are full of greed and self-indulgence. Blind Pharisee! First clean the inside of the cup, so that the outside may become clean too! (Matt. 23:25–26 NET)

Too many from our revival realized too late that no degree of separation would protect our children from the sin on the inside. Often these "innocent" environments forced our families to simply devise more cunning outlets for sin. When we finally noticed the stains underneath the white-washed tombs of our little houses on the prairie, the stench of uncleanness, hypocrisy, and lawlessness defiled Christ's reputation to a watching world.

Judy and I recently had dinner with two former "little house on the prairians." They found each other a few years after discovering the secret lives of their former spouses. Their happiness together and their restored love for the Lord Jesus eased some of the pain of what their outside-in, keep-out-the-world theories of holiness had done to their previous families.

She told me that I should warn people that "this stuff doesn't work," and I asked her, "Why do you think they will listen to me while they're ordering their lives in a way that removes all risk and refuses to face reality? If you recall, Judy and I tried to warn you, but you wouldn't listen until it all fell apart."

I have no problem with people who say, "We're not going to expose our children to such things," just as long as they're not using that as justification for not dealing with the truth about their inner lives. But the current state of unholiness among Christians tells us that too many of us need an inner-cup cleansing.

Some of my closest friends from the Jesus Movement are still trying to get away to their "little house." Only now they've made enough money to run a lot farther and deny a lot more than they could in their younger days. What they can't outrun is the impact of their preoccupation with the outer cup on the next generation.

If you're wondering why your children aren't as fired up about Jesus as you were at their age, it may be that they haven't seen the fire in you. The best way, the only way, to impress them with the reality of Christ's power in this world is to rekindle the fire in your own life.

Once you begin honestly assessing what your preoccupation with the enemy has cost your children, you are ready to admit what it has cost God's kingdom.

From Explo '72 to Implo '92

Explo '72 was the "Christian Woodstock" of the Jesus Movement. Young people from all over the world filled the Cotton Bowl in Dallas, Texas, from June 12 to June 17, 1972, to learn how to share their faith and to pray about the possibility of entering vocational ministry. Billy Graham spoke six times at the event, sponsored by Campus Crusade for Christ.

Nearly two hundred thousand people attended the conference that many view as the birthplace of Christian rock. Artists such as Love Song, Larry Norman, Randy Matthews, the Archers, and even Johnny Cash and Kris Kristofferson attracted not only huge crowds, but also the condemnation of many conservative church leaders.

Joe Losiak, a Polish-American student, was just one of the thousands who left Explo '72 with a vision for what the love of Christ meant for his world. He shared the concepts with his cardinal in Poland, who introduced them to the Catholic Church as the first non-Italian Pope since the 1500s—Pope John Paul II.

One of my best friends from seminary was also a part of that capacity crowd in 1972. In the Cotton Bowl, God so burdened him for a particular continent that he redirected his life toward the mission field. He prayed for and God gave him a wife who shared his burden, and the two of them arrived at Dallas Seminary the same year as Judy and me.

We instantly knew that these two were destined for greatness in the kingdom of God. Articulate, talented, and deeply passionate about worldwide outreach, they organized prayer groups for the people groups of their continent and took every opportunity to tell fellow students about their burden.

I have met few Christians before or since so sure of their calling, and so competent to pursue it. We delighted in their reports from the field the first few years of their missionary service. We prayed with them through the challenges of their work and begged God to give them open doors for the gospel. We marveled at their willingness to immerse themselves in such a godless and decadent culture for Jesus' sake.

A few years later, they returned to the United States disillusioned and worn out by the combination of intense spiritual warfare and unfortunate missionary politics. Their burden for people overseas remained strong, but they were learning hard lessons about failure and despair.

He still felt strongly that God was calling them back to the dream God planted in his heart at Explo '72. That required a lengthy process of trying to recover from the hurt of their first tour of duty and finding another mission agency with whom to partner.

They sent updates to their prayer-support team. We all began to sense that the Lord might be asking them to establish a ministry of their own. Every mission organization door seemed to close, until he was accepted into a very selective professional graduate school that would provide great opportunity for influence.

Every month, we joined them in asking God to keep the fire for the people burning in their hearts. Then we prayed for his studies, their neighbors and fellow students at the professional school, and their growing family.

By the end of the first year, I noticed a significant change in the content and tone of their prayer requests. We saw fewer references to the world's desperate need for Christ and more reports of the world's wickedness and opposition to Christ. Their bold desire to charge into Satan's territory winning souls for Christ in this great big world diminished as their hand-wringing apprehensions over Satan's influence in their little world increased.

In the fall of 1992 they stayed in our home on their way to the life they now lead in an extremely remote part of our country. Their vision shifted from establishing a beachhead for Jesus in a godless land to building a fortress of godliness for their family and selected friends.

Are they a wonderful Christian couple? Yes! Does the Lord Jesus appreciate their devotion to Him in his professional life and their business? Absolutely! Will God affirm their dedication to their family and little community of Christians? Of course!

And yet the continent God burdened them with thirty-five years ago still languishes in the hopeless darkness of paganism. It's not that their lives today don't count for the Lord Jesus; it's just that they could have counted so much more.

Only God knows how many hearts exploding with enthusiasm for reaching out to the lost have imploded—collapsing in on themselves from the crushing weight of fear and anger toward outside forces of evil.

If you have ever heard God's calling, or had your own personal dream of significance in His kingdom, or felt His burden for a portion of this lost world, you know already how the pressures of fear and anger can feel. In fact, you might be wondering how you ever lost the fire. If so, you're probably wondering where you went wrong and how your caring heart got turned in on itself.

Our separation anxiety and our incorrect thinking about our enemies stem from two serious and correlated misunderstandings: We misdiagnosed the longing of our hearts while misreading God's purpose for our lives.

What Do I Long For?

I hear Christians say that they can't wait for heaven because they're tired of having to live around all this sin and pain. The remark reveals a longing for a place far removed from the wickedness that touches our lives every day in a million ways.

The Bible says that heaven will be void of evil, but that's because it's full of something else—the presence of the Lord Jesus Christ (Rev. 21:23). I expect the absence of wickedness to thrill our hearts, but that's not the main attraction. What pulls our redeemed hearts to heaven is the promise of face-to-face intimacy with Jesus (Rev. 22:4). Biblically, "going to heaven" isn't running *from* the presence of the evil of this world, it's running *to* the presence of the Lord Jesus Christ.

Confusing our heavenly desire for the joy of intimacy with Christ with the side benefit of no exposure to wickedness has led many of us to believe we deserve the absence of evil on earth. Clamoring for what we can never have on earth, we neglect our family's only hope for overcoming the world, which is a relationship with Jesus Christ (John 14:15; 1 John 5:4–5).

The week before our son Bob deployed to Iraq the second time, we had dinner with the then-president of Biola University, Dr. Clyde Cook, and his wife, Anna Belle. Clyde is in heaven now, but on that afternoon, he really helped our family remember God's definition of security. This great man of God was very purposeful to sit next to Bob and to speak truth into his life. He looked Bob in the eye and said, "Here is something I want you to remember in the war zone: 'Safety is not the absence of danger but the presence of the Lord.'" He repeated that sentence throughout the meal, "Safety is not the absence of danger but the presence of the Lord."

During Bob's twelve months in Baghdad, we often heard or read reports of casualties in the areas we knew our soldier served. Every time, we would hold our breath, praying for his safety. After each of these minicrises, Clyde's words would remind us of what really mattered, "Safety is not the absence of danger but the presence of the Lord."

We knew that it was much better for us that Bob was in Iraq walking with Jesus than it was for a lot of our friends whose children were "safe" in Southern California walking away from Jesus. And though we couldn't keep from worrying about our son, Jesus' strong presence in his life brought a God-made peace to our hearts no parent-configured security strategy ever could.

You may be thinking, "Well, my son or daughter will never be dodging bullets and mortars in a war zone." Yes, you can keep your children out of the military and the threat of physical harm from the hot lead of battle, but you cannot keep your children out of the line of fire of their spiritual enemies—Satan, the world, and the flesh.

Let me ask you, do you think you can outrun evil? Do you believe your family's spiritual health is influenced more by the absence of wickedness or the presence of Jesus within them?

I've observed that Christians who grew up in these run-from-evil homes lose their spiritual breath when they hit the real world in the same way that we gasp for air when diving into ice-cold water. Almost all of them become temporarily disoriented, but many lose their way for months or years and even decades.

What's most alarming to me is that many of these perplexed Christians— my students in Christian colleges and universities, young people I talk to at Bible conferences, even some I know personally—are children of Jesus Movement believers! If ever a generation of parents should have made the connection between the inner strength of our children's relationship with Jesus and their spiritual survivability factor, it should have been us.

And let me ask you: Which strategy have you embraced to protect your family from the evil of this world and our spiritual enemies?

Think about the message you're sending your family about the power of the living God over His enemies. If your fear of evil's potency is stronger than your faith in Jesus' strength, doesn't that give them a wimpy view of God? If you're living as if Jesus really is all you need to overcome the world, wouldn't that dramatically change the way they live their lives and how they think about God?

You simply cannot satisfy the longing of a believer's heart by running away from darkness. The message of Christianity is the exact opposite. We're the ones whose joy is full only when we are having deep intimacy with the Father and His Son, Jesus Christ. We're the ones who declare that God is light and in Him is no darkness at all (1 John 1:3–5). We're the ones whose deepest need is not the absence of danger but the presence of the Lord.

God's Spirit won't tell you that your comfort zone is your safety zone. And God's Spirit won't tell you to run from this world. He will tell you to run to the battle.

What Am I Here For?

Until we go to heaven, our present assignment is to represent heaven on earth. Paul says we are ambassadors for Christ (2 Cor. 5:20). What do you think our president would think of an ambassador for the United States who refused to leave the U.S. embassy because he or she didn't want to come into contact with the people or the culture of the foreign station? What do you think Jesus thinks of His ambassadors who refuse to leave their holy compounds, afraid to engage with the people and the culture of their alien assignment?

Jesus didn't say, "Gather in protected places and think about Me." He said, "Follow Me" (Matt. 4:19; Luke 5:27; John 1:43). And then He waded into a culture ferociously hostile to Him and His message.

If disciples are anything, they are followers. Walking with Jesus never puts us on a trail to seclusion and separation. Jesus had a reputation for hanging out with the wrong crowd. The religious people of His day accused Him of being a glutton and a drunkard, a friend of sinners (Luke 7:34).

A few years ago our church sent a missionary family to Holland. Some of their friends were appalled at this couple's willingness to expose their children to such a godless culture. "Isn't Amsterdam the city with the largest red-light district in the world? How could you go to a place that actually prides itself on its tolerant attitude toward drugs, pornography, and prostitution?"

But Eric, the father, has a different view of the Dutch people. He doesn't think of them as the enemy. He feels they are exploited and wounded by the enemy. He's not alone in his opinion. Embedded in Amsterdam's red-light district is The Cleft, a building owned by Youth With a Mission. Every day, the staff reaches out to the prostitutes, homeless, addicted, hungry, and even the men coming to see the women. In the name of Jesus, they bring coffee, tea, prayer, and friendship to the women in the window brothels, build relationships with the street addicts and prostitutes, counsel, hold evangelistic street meetings, feed the hungry, and visit these sexually broken people in hospitals and prisons.

Do you think Jesus wants more Christians like Eric and the staff of YWAM's The Cleft, or more Christians like the ones challenging them from their holed-up, gated, barbed-wired enclaves in the suburbs? Where do you think the footsteps of Jesus lead His followers: toward the lost and hopeless, or away from them?

It's a critical insight from Scripture that unbelievers aren't the enemy—they are victims of the enemy! Paul said that the god of this world is blinding the eyes of unbelievers (2 Cor. 4:3–4) and that we reach out to them so that they may come to their senses and escape the snare of the devil (2 Tim. 2:26). A New Testament view of the world drips with Jesus' compassion for the lost because we see them as He sees them—blind and ensnared by Satan's lies and power.

Maybe the truest indicator of authentic revival is that it's all about the harvest. Jesus told us that there's nothing wrong with the harvest; it's the shortage of harvesters that limits the yield. Jesus never told us to build large plantation homes removed from the risk, pain, and struggle of harvesting. Our place is in the fields, backs bent and hands in the dirt, begging the Lord of the harvest to send out more laborers to join us (Matt. 9:37).

So let me ask you, are you afraid to enter the very field the Lord Jesus sent you to harvest? If you aren't purposefully and fervently connecting your life to this lost and dying world, you will never know the thrill of revival.

Jesus' will for you in the harvest of souls is clear: probably risky, certainly messy, but completely redemptive. Don't wait until you feel like you're not afraid of those you formerly viewed as the "enemies" of Christ, because that day may never come. Listen to Jesus instead of your fears. Trust in His power instead of your plans. Look at the walls you've built around your life and identify them for what they really are: These aren't God's way of keeping evil people out; these are Satan's way of keeping you in, where you will never know the joy of the harvest.

Checkpoint Charlie

In 1977, while I was serving as an army officer in Europe, our unit trained in Berlin for a week. The most significant day of training wasn't the day we practiced defending the West Germans from the Soviet Empire, neither was it the day we drove our tanks around a course teaching us the skills of fighting in urban warfare. The single most life-changing moment occurred the day we passed through Checkpoint Charlie.

Checkpoint Charlie was the name Western Allies assigned to a border-crossing point between East Berlin and West Berlin during the Cold War. The Berlin Wall separated the two—twelve feet of concrete topped with barbed wire and supported by machine gun positions and sharpshooters.

The Soviets didn't erect the wall to keep the West Germans out. They built it to keep the East Germans in. The machine gunners and sharpshooters only shot and killed those trying to escape to freedom.

Whatever doubts we may have had about whether we were fighting on the right side evaporated that day. West Berlin was a thriving metropolis; it reminded me of Los Angeles—streets alive with the sounds of freedom. East Berlin was a gray and dreary place; only the police walked the streets; everyone else hurried between destinations with fear in their eyes.

Even the mighty propaganda machine of the Soviet Empire couldn't explain that reality away. Nothing they said about the benefits of Communism or the superiority of their way of life could deny that one glaring inconsistency: They had to quarantine their people, afraid of what they would do if they ever saw the other side of the wall.

If Jesus chose spiritual freedom for us and expects us to use it to reach the world rather than run from it, how do we find authentic spiritual fulfillment behind our Christian walls? How do we explain our fears and quarantining strategies to our children?

The answer is this: We don't. We lose them to the very world we are vainly trying to wall out.

On June 12, 1987, President Ronald Reagan stood at the Brandenburg Gate on the free side of the Berlin Wall and challenged the general secretary of the Communist Party: "Mr. Gorbachev, tear down this wall!"

It's time for Christians whose hearts long for revival to denounce the lie that the enemies of Christ are more powerful than His life within us. It's time for harvesters to move into the fields of opportunity made ripe by the Lord of the harvest. It's time to shout, "Christians, tear down this wall!"

Is it time to tear down the walls in your life? Are you hearing God's call to move boldly into enemy territory with His promises in your heart? Have you been misrepresenting the awesome power of the living God to your children? Do you want them to see what He can do? How He can overcome all His foes?

Then tell Him:

> Oh, my Father in heaven, I'm tired of being afraid of this
> world and I'm weary of these futile, desperate strategies
> of separation. I'm tired of living as if I'm ashamed of the
> gospel and its power to deliver. I want to strap on Your
> armor and run to the battle. I don't want my children to
> think of me as one who cowers behind the lines in fear. I
> want them to see me raising Your banner high and planting
> it in enemy territory. Forgive me for not believing in Your
> Son's resurrection power, for disrespecting His claim to be
> greater than all my enemies and His promise to overcome
> the world. Oh my God, just give me another chance to
> fight. Let me live from this day forward as a soldier of
> Christ, a warrior who will be able to look my loved ones
> in the eye from my deathbed and say, "I have fought the
> good fight, I have finished the race, I have kept the faith"
> (2 Tim. 4:7).

If you want to be a revival warrior, there's one more lie you must
renounce. Soldiers travel light, carrying only the essentials with them. You
won't be able to fight with your arms full of the stuff you can never take
with you to heaven anyway.

Chapter 9

It's All Mine

If someone asked you to describe the financial choices and spending habits of a sold-out, revival-hearted Christian, what words would you use? Here are a few I'm sure you're thinking of: sacrificial, unselfish, generous, purposeful, responsible, cheerful, trusting, obedient, and transcendent. Here are a few that do not come to mind: self-indulgent, miserly, impetuous, reckless, grudging, independent, rebellious, and myopic.

In the early years of our revival, I believe the first list of words described us. We had very little and gave away most of the little we had. The wrecks we drove around town were full of kids we were discipling. Who had money for a car payment? Most of these unsaved kids didn't have a Bible or the money to buy any of the resources we used to teach them about Jesus. We took them to breakfast and lunch two or three times a week, and we had to save every penny to pick up the tab. We wouldn't want a dollar to stand between one of our clubbers and Christ. Our churches needed money to tell people in faraway places about our Jesus. Those were our priorities and a far better use of our resources than shopping and spending.

Today the embarrassing words of the second list could explain the financial attitudes of too many of us. We drive luxury cars and spacious SUVs, live in expansive homes in the suburbs, eat in the top restaurants, smoke the most expensive cigars, and drink the finest wines, play on premium golf courses, shop in trendy stores, cruise the seas and fly with the beautiful people to faraway places, while most of our churches struggle to meet bare-bones budgets and cross-cultural Christian workers live hand-to-mouth.

We've accumulated more wealth and prosperity than any generation in church history. And unless something changes, we will leave this earth in its sin-stained decadence and enter heaven empty-handed, because we have invested most of our resources here rather than there. Do we really need to swim with the dolphins or visit Paris one more time before we die?

This last lie may be the one we most wanted to believe: *It's all mine!* We listened too approvingly to teachers who made the hard sayings of Jesus about finances easy. We gave what we "could" or what we could control. And we wonder why the postmodern Christians aren't listening to us?

Why is it that we're so careful when we read the Bible's instruction on marriage, family, morality, culture, creation, and church, but so sloppy when we interpret Jesus' lessons on money? We explain away His hard sayings with complicated interpretations, and excuse our disobedience with absurd reasoning. But I think Jesus would have some tough questions for us if we offered these explanations and excuses to Him. The same questions He asked the large crowd clamoring for His attention and favor in Luke 12 when the subject of money came up.

How Do You Define Meaning in Life?

The man who initiated the discussion of money pushed forward in the crowd to get Jesus' attention, "Teacher, tell my brother to divide the inheritance with me" (Luke 12:13). His brother must have been there with him, so the crowd was expecting the usual—charges and countercharges, inquiries, and an attempt to settle the dispute according to the Law.

Instead, Jesus saw right through the brothers' dispute to their true motivation: greed! Refusing to arbitrate their disagreement, He warns them, "Beware, and be on your guard against every form of greed" (Luke 12:15a NASB). But then Jesus goes even deeper, exposing their core problem: their values! He advises them both to rethink their definition of life's meaning: "For not even when one has an abundance does his life consist of his possessions" (Luke 12:15b NASB).

A greedy heart is a disoriented heart—a heart that views life as consisting of the stuff we own. For the greedy heart, life is about owning a nice home in a neighborhood with good schools. Life is about taking nice vacations every year. Life is about sending our children to the college of their choice. Life is about driving that luxury car I always wanted. Life is about season tickets, upscale restaurants, shopping at Nordstrom's, the second home at the beach or in the mountains, the cruise, the expensive hobby, the boat, the ski trips, the …

I'm not saying that any of these possessions or activities is wrong, as long as they're not a part of our definition of what matters most in life. But before you conclude too quickly that you don't define life this way, remember what upset this man the most in Luke 12!

With the *Son of God* and *Messiah of Israel* as his audience, and with the opportunity to ask Him for anything he wanted, to seek any comfort, his preoccupying thought was *money*. That's what bothered him most; that's what he wanted to talk to God about.

So what preoccupies your thoughts right now? Do you think about the millions of souls around the world slipping toward a godless eternity because they've never heard the name of Jesus, or the type of marble you need to choose for your new countertops? Do you think about the neighborhoods in your city where poverty distances people from tangible evidence of the love of Christ, or how you're going to get tickets for the concert or the big game? Do you think about the starving millions around the world, or the healthiest options and most effective workout to maximize your personal health? Do you think about the young families in your church trying to walk with Christ with no godly models, or your research on the Web trying to determine the very best car, computer, RV, watch, barbecue, HDTV with surround sound, pool and spa, wallpaper, paint, or whatever toy you're pursuing right now?

Even more revealing is what upsets you most. Is it the lack of commitment in the church today or the lack of funds in your bank account? Would it be the lies about Christ circulating in the world or the lies the contractor told you during your latest remodel, upgrade, or landscaping project?

And maybe the most probing question, do sermons on giving and appeals for money from Christian leaders bother you? Is this chapter upsetting to you? Why?

I'm preaching through the book of Proverbs right now, and the book says a lot about money. Sometimes I catch myself buying into the "It's all mine" mentality even as I prepare for next week's sermon. "Okay, Lord, they get it. This is going to get old, week after week. It feels like all I'm doing is talking about money."

When you and I begin to accuse God of overemphasis, it has nothing to do with His inerrant Word. Sixteen of the thirty-eight parables Jesus taught deal with money, and one out of every ten verses in the New Testament addresses the subject of our finances. There are only five hundred verses on prayer and less than five hundred on faith in the New Testament, but over two thousand verses specifically dealing with money! God never overemphasizes; He always tells us what we need to hear in perfect proportion to what is important to Him.

It's important to God that we define life in terms of His glory and significance in His kingdom rather than ease and pleasure.

God made our churches and our missionaries dependent on our attitude toward money on purpose—to protect us from the temptation of our flesh to define meaning in life by the things in this life. In Christ's church, the believer's definition of life is evident in his or her attitude toward giving. When we succumb to this world's evil pull of greed, it's more than a selfish setback; it's an expression of what we truly believe about life.

By now you may be asking, "Okay, Ed, I'm convinced. I look at the rock stars and sports heroes with their millions and see it: Accumulating wealth does not produce life. But I'm not trying to get rich; I just want to provide for my family. I'm not materialistic; I would give more if I could. Shouldn't I provide for my future, my family's future?"

I understand the question. The Bible is full of exhortations to prepare for the future. But our planning must be based upon Jesus' definition of financial security, not our own.

How Do You Define Financial Security?

I believe the man who asked Jesus to arbitrate his inheritance was ready to ask Jesus this question: "But what about my financial security? If my brother gets all of our inheritance, I'm not going to make it!"

Before he could object, Jesus again corrected the thinking behind the question. Apparently, losing his inheritance wouldn't have left this man homeless. If he looked at his life honestly, he would have to admit that his security wasn't in jeopardy. What he really wanted was "more" security. But it's his definition of "more" that Jesus challenged through a parable of another rich man in Luke 12, verses 16–21, whose ideas of more security caused him to prepare foolishly for his retirement.

The rich fool's land was so fertile and his harvests so bountiful that he ran out of places to store his crops (Luke 12:16–17). Talk about a portfolio! This guy's investments paid off so well, he couldn't find a bank large enough to deposit his money.

Jesus took us into the thought process of the rich fool and allowed us to eavesdrop on an amazing internal struggle. *Wow, I don't have anywhere else to put this stuff. What should I do?* he asked himself. *Oh I know,* he happily concludes, *I'll just tear down the old barns and build newer and bigger ones. Then I'll be able to hoard even more. Yeah, that's it. Then I'll really have it made. Once these big barns fill up, I'll be set for life. Retirement, here I come—years of doing whatever I want, when I want, and in whatever way I want* (Luke 12:17–19).

Does the rich fool's shallow reasoning and errant conclusion remind you of anyone? How about us? Our foolish "It's all mine" mentality differs very little, if at all, from his!

Never imagining that our problem may be that we have too much stuff, we fill our garages with so much stuff that we have to park our cars in the driveway, rent storage units, and put on garage sales to get rid of the stuff we don't want anymore so we can get some money to buy more.

We rarely consider that our definition of security doesn't agree with God's; instead we worry over our investments and plan for the future we feel we deserve rather than the future God might want to give us. Too many of us view our retirement in the same way the rich fool did—a time for *me,* when I can finally have things my way and enjoy life as I've always deserved to enjoy it. After all, I worked hard for this!

Now that we know how the rich fool thought about his security, Jesus lets us hear what God thought: "But God said to him, 'Fool! This night your soul will be required of you; then whose will those things be which you have provided?'" (Luke 12:20).

There's a question for our "It's all mine" attitude toward money and financial security: "Then whose will those things be which you have provided?"

Seems like it's true: You can't take the stuff that doesn't matter to God with you to heaven! You and I, like the rich fool, will leave it *all* behind.

Failing to factor God into our definition of security is a big mistake. He numbers our days. He knows what the future holds. And He will decide how much of our precious "stuff" we get to personally enjoy.

You may resist all the verses, sermons, and letters asking you to live unselfishly with your finances—to give to your church, to Christian workers, and Christian causes around the world, to give to the poor in the name of Christ, to share your resources to the glory of God, and to build His Son's church. You may persist in your "I worked hard for this, it's my money, no one is going to separate me from my money" way of thinking. But the day will come when God will absolutely separate you from all of your earth-invested money. The day He has appointed for you to die.

Then what? That money won't be yours anymore; you left it behind.

Jesus says so when He applies the parable to every "It's all mine" thinker who "lays up treasure for himself, and is not rich toward God" (Luke 12:21).

Here, in just one parable, Jesus crushes three common miscalculations of the "It's all mine" lie that has sidetracked us, His people:

> 1. *How Did You Get Your Treasure? I earned it by working hard or investing smart.* Jesus is careful not to say anything about this man's intelligence or diligence. The only reason for his barns bursting with grain was that this man's ground "yielded plentifully." He wants us to know that our wealth comes from God.

> 2. *For Whom Is Your Treasure? I need to store this up, use it for me, and save it for me.* When his barns could no longer hold his wealth, it never occurred to him to give it away to the poor, or to the temple, or the synagogue. Jesus never encourages His people to be selfish, only selfless. The

question for the follower of Christ should never be, "How can I spend this money?" The question is, "How does Jesus want me to spend this money?"

3. *Where Should You Invest Your Treasure? I will be secure when I have enough money to live the rest of my years without working.* The rich fool was sure that he had achieved his goal to live the good life, the easy life, to "eat, drink, and be merry." If your view of the future stops short of the future kingdom of God, your security plan will not survive your death. The sad truth is that you have invested your treasure in the wrong place for the wrong reasons.

When you read this list, you might identify some shortcomings in your own understanding of security. You may be hearing the Lord tell you to stop building that bigger barn and start emptying the one you have by investing your resources into the things that matter most to Him. Or you might read the list and feel pretty good about yourself: *Good for You, Jesus. I've noticed that rich people really are greedy. They're always suing one another and hoarding their wealth for their own selfish purposes. If I ever get rich, I'll be sure to deposit a lot of my resources in heaven.*

Before you relax too much, read what Jesus says to some of the poorest people in the crowd that day, His disciples. What the rich young man worried about exposed his wrong thinking about money. But it's what the poor disciples worried about that would expose their own wrong thinking about money.

What Are You Worried About?

I've observed that believers who take the first steps away from the greediness of materialism usually hit the worry wall hard. After a few months of sacrificially committing their resources to Christ's work, they face a financial crisis. Though they understand that being upset over not having everything they want is a clear indicator of a wrong definition of life, they feel quite justified to worry about how they're now going to make ends meet. They'll say, "I'm already stretched to the limit. I barely get by as it is." Or, "I've got kids to take care of, a mortgage to pay, doctor bills, and look at this economy. I'm trying to live for Jesus, but how could He possibly expect someone like me to give any more of my money away?"

I had some of the same feelings when Judy and I began submitting our finances to God. I was more than willing to give, even give a lot. I just couldn't understand why God didn't take better care of me, why He refused to take some of the pressure off. Some of our most heated marital arguments were over money—how much we should give or whether we really had the money to give this month. I would lie awake for hours, worrying about money.

Jesus' command in Luke 12:22 and exhortation in verse 23 helped change my thinking:

> Then He said to His disciples, "Therefore I say to you, do
> not worry about your life, what you will eat; nor about the
> body, what you will put on. Life is more than food, and the
> body is more than clothing."

The rich fool had to learn that life is about more than accumulating wealth. The committed disciple needs to learn that life is about more than what it takes to "get by" or "make ends meet." Worrying about having enough to eat or adequate clothes to wear is foolish for the same reason— these things are not important in life.

In verses 24 and 27, Jesus uses two illustrations from nature, the raven and the lily, to demonstrate God's provision of food (raven) and God's provision of clothing (lily).

The raven doesn't have any resource to grow, harvest, or store the crops it needs to survive. The lily's magnificent apparel is all a work of God because it has no capacity to "toil." If God cares for insignificant ravens (an unclean bird to the Hebrews) and short-lived lilies so well, don't you think He will care for Christ's disciples—His cherished children?

Jesus' point in verses 24 and 25 is that worrying doesn't change a thing. You can't worry yourself taller or worry your life longer, so why do you think you can worry yourself a meal when you're hungry or a coat when you're cold?

Worrying doesn't work! It's a waste of time. Worrying about your finances will not solve any of your financial problems or ease any of your sleepless nights. You just wake up the next morning with the same challenges you had the night before. In fact, I have found that worrying usually only makes things worse.

> If then God so clothes the grass, which today is in the field and tomorrow is thrown into the oven, how much more will He clothe you, O you of little faith? And do not seek what you should eat or what you should drink, nor have an anxious mind. For all these things the nations of the world seek after, and your Father knows that you need these things. (Luke 12:28–30)

This passage reminds me that worry is the opposite of faith, and faith is what sets me as a Christian apart from everyone else. If I worry about my finances, it's because I really don't believe that He is as good and powerful and caring as I say He is. I'm no different from my neighbor who doesn't believe in God if we both go to bed at night with anxious minds. I need to remember that my heavenly Father knows what I need.

I wonder how many Jesus Movement Christians go to bed every night worried to distraction about how they're going to pay their bills, make payroll, send their kids to college, or provide for their retirement.

I wonder how long it will take us to realize that all our worry does is tell our watching children and our waiting God that we really don't believe He is our loving Father. Worrying says that we really don't view Him as the one who can meet our every need.

I wonder how often we think back to the days when we didn't worry about what we would eat or what we would wear. To the days when we pooled our gas money to go to a retreat and skipped meals because we had given our last penny to the kid who didn't have enough to go to Young Life Camp.

I wonder how we could forget that we didn't have any idea how we would pay our tuition and still give to our local church, but since the Lord led us to college, He would take care of us … and He did!

I wonder if you're thinking about the last time you fell asleep not worrying about money.

If you're honest, you have to admit it was a time when you were closer to God and leaning on Him. I'm sure it was a time when you weren't so preoccupied with the things of this world. There was the hope of a better life now, a better world, and a future world that would be glorious—a coming kingdom that had captured your heart.

If you can't remember a time like that, it may be that Jesus' words have never before pulled your heart toward all that really matters in life—His coming kingdom.

What Are You Living For?

Jesus finished His teaching on meaning in life and financial security by turning His disciples' attention from what will never bring financial security because it is based on the world's view of life—worrying about money—to what will always result in financial security because it is based on His view of life—trusting His Father to care for kingdom-seekers:

> But seek the kingdom of God, and all these things shall
> be added to you. Do not fear, little flock, for it is your
> Father's good pleasure to give you the kingdom. (Luke
> 12:31–32)

Once believers understand that worrying about their material needs is always futile and a failure of faith, a radical new way to financial well-being opens up: *Claiming Jesus' promise that His Father will care for them if they will devote their resources to His kingdom.*

One of my greatest Christmas morning frustrations as a loving father and grandfather is the ridiculous preoccupation toddlers have with the box their presents come in. Judy and I carefully select the perfect gift to express our love for them, wrap it, and put it under the tree. As Christmas draws near, we anticipate their joy when they unwrap our gift and discover all the wonderful things inside. The older children do just what we want them to do—they tear open the box, cast it aside, and rejoice over all that our heart desired to give them. The toddlers, however, react in exactly the wrong way—they turn the box upside down, dump out all the good stuff, and sit in a corner, preoccupied with the lousy box we found in the garage to contain the wonderful manifestations of our affection for them.

Most Christians never get past the toddler stage when it comes to opening the gifts of grace God loves to give His children. So preoccupied with the "box" of their physical needs, they never notice the breathtakingly supernatural kingdom-building treasures of opportunity and blessing He really wants to give them.

It isn't that God doesn't care for your physical needs and your financial hardships; He does. It's just that these things aren't what He most wants to give you. He wants to give His flock entrance into His kingdom. Not only does He want to give it; it brings Him great pleasure to give!

I believe that this offer of the "kingdom of God" is a real offer of life now. It is a life full of eternal significance and meaning known only to those who live to see His glory displayed here on earth (Matt. 6:33). It is a real offer of reward in Christ's future kingdom, where faithful saints and kingdom-seekers will rule and reign with Him (Rev. 22:12).

This is why Jesus tells us to make Him our number-one priority, to seek His kingdom. It's as if He's saying, "Why are you so worried about the box? Grow up! If you'll just take the time to look inside, you'll find experiences of grace, eternal opportunities, and spiritual power you never imagined—everything My Father really wants to give you. But you must seek His kingdom before He will give you another eternal treasure in a brown earthly box, because you can't seem to get past the box!"

It's one of the most countercultural, paradoxical principles in the Christian life. Hoarding wealth or worrying about money is not the way to financial security: *Seeking the kingdom of God is the only sure way to the security of knowing that God is underwriting your finances.*

Saying you believe this to be true isn't enough. Jesus' next command to His disciples is one of those "prove it" challenges He often adds to His teaching on the faith it takes to follow Him:

> Sell what you have and give alms; provide yourself money bags which do not grow old, a treasure in the heavens that does not fail, where no thief approaches nor moth destroys. For where your treasure is, there your heart will be also. (Luke 12:33–34)

This is Jesus' invitation to start seeking the kingdom of God by emptying our barns. He doesn't tell us to give everything away. He tells us to sell "what we have" (things that are valuable) and redirect that money toward the poor and needy, and therefore, into investments (money bags) that will never fail to appreciate to our account—Christ's kingdom-building work.

This is also Jesus' declaration that we can't hide the true meaning of our refusal or fear to invest in His kingdom—the idea that our heart just isn't in it. Over the years, I've offered a few and heard just about every excuse not to give generously to Christ's work.

"We're just not in a place where we can give much right now, with the doctor bills and the cutbacks at work."

"I'm going to give as soon as I get out of debt."

"I would give if I could find a church that does things the way I think it should."

"If God would just take better care of me financially, I would be happy to give."

Jesus would say, "No, the problem isn't your doctor bills or your working conditions; it's your heart. It's not your debt; it's your heart. It's not the church; it's your heart. And it's certainly not My Father's fault … it's your heart!"

And the only way to reorient your heart is to redirect your resources. Jesus says that your heart and your money are inseparable: "For where your treasure is, there your heart will be also" (Matt. 6:21).

You see, God already knows what you're living for: either yourself and all this world has to offer, or Him and all He promises to kingdom-seekers. Whether you realize it or not, you've been telling Him for years—by where you invest your money.

I have a very simple rule of theology that has never failed me: *God is smart!* The corollary to that is: *God is not stupid!*

If you and I really want to be a part of another revival like the Jesus Movement, we must remember that *God is smart*—He would never pour His revival-generating power into hearts that care more about this world than they do about the world to come.

He's so smart, in fact, that He's prepared a test that we must pass before He lets us get involved with the things that mean most to Him. But He's also gracious, so this isn't some surprise test that we can't prepare for. His

Son told us plainly what was "on the test" in a familiar verse most of us know, but few of us have understood in its context.

The Test: A Little for a Lot

By turning a few pages from Jesus' teaching on money in Luke 12 we find another passage on how God views our use of money. "He who is faithful in what is *least* is faithful also in *much*" (Luke 16:10).

If you stay within the story itself, you will find the keys that unlock this verse's meaning. The issue is the faithfulness of a steward—someone who is managing someone else's resources. The shrewd steward of Jesus' parable kept his master's business intact by sacrificing his own money, removing his personal commission from the price, and making the master's customers happy (Luke 16:1–8).

The *little* is the steward's small commission, which meant everything to the steward, but very little to the master. The *much* is the master's overall enterprise, which meant everything to the master. The test from the master's perspective was, "What will the steward do with what is not important to me, my *little?*" The reward was, "If he passes this test, then I'll know that I can trust him with what I really care about, my *much.*"

As you read on, the application is revealed: If you and I have been faithful in our stewardship of the physical resources God gives us— unrighteous mammon, *mere money,* God's *little*—then He will entrust us with true riches—His redemptive kingdom work in this world as His Son builds His church, or God's *much.*

I believe God is looking for faithful stewards to call His people back to revival. I believe that many of those He's calling were, like me, a part of the last great American revival—the Jesus Movement. But I also believe that our materialism, our hoarding of money, our myopic, self-centered spending habits, and our failure to invest in the kingdom of God are our greatest barriers to seeing another worldwide movement of God's Spirit.

That is why I saved this chapter for last in this section exposing the six lies that stalled our revolution. The other five lies—*More Is Better,* *"Churchianity" Is Enough, Power Is Good, Bigger Is Better,* and *Enemies All Around*—pulled us away from the path to revival. I hope this book is helping you see where we made a wrong turn. But this lie—*It's All Mine*—didn't cause us to lose our *way* to revival; it caused us to lose our *right* to be a part of one.

We have so mismanaged God's *little,* our money, that He is passing the stewardship of His *much,* revival, on to others whose hearts are fixed on His kingdom … *unless we repent.*

Repentance is turning to God—trusting who He says He is and what He says about life rather than trusting in our futile attempts to make life work without Him. The act of repentance that tells God we trust Him with our finances (our little) so that He will trust us with revival (His much) is to invest the money He gave us and rightfully owns, into His kingdom.

Because you're still reading this chapter on money, I believe you share my desire to be a part of a revival that turns the world upside down again for Jesus Christ. And I think you'll want to join me in this prayer.

Oh, but before we pray, let's pull out our checkbook or debit card and spend a few minutes asking God how much He wants us to invest. You'll probably be shocked by His answer because He's asking you to empty a lot out of your barn, or even sell some of your possessions. But don't argue with Him. Remember, He's not stupid and the stakes are high. He's deciding who will lead His coming revival.

> *Father, I so want to be a part of a revival, but I have disqualified myself by my unfaithful stewardship. My barns are full and I've been hoarding money for myself. Worse yet, I have wasted so much time worrying about my finances while disregarding Your promise to meet my every need. If only I would manage my money the way You have directed. I know*

I've failed the test that opens the door to greater opportunities to serve Your Son. I'm telling You now that I want to change all that. Please accept this gift as my first "revival offering." This is only the beginning, Lord, but I had to start somewhere. I'm asking You now to give me the courage and the faith to say no to my selfish desire to invest in my own life and yes to Your selfless call to invest in Your work. Oh God, please let me be a part of Your coming revival. I beg You to use me powerfully as I demonstrate to You that I am a steward worthy of Your trust. In Jesus' name, amen.

If you just prayed this prayer and showed God that your heart is turning toward heaven again, keep reading. And, welcome back to the road to revival.

Now, write the check!

Then How?

If the last six chapters discouraged you, I join you in that discouragement. It's a tragic story of lost opportunity and neutralized lives on a massive scale. However, if your discouragement is causing you to throw up your hands and say, "I guess that's it. It's over. We blew it," you're wrong.

I believe that God's Spirit is calling the spiritual revolutionaries of the 1960s and 1970s back to the radical Christianity that spawned our revival. Virtually every Jesus Movement Christian I've talked to about our sidetracked revival has told me how disgusted they are with what we've become, and how God has awakened a craving in their heart to finish what we started and begin living out the revival of our youth again.

I believe that God's Spirit is also moving us to reach across the theological, cultural, and generational dividing lines of Christianity to lock arms with a remnant of believers who, like us, are ready to make a radical commitment to the Lord Jesus because their hearts long for revival.

I believe that God's Spirit is especially focused on the authentic core of the passionate men and women gathering together at the conferences and in the promising young churches of what is popularly known as the "emerging church."

If you would place yourself in any of these revival-hearted categories, I invite you to think with me as I answer the question: "If I could do it over again, what would I do differently?"

I'm convinced that the answer to that question will not only get our sidetracked revival back on track and awaken our wild hearts, but will put us all on the road to revival *together*. The critical insight for the next five chapters comes from a sentence in the preface of this book: *We knew little but believed much, and God used us mightily.*

If I could do it over again, I would pay more attention to the *name* of our revival. We weren't the Bible movement, the charismatic movement, the theology movement, the church movement, the conservative political movement, the megachurch movement, the holy-neighborhood movement, or the prosperity movement. We were, simply, *the Jesus Movement.*

It was all about Him—learning about Him, talking about Him, listening to Him, walking with Him, following Him, gathering in His name, and worshipping Him. *Jesus was the one who got us moving, and He is the only one who can get us moving again.*

The only way back to revival is through Him. Our relationship with Jesus must once again define our lives. When we put Jesus back into the Jesus Movement, He will finish what He started through us. When you put Him back into the center of your passion for revival, you will join our spiritual revolution.

If I could do it over again, I would pay a lot more attention to the very simple words of Jesus and a lot less attention to the convoluted teachings of men. I listened to their "enlightened" explanations of why we couldn't take

Jesus' words at face value, why they don't apply to us today, and why they're not as radical or dangerous as they seem at first glance. I wish I would have trusted my first pure understanding of His radical words rather than their taming clarifications of "what He really meant."

When we reembrace the simple but transforming words of Christ, when you and I, no matter what our age, believe them as much as we did back then, then we will all begin to experience revival again.

The six lies sidetracked us and gentled our wild hearts, but we can get back on track by believing five simple truths from our Savior that guided our revival and radicalized our hearts.

Part Three

A Revolution Reborn

Call to Radical Commitment

Chapter 10

Our Only Hope, Our Only Hero

I am the way, the truth, and the life. No one
comes to the Father except through Me.
—Jesus Christ, John 14:6

First-century Christians embraced the Greek spelling of the word *fish* as
the symbol of their movement. They saw in the five ordinary letters of
that everyday word—*iota, chi, theta, upsilon, sigma*—the first letters of the
confession of our faith: *Jesus, Christ, Son of God, Savior.* Early Christians
used the symbol of the fish to identify one another during the vicious
persecution of the Roman emperor Nero. We display it proudly as our

reminder of their revival and our identity in Christ now, two thousand years later.

If there was a symbol of our revival during the Jesus Movement it was the "One Way" street sign. We pasted One Way bumper stickers to our cars, posted One Way signs in our dorm rooms, and wore One Way T-shirts with images of the cross or Jesus in the background. We saw in the message of that ordinary road sign in every city—One Way—the bold and uncompromising claim of our faith: Jesus is the only way to heaven. Call us naive; call us insensitive; call us politically incorrect; but we took Jesus' simple sentence in John 14:6 literally: "I am the way, the truth, and the life. No one comes to the Father except through Me."

As the early Christians did, we used a simple but meaningful symbol as our stealthy way to identify one another. I remember making eye contact with fellow believers sitting in a college class as the professor ragged on Christianity as a myth or as the worst thing that ever happened to the world. A simple gesture of pointing the index finger to heaven communicated, *I'm not buying this either. Jesus isn't the problem, but the solution. One Way, man. Jesus is the only way. I'm your brother.*

When we gathered in groups, we pointed to the air together and shouted, "One Way!" It was our "amen," our motto, our benediction.

If I could do it over again, I wouldn't take down my One Way signs or scrape them off my bumper because it wasn't "sensitive" to seekers. I'd believe John 14:6 a lot more and believe the warnings about our culture's inability to receive such a brash claim a lot less. I wish we wouldn't have become so sophisticated that we were embarrassed to shout it: "One Way, man. John 14:6, man. Read it! Jesus is our only way to God … our only hope, our only hero."

Somewhere along the way, we forgot that Christianity is a personal relationship with Jesus Christ. We forgot that He is our only hope and began to hope in other things, like our theology, our churches, our politics, our families, and our money. We forgot that He is our only hero and began to worship other heroes, like our radio preachers, our television personalities,

our ministry leaders, our megachurch pastors, our authors, and our politicians. We must become, once again, a "personality cult" of One. Our faith
begins and ends with Him.

Our radical commitment to Jesus defined our movement and it's only
a radical recommitment to Jesus that will get it moving again. The first
step back to revival is to remind ourselves of the one who called us out of
darkness: *Jesus*.

In chapter 4, we saw how the great Asian revival centered in Ephesus
(Acts 19:10) lost momentum when they moved Jesus out of the center of
their movement. When Paul heard about the problem, he knew exactly
what to do. He didn't shame the church or try to teach them a lot of new,
cutting-edge insights about Jesus. He simply reminded them of what they
already knew.

Paul's Praise Song

Using the words of one of their favorite praise songs, a simple hymn they had
sung together around campfires, in small groups in their homes, and in larger
gatherings all over the New Testament world, Paul reminded them of Christ.
The apostle wrote as the Holy Spirit directed him, and the result is a literary
masterpiece that Christians rightly consider one of the most beautiful and
critical passages in God's Word. Paul's message to the sidetracked Colossian
believers is clear: Remember who Jesus is and what He has done! This Jesus
who is able to save your soul and present you acceptably to God is the Lord
(Col. 1:12–14). But before his readers had the chance to underdefine His
lordship, two stanzas of this familiar song present Christ as *the* Lord of
Creation (Col. 1:15–17) and *the* Lord of the Church (Col. 1:18–20):

> He is the image of the invisible God, the firstborn over
> all creation. For by Him all things were created that are

in heaven and that are on earth, visible and invisible, whether thrones or dominions or principalities or powers. All things were created through Him and for Him. And He is before all things, and in Him all things consist. And He is the head of the body, the church, who is the beginning, the firstborn from the dead, that in all things He may have the preeminence. For it pleased the Father that in Him all the fullness should dwell, and by Him to reconcile all things to Himself, by Him, whether things on earth or things in heaven, having made peace through the blood of His cross.

The term *firstborn* translates a key Greek word that appears twice in this hymn: *prototokos,* meaning to be first in time, priority, and rank. Christ Jesus is the Supreme Being of the universe and the Supreme Being in the church.

Paul selects some of the most majestic terms in Scripture to present Christ as the Lord of Creation in verses 15–17. Our only hero is the pre-eminent One of the universe—the express image of God. Christ is like God in every way (Heb. 1:3), represents God to us (2 Cor. 3:18; John 1:18), and manifests God to us (2 Cor. 4:6). He was not made in the image of God like us; He *is* the image of God (2 Cor. 4:4).

When you and I believed in Jesus, we entrusted our lives to the Lord of Creation: Jesus Himself created the universe through His divine effort and for His purposes (Col. 1:16). Jesus Himself preexisted the universe He now sustains and holds together (Col. 1:17).

Who is Christ and *what* has He done? He made everything you see, everything any human ever has or ever will see through any expedition to the depths of the oceans or the most remote corners of our planet, our solar system, and beyond. He made it all and keeps it all together! Him, the one you met when you believed in Him personally, *personally* brought the universe into existence and now ensures its continuing survival.

Think of one of your favorite places to go to simply take in the wonder of God's creation. For me, it would be a string of high-country meadows in the eastern Sierras called the Golden Trout Wilderness. I never walk through these meadows without stopping to think, *I know the One who made these golden trout, this stream, this meadow, these mountains, every ecosystem and lifeform they support, and every star and galaxy I will see tonight from my campfire as I gaze into that pure alpine sky.*

His name is Jesus, and nobody compares to Him. Nobody! He said it Himself: "I'm the only way to God!"

In the last three lines of his hymn, Paul presents Christ as the Lord of the Church, the preeminent one of resurrection life. He is the head of the church, the powerful originator and trailblazer of resurrection power, which gives Him primacy over all things concerning this new life (Col. 1:18; see also Heb. 10:12). Christ was the first person to rise from the dead with a glorified body so that we would never die again.

When you and I follow Christ, we're following the God-man, the one whom the Godhead chose to reconcile the entire universe to Himself (Col. 1:19–20; see also Rom. 8:18–22).

Who is Christ and *what* has He done? He is God in the flesh whose work on the cross not only reconciled me, but all of creation, to Himself.

Have you ever broken a bone or hurt your back? If you have, then you can understand the word *reconcile*. It means to restore something back to what it was, to effect a thorough change back. The origins of the word speak of resetting a bone. Something is broken and it needs to be fixed in order to ease the pain, to get a new start.

What a picture of the mighty work of Christ! The entire creation He wrought (Col. 1:15–17) was devastated by the sin of humanity and groaned with grievous intensity. So, the Creator died on the cross and made things right (Col. 1:19–20).

Our personal reconciliation is part of a much greater work that occurred on a specific day in history, and in a specific place on earth. Someone died on a cross, was buried, and rose again to fix this mess of a universe. He came to deliver us from our sin and lead us in a new way of life—resurrection life.

Again, His name is Jesus, and nobody compares to Him. Nobody! He said it Himself: "I'm the only way to God!"

So what were we thinking? Why did we cultivate a culture preoccupied with radio preachers, converted politicians, redeemed athletes, and repentant movie stars? Why did we grow churches around the personalities of dynamic teachers and compelling pastors?

The answer is: We weren't thinking biblically. Maybe it wasn't such a good idea to take down our One Way posters. They might have warned us that we were drifting away from the only hero worthy of our worship and the only hope for this world.

If we had been thinking biblically, we would have remembered not only *who* Jesus is and *what* He has done, but also *where* He is right now.

High and Lifted Up

In 2006 our church spent the entire year studying the book of Acts, Luke's sequel to his gospel. We were looking for the answer to one question: "How can we be more like the first Christians who turned the world upside down for Jesus Christ?"

Throughout his account, Luke presents Christianity as an irresistible force in the face of great opposition and persecution. Nothing could stop the work of Christ by the Spirit through His church. Our church struggled with the same issues you and I have been considering in the chapters of this book.

If we want to live the way the early church lived and see the revival the early church saw, what do we need to change? What did they have that isn't true of us? Are we missing some insight, some belief or experience that would propel us as it did them across the threshold of revival?

A big part of our answer came right away, in the first fourteen verses of Acts.

If you and I could sit across a table with Dr. Luke and say to him, "I'm excited about your book; this is what I want! What do I need to change to live the type of life you describe in Acts?" I believe he might ask, "When you think of Jesus, how do you think of Him?"

Most of us would answer, "I picture Him as a helpless baby in a manger in Bethlehem who became the mighty miracle worker and most profound teacher who walked among men. The next scene in my mind's eye is Jesus dying for our sin on the cross. The final scene I see is the resurrected Jesus, appearing to His followers for forty days after He was crucified."

Then, I believe Luke would say, "Your perceptions of Jesus are correct, but they are incomplete because you are concentrating on how Jesus *was* during His earthly ministry. If you want to live the way we did in the first century, you need to think of Jesus in a different way. I thought I made this clear by emphasizing His *ascension*. I went out of my way to highlight it twice!"

When we look again at Luke and Acts, we discover that he told the same story two times—first, as the last event of Jesus' life on earth from the real-time perspective of his gospel, and second, as the first event relevant to the church from the retrospection of Acts:

> And He led them out as far as Bethany, and He lifted up His hands and blessed them. Now it came to pass, while He blessed them, that He was parted from them and carried up into heaven. And they worshiped Him, and returned to Jerusalem with great joy, and were continually in the temple praising and blessing God. Amen. (Luke 24:50–53)

> Now when He had spoken these things, while they watched, He was taken up, and a cloud received Him out

of their sight. And while they looked steadfastly toward heaven as He went up, behold, two men stood by them in white apparel, who also said, "Men of Galilee, why do you stand gazing up into heaven? This same Jesus, who was taken up from you into heaven, will so come in like manner as you saw Him go into heaven." (Acts 1:9–11)

Before they watched Jesus of Nazareth disappear into the sky on that day, they looked and acted like any other group of confused and cowering followers who had just lost their hero (Luke 24:36–43). After witnessing the ascension of the Son of God, these same disciples walked the two miles back to Jerusalem from Bethany worshipping Jesus Christ with great joy.

Talk about bold; they walked right into the temple they had been trying to avoid, praising and blessing God. It was as if they were saying, "All right, bring it on. Don't tell us He's not the Messiah. We just talked to some angels about Him and saw Him shoot into the sky like a … come on, help me here … like a … I don't know … but it's something you've never seen before. Anyway, you're going to have to deal with us. Game on! And don't think we'll get over it, because we won't." This went on for ten days (Luke 24), before the coming of the Holy Spirit!

It's a stretch, but my Jesus Movement heart pictures them running back to Jerusalem shouting, "One Way, man; One Way. Jesus, He's the One. He's our hero. One Way! Can you dig it?"

Their circumstances hadn't changed. Jerusalem was still a dangerous place for followers of the Way. Their view of Jesus had changed, and it changed radically. On the day of His ascension the disciples quit viewing Christ as He was on earth—self-limited in power and glory—and began viewing Christ as He is now in heaven—unleashed in power and glory. And their shift in perspective radicalized their hearts and behavior because from that day forward, they knew that *Jesus is high and lifted up, regardless of what's happening on earth!*

There was a time when I thought of Jesus this way. I remember the night Bobby, Phil, and I stealthily turned off the lights of our old car and coasted into the empty bank parking lot across from Bakersfield College. We had about a hundred black-and-white, eight-by-ten-inch posters with the Jesus Movement's favorite picture of Christ on them—the one that made Him look like a handsomely rugged revolutionary—and John 14:6 underneath: *I am the way, the truth, and the life. No one comes to the Father except by Me.*

Like three commandos on a mission from God, we ran across the street armed with our posters and a roll of Scotch tape. As the night watchmen chased us all over the campus, we scurried around and posted our John 14:6 posters on every pole, signpost, and bulletin board. The next morning, we walked onto campus and the steel in our hearts got a little harder every time we walked by one of "our posters."

Of course it was stupid. Of course most of the signs were torn down by midmorning. Of course it was bad evangelism that probably turned off more people than it turned on. But I'll tell you what it wasn't: It was not wimpy. It was boldness in the hearts of three brand-new Christians who understood that Jesus is high and lifted up, and passionately believed He is the way, the truth, and the life.

Though we couldn't have articulated the theological and practical implications of His ascension, we thought of Him as the one who was in total control, the ruler of the universe. There was nothing *He* couldn't do, no problem *He* couldn't solve, no world tragedy *He* wasn't aware of, no wickedness in our culture or pain in marginalized people *He* didn't care for, no turn of history *He* did not anticipate. Nothing on earth *was greater than Him*. We knew that our Savior was *high and lifted up, regardless of what happened on earth.*

So bring it on. Arrest us if you must, call us Jesus freaks if you want, but we're hanging up these pictures of Jesus. One Way, man!

We've got some of that going on right now in the schools of Glendora, California. Our student ministries pastor walks boldly onto the campuses preaching Jesus. He meets with kids, teaches the Bible, and even speaks at large gatherings set up for him by the Christian Club. What he doesn't say is, "There are a lot of ways to God." He tells them about the only way to God, through Jesus Christ our Lord.

Interestingly, it is not the boldness of the students that wavers—it's some of the Christian parents and teachers! They're afraid that our church or their children might get in trouble, get sued, or make the local papers.

Where's the boldness? What happened to proclaiming Christ? Don't we still believe that He's the only way to heaven? How did it come to this?

I believe that we wouldn't have so hastily pushed Jesus aside if we viewed Him where He really is today: in a real place called heaven, seated at the Father's right hand. We wouldn't push Him aside if we respected Him as He really is today: reigning shepherd of His people. I believe we would be much bolder if we had more faith in Him as He is and less faith in our idols: our theologies, our religious institutions, our vote, our big churches and big personalities, and our money.

When you think of Jesus, how do you think of Him? Would you have to admit that you're more like the confused and cowering disciples of Luke 24:36–43 who only knew of His birth, life, death, and resurrection? Do you identify more with the worried parents and teachers than you do with the bold high-school students? Is your Jesus too earthbound to trust with the deepest fears and hurts of your life, and the greatest injustices and most dreadful evils of this world?

It's time to start thinking of Jesus on the throne again, seated at the right hand of the Father, ascended high and lifted up above all principalities and powers. He is the shepherd who cares for His sheep from a position of power over the universe.

But understanding Jesus' present ministry as our exalted shepherd is only the beginning of what the ascension means to His people. Viewing Him where He is today becomes our constant reminder of His next move— He's coming back!

The King Is Coming

I had been attending Fruitvale Community Church for just a few months when it happened—my first over-the-top worship experience. Since I knew nothing about Jesus before I believed in Him, Ted's sermons unfolded the wonder of new life in Christ every Sunday. But this particular Sunday was special.

Ted taught on the rapture—that future event when every living Christian would meet Christ in the air. I remember thinking, *You've got to be kidding me! This just gets better and better. Jesus is the only way to heaven. He loves me. He died for me. He gave me new life. And now you're telling me that He's coming from heaven to get me?*

And then Ted's wife, Jo, sat at the piano and started to sing the wonderful song "The King Is Coming," written by Bill Gaither, Gloria Gaither, and Charley Millhuff.[7]

I could see it in my mind's eye. Suddenly nothing mattered because Jesus just showed up. I remember thinking Jo sounded like an angel when she sang the chorus:

> *Oh, the King is coming,*
> *The King is coming*
> *PRAISE GOD,*
> *He's coming for me!*

This was all too wonderful to take in cognitively—I could only stand and sing and cry. Not only is Jesus the only way. Not only is Jesus the king. Not only is He coming back to make things right. He's coming back *for me*. Jesus was coming back for me, and I needed to get to work for Him.

I can't remember the exact timing of it all, but I honestly wonder if it wasn't soon after that Sunday that we three crazy Jesus-freak saboteurs launched Operation Jesus Poster at Bakersfield College.

I don't think it's an accident that our revival occurred during a time when the church and the world seemed preoccupied with biblical prophecy. Everyone, Christian and non-Christian, seemed to be asking questions about the return of the Lord. Hal Lindsey's *Late Great Planet Earth* was the largest-selling nonfiction book of the 1970s, and we virtually memorized it. Citywide prophecy conferences sprouted up in every major metropolitan center. Little Israel was back in the Promised Land, and the only explanations for her amazing victories in the Six-Day War of 1967 and the Yom Kippur War of 1973 that made sense were the prophecies of Daniel, Isaiah, and Ezekiel.

You may believe that prophecy is irrelevant today and feel that the church should be about the more immediate needs of humanity. You're probably thinking about all the excesses of our movement, and I would have to admit that they were there. Some of us dropped out of college and quit our careers because it just made no sense to care about this world when Jesus' coming seemed so imminent. We argued too much about when and how He was coming. Rapturists divided into three camps: post-, pre-, and midtribulationalists. Nonrapturists challenged the idea that Christians could avoid the wrath of the tribulation. Others viewed all this talk about a literal tribulation and millennium as theologically naive and dangerously distracting—and, as was our bent, we allowed the enemy of the church to divide us too easily.

But it seems reasonable to ask if there is any connection between prophetic teaching and revival.

It's impossible to separate the explosive growth of the church in Acts from its prophetic hope. The early Christians who turned the world upside down for Christ hoped in Jesus' coming. They did not believe their world would ever get better apart from the resurrection power of Jesus. They did believe that they were a part of God's ultimate rescue of their world in Christ. Paul said that he endured the suffering of serving Christ because he knew that the church is part of God's glorious plan for the future—the glory to come when all that creation groans for and all that we experience in the delivering power of Christ's resurrection will be realized (Rom. 8:18–25). They knew that Jesus would finally secure all that He accomplished through His cross and resurrection—the redemption and renewal of all that He created—when He returned. The early church prayed constantly for and looked forward to the return of Jesus.

They knew their king was coming.

It is impossible to separate God's message in His Word from its offer of prophetic hope. One-fourth of the Bible was prophecy when it was written. Surely God meant for us to look into the future with eyes of hope, knowing His good plans and redemptive purposes for humanity and for the universe. Although Christians can't agree on all the details, our common hope for the future should never diminish. Unlike heathen religions, Christianity's hope is brilliant and plain—we will not always feel the way we feel today and this world will not always be the way it is now. The life to come is better than this life, and the world to come is better than the one we live in today.

The Bible says that our king is coming.

And it's impossible for me to separate our zeal for Christ in the Jesus Movement from our prophetic hope. I can't know exactly how God used prophetic hope in the return of Jesus to fuel other revivals, but I do know how He used it in ours. He restored our belief in the purpose of life on earth, emboldened us with a confidence we had never before known, and burdened us with an urgency to tell others about Christ because our king was coming!

Suddenly, Jesus' life in us, and His Word to us, introduced us to a new reality. We no longer viewed this as a purposeless, impersonal world calling us to fight wars we didn't understand, forcing us to follow rules we didn't value, and asking us to overlook the prejudices and injustices we couldn't ignore. Ours was a world being rescued by the power of the living God, and we were His people. We were given a responsibility to represent a king who would never let us down and whose power could transform lives and influence cultures. Ours was a call to touch lives with His mercy and grace, to love in His name by reaching out to the desperate, the powerless, and the marginalized. Ours was a cause moving history toward its final conclusion.

Our king was coming.

Suddenly, Jesus' power in us and His promises to us meant that we had the answers to life's most important questions! We were the people unashamed of the only radical message that would make any real and lasting difference. We were the people with the only offer that broken lives, neighborhoods, and cultures could cling to. We were the people of the king.

And our king was coming.

Suddenly, Jesus' temporary place at the Father's right hand and soon-to-be seat on His rightful throne to judge and rule this world focused our minds on all that matters most in this life. We rightly viewed everyone we met as someone on his or her way to heaven or hell. We rightly viewed our days here on earth as limited—either by our ultimate death or the coming of our king. We rightly viewed every relationship, conversation, social gathering, and every day, even every minute, as possibly our last opportunity to tell someone that they didn't have to fear the coming of the judge of heaven and earth. They could join the winning side by believing in our king.

Oh yes, our king was coming.

The return of the king was surely on my mind the evening Gary stopped by to say hi during his spring break from college in Northern California. We grew up together, but we weren't very close. Once, during my drinking days, we squared off to fight, but friends pulled us away from one another. Before Christ changed me, I wouldn't have given a guy like Gary the time of day. Oh, I would have been somewhat civil, but he just wasn't cool enough for our crowd.

I remember being somewhat bothered that he interrupted my night. Then the Spirit reminded me that Gary probably wasn't a Christian yet and asked me how I would feel if this were Gary's only opportunity to hear about the love of Christ before Jesus returned to earth. We sat in his new Chevy Super Sport in my driveway, listening to eight-track tapes. I pulled out my trusty "Four Spiritual Laws" booklet, and Gary prayed to receive Christ.

My experience with Gary was representative of how the Spirit moved throughout our revival. You could multiply it thousands of times. Our hope in the soon return of our king brought an urgency to our efforts to share the gospel, explained only by the prophetic fervor of our day.

Do you need a "refresher course" in prophecy, a restoration of your hope for the future that will give you the purpose, confidence, and urgency you need to rekindle the revival fire in your heart?

Four biblical truths should suffice:

- Christ ascended on high to prepare a place for His people, the church, in heaven, His "Father's house" (John 14:1–3).
- Christ ascended on high to execute judgment by resurrecting all people by calling them from the grave—believers to life and unbelievers to condemnation in hell (John 5:22–30).
- Christ ascended on high to reward all people—believers at His Judgment Seat (2 Cor. 5:10) and unbelievers at His Great White Throne (Rev. 20:11–15).
- Christ ascended on high to return as the ruler of His kingdom (Rev. 19:16).

God has a future plan for the earth and a future plan for His people. His Son is coming back to rule and to reign. If you're one of His people, your king is coming. The long-awaited fulfillment of God's promise to establish the righteous rule of His Son and our hero, Jesus Christ, to reign with His people is the most sure coming event of prophecy. Until then, our privilege is to fall in love with our king as we wait for Him, the One who is our only hope.

Love Story

The primary question of this chapter is, "How can we rekindle the revival fires by moving Jesus back to the center of our lives where He belongs?" And its corollary, "How can we put Jesus back in the Jesus Movement?"

The simple words of Jesus in John 14:6 turn our eyes back to Him as our "One Way," our all-in-all, our only hero, and our only hope. And if He is our only way, the one who sits at the right hand of the Father and is coming for us someday, then it only makes sense that we should be falling in love with Him a little more every day.

Paul says that if that's true of us, if we are becoming more enamored with Him every day, then we will "seek [and set our minds on] those things which are above, where Christ is, sitting at the right hand of God" (Col. 3:1).

Truly spiritual and authentically revival-hearted Christians are pre-occupied with Christ. Are you? They fill their days with the pursuit of Him and fill their minds with thoughts of Him. Do you? If not, there's a problem with your claim to be passionately in love with the one who is your one way to God—your only hope and only hero.

From the day I met Judy Christman, now Judy Underwood, she pre-occupied my time and my thoughts. Sometimes I embarrass her and the kids with my demonstrative love. If the kids think this is bad, they should have seen me when I first fell in love.

Even though I was "going with" the skier girl, Judy Christman was the focus of my life. I memorized her schedule at South High School in our hometown of Bakersfield. I was a senior and she was a sophomore. She must have thought I was a stalker. Everywhere she went, I was there. I worked in the school office one hour a day. I made sure that every note to French class was hand-delivered by me so that I could see her one more time. Once I even swallowed a snail she fed me in French class with the tobacco I had hidden in my cheek. Those drop-dead beautiful green eyes mesmerized me. It didn't even matter that a few minutes later, I was puking up all the contents of my stomach—breakfast that morning, snail, and tobacco. I got to be close to my love and that was enough! Every night, I would pore over every picture of her in the yearbook … for hours. I drove by her house, sometimes ten times a day. And she lived on a cul-de-sac!

I lost my mind.

My point? True love changes everything. When you are in love with someone, it consumes you. You can't get enough of that person. Your mind is filled with thoughts of her, and your days are spent pursuing her.

Have you "lost your mind" over Jesus? Or are you still sensible and sane and reserved in your devotion to Him?

Is it time for you to start writing a new chapter in your love story with Jesus? I believe that the more your story of faith revolves around Him, the more your story will be about revival.

The story of the Jesus Movement will end well if we finish the story with chapters that look more like the chapters of our first decade—stories of how His simple claim in John 14:6 caused us to fall in love with the greatest person we ever met.

He's Everything to Me

If you had been a part of the Asian revival of the first century, Paul's reminder of all that Christ used to mean to you in Colossians 1:15–20 would have moved your heart powerfully. The memories of singing that praise song would have brought tears to your eyes as you recalled the places you were, the friends you were with, and the impact you had for Christ back then. That song would have called your heart back to Jesus Christ—your only hope and your only hero.

If you were a part of *my* revival the song that would bring wonderful memories of the love for Jesus you shared with friends so taken by Him you could do nothing else but serve Him radically and trust Him with abandon would be "He's Everything to Me," by Ralph Carmichael.[8] It was the praise song that expressed our fervent belief in John 14:6:

> *Now He walks beside me day by day,*
> *Ever watching o'er me lest I stray,*
> *Helping me to find that narrow way,*
> *He's everything to me.*

"He's Everything to Me" was the closing song to most of our Young Life meetings and camps. "He's Everything to Me" ended our prayer meetings and our time together around a campfire. We sang it driving down the road in our cars and belted it out when some of our churches risked the wrath of the traditionalists to "sing one for the young people." Judy and I loved it so much a friend sang it at our wedding!

It only makes sense that the movement so identified with Jesus would choose such a piece as its defining hymn. He was *everything* to us.

I believe that's the first step toward getting our revival back on track or sparking yours. He must become everything to us again.

I believe that's the first message God's Spirit would send to any heart longing for revival: *He must be everything to you.*

Isn't it amazing that Jesus allows Himself to be pushed out of our lives? It's hard to grasp His patience as He deals with our disregard of Him, our frivolous pursuit of everything and everyone else, and our unjustifiable exploitation of His grace. Yet He stands waiting to be our *everything* so He can use us mightily!

We don't represent an idea, a body of truth, a political party, a religious institution, a denomination, a race of people, or even a nation. We represent Jesus. Sooner or later, every generation of Christians must come to grips with the truth that we are, in the final analysis, *the Jesus Movement.*

Is Jesus everything to you? He should be, but if you really mean it when you say you want to be a part of a revival, He must be everything.

I encourage you to tell Him the ways you have pushed Him aside in your life, how you have apologized for His narrow claim in John 14:6, how you have disregarded His call on your life, and how you have neglected your relationship with Him. Tell Him exactly how you have been sidetracked and why. Ask for His forgiveness. Tell Him you want to read the next chapter as the type of Christian He can use in a revival. A John 14:6 Christian, your version of a "One Way, man" radical. Tell Him that He is indeed everything to you.

> Lord Jesus, I'm ashamed to admit that I have forgotten in so many ways that Christianity is a personal relationship with You. I remember the day when You were everything to me. But I must confess that I have allowed issues and people to take Your rightful place as the center of my life, my Lord of Creation, my Lord of the Church. I have replaced You with other heroes and hoped in what could only disappoint. But I'm asking You to believe me when I say, "I'm back." Please ask Your Father to empower me with Your Spirit so that I can deliver on this promise: "I will fill my time with the pursuit of You and fill my mind with thoughts of You. You're everything to me, Jesus. Heavenly Father, Your Son is everything to me. Please make me a part of Your coming revival. In Jesus' name, amen.

You've just turned away from compromise and toward revival. Jesus has moved back to the center of your life as you see Him high and lifted up, sitting on His throne awaiting His Father's command to come for you. If you think you're fired up and ready for revival now because you know He is coming quickly, wait till you hear what He's bringing with Him!

Chapter 11

Our Only Goal, Our Only Gold

And behold, I am coming quickly,
and My reward is with Me,
to give to every one according to his work.
I am the Alpha and the Omega,
the Beginning and the End, the First and the Last.
—Jesus Christ, Revelation 22:12–13

In 1980, I was sitting in a theology class at Dallas Seminary. I had been a Christian for over ten years. From the first day I believed, I was a serious student of the Bible, listening to hours of sermons, filling in the blanks of discipleship books, and spending time with just about anyone who impressed me with their knowledge of the Scriptures. I had led Young Life Clubs, taught Officers' Christian Fellowship Bible studies, even preached a sermon in the First Armored Division chapel in Katterbach, Germany.

Then the professor used a word I had never heard before—*bema*—the Greek term the New Testament uses to represent the Judgment Seat of Christ. I looked around the room to see if anyone else seemed as surprised as I was by this revolutionary concept. Nobody seemed overly stunned or agitated. He went on to explain that earthly *bemas* were raised, throne-like platforms on which judges and rulers sat when evaluating those who stood before them. And the day is coming, the day of Christ, when millions of believers from the church age will gather before Him, anticipating the rewards He will give.

Rewards! I remember shouting in my mind. *What rewards? Judgment Seat of Christ, what's that? I thought Christians wouldn't be judged!* I felt an initial aversion to the whole idea of serving Christ because He would some-how repay me. Wasn't His death on the cross enough?

As our professor cited passages from the gospels and epistles, I had to admit that it seemed the Bible said that every Christian would stand before Jesus as Judge to receive rewards. And then he turned us to a verse I thought I knew, one of the key verses of the Jesus Movement—Revelation 22:12. The first six words had been one of our slogans: "And behold, I am coming quickly." I sat stunned as I read the rest of the verse: "And My reward is with Me, to give to every one according to his work." *How did I miss that?* I asked myself, *Why didn't I read on?*

When I think about our revival and what sidetracked us, my questions become more comprehensive: How did *we* miss it? Why didn't *we* read on? How could it be that a generation so focused on Jesus' soon return didn't think that much about what He would bring with Him?

The more I studied rewards, the more I realized that this is indeed a major theme of the New Testament. The more the Spirit deepened my understanding of my accountability to Christ at His Judgment Seat, the more it transformed my life. The thought of Jesus bringing His reward with Him not only deepened my longing for His return, but it also reradicalized my revival heart. The doctrine of rewards made me more willing than ever to sacrifice for the Lord Jesus, more willing to do the hard things, more willing to pay the price for discipleship.

The years since have convinced me that the doctrine of eternal rewards is one of the most undertaught and underappreciated truths in the modern church. Maybe the most striking contrast between the church today and the early church is that they lived with a deep awareness of their accountability before Christ.

If I could do it over again, every time someone said, "Jesus is coming again. He said Himself, 'Behold, I am coming quickly,'" I'd say, "Yeah, but it's even better than you thought. Read the rest of the verse, look what He's bringing with Him: 'And My reward is with Me'!" If I could do it over again, I'd teach rewards to brand-new Christians, motivating them to walk the sacrificial path of a disciple.

I believe that the sure knowledge that Jesus is bringing His reward with Him is the single most convincing and theologically balanced answer to one of the first questions new believers ask, "If I'm saved by grace and I know I'm going to heaven, then why should I endeavor to serve Jesus sacrificially here on earth? If discipleship is costly, why should I pay the price?"

Knowing that we will stand before Him at His Judgment Seat is the part of the answer to that question most Christians have not heard. If this is all new to you, you may be wondering what this has to do with revival. What you're about to learn has the potential to revolutionize and focus your life like no other spiritual truth. It was the one biblical reality that was missing from our revival that I feel would have made us even more radical. Who knows, it may have kept more of us on track. It is the compelling truth that could energize and sustain the revival you've been asking God for since you started reading this book.

But none if it will make sense if your concept of biblical judgment is flawed.

Biblical Judgment

I suspect that one reason we may not have read past "I am coming quickly" to "and My reward is with Me" was our aversion to the whole idea of judgment. Remember that ours was a revival that stood against the prevailing legalistic Christian culture of our day. Interestingly, I've detected this same aversion in conversations with younger, emergent-type believers. Just the words *biblical judgment* cause most people to shudder as they picture God in flowing robes standing on a cold stone throne against the backdrop of a dark storm of swirling clouds and lightning, scowling at a crowd of horrified men and women. It's as if the only role of a judge is to determine failure and loss, condemnation and punishment.

There's no question that everyone standing before Christ on his or her judgment day will feel some failure and loss. The condemnation of the unbelieving will result in everlasting punishment. But I don't see that as the *primary* purpose of the two great and future judgments that everyone reading these words will be a part of—either the Judgment Seat of Christ (Rom. 14:10; 2 Cor. 5:10) or the Great White Throne Judgment (Rev. 20:11–15).

What will be tested at both of these judgments are our *works,* and the issue is whether or not Jesus is *justified* to give us what He wants to give us: all that His mighty work on earth secured for every human being. Jesus had you and me in mind when He came to earth, died on the cross, was buried, rose again, and ascended to His Father's right hand. He did all of that so He could give us two things *freely:* His life (eternal life) and our inheritance in His kingdom (our reward).

At the conclusion of the old earth, and just before the beginning of the new earth, all who have persisted in their unbelief will be raised and judged. Those who rejected Jesus' free offer of eternal life will be judged. Jesus speaks of their resurrection of judgment in John 5:29. They will stand before a Great White Throne (Revelation 20:11–15) and their Judge, the Lord Jesus (John 5:22, 27).

This is the judgment you do not want to be a part of because it is there that you will see that your name is *not* written in the Book of Life. This book contains the names of all of us who have placed our trust in Jesus' work on the cross rather than our own good works. Then Jesus, who died on the cross to pay the penalty of your sin and give you eternal life, will open more books. He will open the books of works (Rev. 20:12). He will find your name and the list all of the works you have done over your entire life, both good and bad. Jesus will evaluate your works fairly, and even sorrowfully, because you will know then for sure what I'm begging you to realize now: *Your works will never measure up to His standard.*

So rather than giving you and the millions standing with you what He desperately wants to give you—eternal life and your place with Him in heaven and the New Earth—He will judge you as unfit for life with Him and cast you into a place that eternally separates you from Him—a place the Bible calls hell and the lake of fire.

But here's the good news: You do not have to stand before Jesus as your Judge at the hopeless judgment of human works to secure eternal life, the Great White Throne Judgment. You can know for sure that you will not be there by placing your faith in Him and His work to secure eternal life for you right now. Jesus said you don't have to come into this judgment of death. You can pass from death to life at this very moment by believing in Him:

> Most assuredly, I say to you, he who hears My word and believes in Him who sent Me has everlasting life, and shall not come into judgment, but has passed from death into life. (John 5:24)

If you will hear His Word—*he who believes in Me has everlasting life* (John 6:47)—viewing Him as the one sent by the Father—*the Father sent the Son as the Savior of the world* (1 John 4:14)—you will not come into this judgment of death.

Have you heard? Have you believed? If so, why not settle it with God right now? Make sure that you will not be standing with the desperate rejecters of God's grace at the Great White Throne. Express your trust in Christ through this prayer:

> Father in heaven, I don't want to be judged according to my works but according to the work of Christ. I want His work to count for mine. I want to pass from death into life. My works will never measure up to Your standards because I am a sinner. I transfer my trust from my works to Your Son, Jesus, right now. I believe in Him. I believe Jesus died for my sins and arose from the dead. I'm trusting in His work to make payment for my sin and I claim His promise that I have everlasting life. Thank You that I have received what Jesus wants to give me, eternal life. In Jesus' name, amen.

Whether you prayed that prayer to Jesus just now, last year, or decades ago, you can be sure that your coming judgment is not one you should dread, but one you can look forward to. This is the time that you will stand before Him at His Judgment Seat, where He will evaluate your works to determine how much of all that He planned for you He can justify giving to you.

What Jesus wants to give you is *significance* in His future kingdom and new earth. What's at stake at this judgment is not heaven or hell, but your personal rewards or the lack of rewards He brings with Him. Your works are not going to be compared to the works of others. The determining factor is how you used your spiritual giftedness to accomplish the works Jesus gave you to do. Your heart's motivation in doing these works will be a supplemental issue. Both good and bad deeds will be exposed, as will both good and bad motives. Then every believer will receive his or her suitable praise from God and fitting assignment in Christ's kingdom.

And remember, *He is coming quickly!*

Paul says that we were created in Christ Jesus to accomplish specific good works God prepared for us to do (Eph. 2:10). The more of these God-ordained and personally fitted works we accomplish through His Spirit's power during our life, the greater our reward. The fewer of these particular works we fulfill, whether due to sin, inattention, or self-serving motives, the less our reward (1 Cor. 3:10–15).

I've met a lot of Christians over the years who consider themselves above all of this and even judge reward-seeking believers as somehow selfish. The early church sure didn't think that way. Maybe if more of us stopped worrying about how "pure" we appeared to other Christians, more of us would start living the way the first Christians did: sold out to Jesus Christ. The possibility of gaining or losing rewards is one of four powerful incentives to sacrificial service to Christ. Most of us are more familiar with the first three motivations.

The first motivation we feel is *gratitude to God* for saving us by His grace. Paul never got over the depth of Christ's love for him demonstrated at the cross, and neither should we. He knew he could trust the words of His Savior who died for him, and so should we (Gal. 2:20). In Romans 12:1–2, Paul begs his readers to give their lives to God in response to His mercies outlined in chapters 1—11.

A second and very practical motivation for growing in Christ is the knowledge that *our heavenly Father blesses obedience and disciplines disobedience in His children.* Like any loving father, your heavenly Father desires the very best for you. He instructs you in much the same way children are taught in a loving home. Being perfect, He never makes a mistake, but He does deal with us in the same manner as earthly fathers. He affirms and blesses us when we please Him, and corrects and disciplines us when we disobey (Heb. 12:5–11).

The third and most personal motivation for serving Christ is *intimacy with Him*. Jesus' clearest and simplest expression of both the terms and definition of friendship with Him is in John 15:14–17. Those believers who do what He says become His friends. He discloses His Father's deepest thoughts to them, uses them to produce a lot of the lasting fruit they ask the Father for in His name, and follow His most special command to love one another.

Jesus' apostles didn't stop there. They also knew that Jesus would return, bringing His reward with Him. God's Spirit used the prophetic motivation of future rewards and significance in His kingdom to move them mightily to sacrificial service to the Lord Jesus. The two principal texts on the coming judgment of believers' works are 1 Corinthians 3:10–15 and 2 Corinthians 5:9–10.

Since this is a book about revival, I want to show you how rewards can fuel revival. Second Corinthians 5:9–10 is the passage that tells us what we should be doing until Jesus comes … if it's true that His reward is coming with Him:

> Therefore we make it our aim, whether present or absent, to be well pleasing to Him. For we must all appear before the judgment seat of Christ, that each one may receive the things done in the body, according to what he has done, whether good or bad.

There's no question Paul believed in the Judgment Seat of Christ. The impact it had on his daily life was clear: Paul made it his aim to be well pleasing to Him.

The Goal: Well Pleasing to Him

If we really believe Jesus will bring rewards with Him and that we will stand before Him to give an account for our life, it only makes sense that we too would live to please Him. What intrigues me is that most of us miss that little word, *well,* that Paul places before the *pleasing.* So when we think of pleasing Christ, our minds tick off some personal checklist: sin less, go to church, work in the nursery, stop lying, don't lust, give some money.

This is the same definition with which we tried to fuel our revival, and it didn't work. It never does work because it's so ordinary, so religious, so unrevival-like. There's a difference between pleasing and *well* pleasing. If you're a parent, you know the difference. There are days your children please you, and then there are days when you are *well* pleased by them.

Like most dads, constantly reminding my son of his duties around the house was part of my daily routine. "Bob, don't forget that you told your mom you would clean your room today. I want it done before I get home tonight." If he had actually done what I told him to do, if he had simply "checked it off" my to-do list for him, I was pleased.

But there were those special moments, like the day I drove into the driveway of our one-acre lot in Oregon. I got out of my truck and stood amazed. Our fourteen-year-old Bobby had, on his own initiative and without me saying a word, mowed the lawn, trimmed it, weeded the flower beds, and even put all of the tools back in their assigned places! I looked around to see if Moses was in the area. It was a miracle. If you've ever raised a boy, you know that at that moment I wasn't just pleased, I was *well* pleased.

To be well pleasing was the aim of Paul's life, and it should be ours. To live our lives in such a way that Jesus knows we have so internalized His values and directions that we live them out in ways that He can really affirm. This goes way beyond some checklist of good deeds to accomplish and bad deeds to avoid. This goes beyond pleasing to well pleasing, beyond everyday obedience and sacrifice to revival-type obedience and sacrifice. This is what happens when we think about that moment when we will stand before our Lord who is bringing His reward with Him.

And He's Coming ... Quickly

If these truths hit your revival heart hard, perhaps you're asking, *Lord, what do You want me to do to be* well *pleasing to You?* He's not going to give you a list of seven holy things you must do every week and six sins you must avoid. He will not tell you which candidates to vote for and which propositions to support, how many hours you should read your Bible or the maximum amount of television you should watch.

Jesus is saying, "Do what My Spirit is prompting you to do. Risk it all for Me. You've received My life; I made you a new creation and gave you My Spirit, My Word, and My church. Live out of the resources I gave you and take every opportunity I bring your way. Sacrifice for Me, obey Me, and accomplish the mission of making disciples of all nations. You know what to do, so do it. Follow Me!"

Well-pleasing Christians follow Him. He used a special word to describe them: *disciple,* His devoted follower. Jesus would say what He said to the great multitudes clamoring after Him in Perea in Luke 14:25–33, "If you want to be well pleasing to me, count the cost of being my disciple!"

Counting the Cost of Well Pleasing

Prior to His final trip to Jerusalem, Jesus spent a significant amount of time east of the Jordan, in the province of Perea. With the cross ahead, our Lord began to teach His followers some tough lessons on what it means to be one of His well-pleasing followers, a disciple indeed.

The days ahead were not for those who had failed to count the cost. So Jesus Christ went out of His way to discourage those who weren't willing to pay the price of following. His words purged the crowds of all who were soft, uncommitted, frivolous, cowardly, or self-serving—all who weren't fit for the battles ahead.

In one of His most pointed lessons east of the Jordan, Jesus spoke in emphatic terms about what it would cost to be His disciple. "Anyone unwilling to pay the price," He warned, "*cannot* be My disciple!" All would-be disciples should seriously consider these hard words before committing to follow their Savior to the cross. They are demands that every Christian who desires to live a well-pleasing life must reckon with.

> Now great multitudes went with Him. And He turned and said to them, "If anyone comes to Me and does not hate his father and mother, wife and children, brothers and sisters, yes, and his own life also, he cannot be My disciple. And whoever does not bear his cross and come after Me cannot be My disciple. For which of you, intending to build a tower, does not sit down first and count the cost, whether he has enough to finish it— lest, after he has laid the foundation, and is not able to finish, all who see it begin to mock him, saying, 'This man began to build and was not able to finish'? Or what king, going to make war against another king, does not sit down first and consider whether he is able with ten thousand to meet him who comes against him with twenty thousand? Or else, while the other is still a great way off, he sends a delegation and asks conditions of peace. So likewise, whoever of you does not forsake all that he has cannot be My disciple." (Luke 14:25–33)

The first mark of a well-pleasing life, the life of a disciple, is total devotion (Luke 14:26). Jesus chooses the most precious relationships of life—parents, spouse, children, and siblings, even our very lives—and tells us to hate them. Obviously this doesn't mean that we should hurry home, scream hatred to our families, and flog ourselves. The Bible often uses the severe contrast between hate and love to describe the deepest devotion. "If anyone compared your love for Me to your love for yourself or your family," says Jesus, "it would look like hate in comparison."

In Jesus' day, these were sobering words. The Jewish believers choosing to follow Him would almost certainly face rejection at home and persecution from the authorities. If you want to live the well-pleasing life of a disciple, expect it to hurt. Your closest loved ones will question your decisions. The culture you live in will, at the very least, regard you as peculiar and likely penalize or even persecute you. And the time will come when you have to stand up to them. When you do, hear the Lord Jesus say, "That is well pleasing to Me."

Jesus' disciples put His interests before their own (Luke 14:27). A too-familiar picture in Palestine in those days was the scene of a neighbor or loved one "bearing his cross" behind Roman soldiers. Whatever the cross-bearer had on his mind the moment before the soldiers lashed the cross to his shoulders—his plans for the day, things he wanted to say to his wife and children, problems at work, dreams for life—suddenly meant nothing. He was a dead man walking; Rome's agenda for his life was all that mattered anymore.

The day you decide to follow Jesus as a disciple is the day you decide that His agenda for your life will replace yours. Whatever you have on your mind the moment before that commitment—the school you will go to, the type of person you will marry, the house you will buy, the career you will choose, the retirement you deserve, the hobbies you'll pursue, the stuff you're going to buy, the schedule you're going to keep—suddenly means nothing compared to the prospect of living well pleasing to Him. His agenda for your life is all that matters anymore.

And when you make that decision, hear Him say, "I am well pleased."

But this isn't a rash decision people make at conferences in the mountains after a scathing or inspirational sermon. It's an emotional decision to be sure, but our mind is thoroughly engaged. Jesus wants disciples who willingly and intelligently decide to commit their lives to Him. The stories of verses 28–32 warn us from moving forward as His disciples until we really know all that it involves: namely, the deep sacrifice of a lifelong commitment.

Too many invitations to follow Jesus are shallow and silly. Momentarily sincere Christians walk an aisle, fill out a card, or stand up and "commit" without really counting the cost. I believe these public displays of simple commitment bring dishonor to Christ. Onlookers mock them and Him because, like the builder who ran out of materials or the king who ran out of warriors, they couldn't finish what they started.

At the end of this chapter, I'm going to ask you to tell Jesus that you want to be His disciple. Don't do it until you thoroughly grasp what you're telling Him. As much as you may think you want Him to return to earth with your personal reward, you need to think it through and count the cost. Wanting to live a well-pleasing life is a great beginning, really the only beginning. Your want-to feelings are responding to the Spirit's deep urging to do this and the Bible's unambiguous promise of rewards if you do. But your want-to feelings have to be informed by the Spirit's cautionary focus on Jesus' unequivocal warning to count the cost. A warning that becomes even more explicit in the next verse:

> So likewise, whoever of you does not forsake all that he has
> cannot be My disciple. (Luke 14:33)

People ask me, "What will it cost me to be Christ's disciple, to live a life well pleasing to Christ?"

I respond with two questions of my own: "Read Luke 14:33 and fill in the blank, 'If I want to be Christ's disciple I must forsake _____.'" and

"If the cost of being a disciple is what you must forsake, then you tell me, what's your cost?"

Sooner rather than later, they look up with solemn insight and answer, "It will cost me *everything*." Then I ask, "Are you sure you really want to earn the reward?"

Any views of the well-pleasing life of a disciple that settle for less commitment than what Jesus asked for are plainly lacking. The gift of salvation is free to you because it cost Jesus everything. The gift of your sacrificed life to Jesus as His obedient disciple will cost you the same: *everything*.

If your goal is to look forward to your reward He is bringing with Him, to live the life Jesus considers *well* pleasing, it will cost you everything.

But, you won't miss any of it.

And He's coming … quickly.

The Gold: "Well Done"

Paul said the aim of our lives is to be well pleasing to Christ and to receive His reward at Christ's *bema* (2 Cor. 5:9–10). Jesus said that the life of a well-pleasing disciple would cost you everything (Luke 14:25–33).

And what are we looking forward to as we count and commit to the cost of discipleship? What is central to the reward He will bring with Him? Something our redeemed heart longs for, two words from the lips of Christ: "Well done!"

Jesus, who knows our hearts, appealed to this longing in the parable of the talents in Matthew 25:14–29, as an illustration of the type of faithfulness that Jesus rewards. Like the master in the parable, Jesus traveled to a far country and left His servants with talents, including large amounts of time, skill, and treasure to invest. The servant who invests most wisely hears this from the Master: "Well done, good and faithful servant; you were faithful over a few things, I will make you ruler over many things. Enter into the joy of your lord" (Matt. 25:21).

What do you think thrilled the servant's heart most? The fact that he was going to receive all that bounty, or the realization that he had pleased the Lord he served?

Jesus seems to think that the *well done* should come first.

Can you imagine what you're going to feel like when you step before Him and look into those holy eyes that have cherished you forever? When you stand before "Jesus Christ, the faithful witness, the firstborn from the dead, and the ruler over the kings of the earth.... Him who loved us and washed us from our sins in His own blood and has made us kings and priests to His God and Father ... [whose] glory and dominion [will be] forever and ever" (Rev. 1:5–6)?

What will run through your mind in that moment you realize that everything He promised you about eternal life is true? What will you feel when you realize that the only explanation for the life you lived before and the life you now look forward to with Him forever is His mercy toward you? What will you think when you realize that the one who made heaven and earth is now going to tell you what He thinks of the life you lived on earth?

Do you think you're going to pull out a tape measure from your pocket to gauge the size of your crown or present an Excel sheet to ensure the accuracy of the dimensions of your inheritance?

I think that just like me, your mind is going to go blank and that deep longing inside you to hear the words only the faithful will hear will overwhelm all other hope and desire.

You will want to bow down, look up into the face of the one who loves you more than any other, the one who so wants to give you everything His heart desired for you when He saved you from your sin. You will want to look up into that face and hear,

> Well done, good and faithful servant; you were faithful
> over a few things, I will make you ruler over many things.
> Enter into the joy of your lord. (Matt. 25:21)

And when you hear *that,* you will know that though it cost you everything, it was all worth it.

And He's coming … quickly.

Until then, there is one essential ingredient that must be a part of your life if you want to know that He's bringing your reward with Him, if you want to please Him.

Without This, It's Impossible

At the Judgment Seat of Christ, every believer will wish he had counted the cost of being Christ's disciple and paid it while he could have!

The dividing line between those who are living as if it's true today and those who aren't is *faith.*

No chapter in the Bible highlights this dividing line better than Hebrews 11. Here the author of Hebrews says that the sacrifices and feats of the great men and women in the Old Testament were due to their *faith* in His promise to reward them. Though none of them fully realized their reward during their lifetime, they persevered, believing that it would come.

No verse in that chapter focuses on the dividing issue more than Hebrews 11:6:

> But without faith it is impossible to please Him, for he
> who comes to God must believe that He is, and that He is
> a rewarder of those who diligently seek Him.

If it's impossible to please Christ without faith, surely it's impossible to *well* please Him apart from faith!

Continuing in the emphatic language of discipleship—*those who do not count the cost* cannot *be My disciple* (Luke 14)—this verse says that it is *impossible* to please Christ without faith. *Cannot* and *impossible* connect in the heart of those pondering the cost of discipleship.

A young man called to tell me that he was dropping out of a discipleship class he had begged me to let him join. When I asked him why, he said that his wife didn't like him being in our group. We had talked enough that I was aware of his wife's irrational fear and control issues. I told him the truth: He needed to stand up to his wife and lovingly, but firmly, tell her he was following Christ. He said he *couldn't.*

No, it wasn't that he couldn't. It was that he wouldn't because he didn't *believe* that Jesus would reward him for putting Him first. He *cannot* be Jesus' disciple because he was *without* the faith it requires to please Him—to love Him more than he feared confronting the problems in his marriage. He had the faith to look forward to Jesus' coming, but he didn't have the faith to sacrifice for the reward Jesus will bring with Him.

Similarly, a busy couple took issue with a friend who told them they were too busy and asked my opinion. I probed into their life to see if I could help. They had decided to quit hosting a small group from our church that met in their home. She had given notice that she would no longer teach children's church, and their son had reported to our pastor of students that his dad said he didn't have to come to Bible study any more. Their schedule was out of control: soccer games, music lessons, school meetings, Boy Scouts, Girl Scouts, and tutoring classes. He had just enrolled in a doctoral course at a local university, and she was getting involved in a home-based business that required at least three evenings a week. I told them the truth—they needed to submit their schedule to Jesus and live His agenda for their life rather than their own. They must pick up their cross and follow Him. They said they *couldn't.*

No, it wasn't that they couldn't. It was that they wouldn't because they didn't *believe* that Jesus would reward them for putting His agenda first. They *cannot* be Jesus' disciples because they are *without* the faith it requires to please Him. They refused to pick up their cross and follow Him—to trust Him enough to live according to His priorities in life rather than their own. They have the faith to look forward to Jesus' coming, but they don't have the faith to sacrifice for the reward Jesus will bring with Him.

Do you see the connection between faith and pleasing Him? Between trusting and following? Between talking about reward and truly believing that Jesus will bring it with Him when He comes? The reason you and I pull back from the threshold of becoming His disciple isn't that we don't know what to do; it's because it's hard, and we're not willing to trust Him to take care of us if we do.

Faith is also the reason we move forward with Him, bearing our cross toward the goal of hearing His *"well done"*: Mark and Michelle moved to California from the Midwest to pursue his career in show business. He showed up at Church of the Open Door with the talent to make it in Hollywood and stars in his eyes. A nominal Christian, he mainly came to church for his wife and daughter. But God grabbed him and began turning his heart toward the path of a disciple. They cleared their schedule to spend time with more mature Christians who mentored them, volunteered to teach children's classes, opened their home to hurting people, a small-group Bible study, and every gathering of their daughter's Christian and non-Christian friends.

Along the way, they faced the hard decision to let go of his Hollywood dreams as they tightened their grip on the dream God laid on their hearts. A few years ago, they sold their home in Southern California, loaded up their life in a moving van, and headed for Dallas Seminary. We're all excited to see what God is going to do with Mark's great heart for people and awesome communication talent and Michelle's relational and hospitality skills.

It's not their choice to go to seminary and become "professional Christians" that Jesus will affirm at His Judgment Seat, but their choice to forsake all to follow Him as disciples. It isn't that they could; it's that they *would*. They really *believe* that Jesus will reward them for giving Him everything. They *can* be Jesus' disciples because they live *with* the faith it requires to please Him. They're trusting Him enough to pick up their cross and follow Him. They're looking forward not only to His soon coming, but the reward He's bringing with Him.

My wife, Judy, leads a small community of faith within our church called His Alone. This group is made up of women who live single for many different reasons. Some of them are widows, grieving the loss of their life partner. Some had spouses who abandoned them for another. Some have never been married and are wondering if living alone may be God's will for them. A few are married to former churchgoers who say they no longer care about the things of Christ Jesus.

What they all have in common is that their lives don't look like they always assumed it would. They pictured a Christian marriage, a lifelong partner who would love and cherish them and help them parent their children. They're a part of the class no Christian woman really wants to be a part of, the His Alone class.

Even though they didn't choose this life, most of them are choosing to trust Jesus in the middle of the pain and confusion. They are becoming courageous examples of those few Christians willing to bear the cross of a disciple of Christ.

It's not that they can stay on the path of honoring Christ in spite of their deep disappointment; it's that they *will*. They really *believe* that Jesus will reward them for giving Him everything. They *can* be Jesus' disciples because they live *with* the faith it requires to please Him. They're trusting Him enough to pick up their cross and follow Him … without a man at their side. They trust Him to be enough for them until God arranges "graduation day" from Judy's class by showing them His choice of the man for them, even if that day never comes.

Jesus is asking you to do something hard right now, isn't He? He's asking you to trust Him for a part of your life you would rather handle on your own. Whatever that hard thing is, *that* is your threshold of discipleship.

That is what will secure your part of the reward He will bring with Him when He returns.

And He's coming … quickly.

But you must trust Him enough to do what He says. Without that kind of faith, it is impossible to please Him. If you won't do that, you cannot be His disciple.

If you will, you're stepping through a threshold of revival.

Revival and Running to Win

What would you think if when the sprinters lined up for an Olympic race and the gun went off, two of the athletes ran down the course straining toward the finish line, but six of them casually stood up and walked down their lanes waving at the crowd, talking and laughing with one another, listening to their iPods and passing a big bag of peanut M&M's back and forth?

Would you be surprised and maybe even a little appalled at their brash disregard for all that the Olympics means? Would you wonder how they could so offhandedly disregard and neglect the great privilege they have as gifted athletes?

If you're upset, what do you think their teammates must be feeling? What about the countries they represent? Can you imagine the disappointment of their coach, and what he might say to them after the race?

This is the exact illustration the Bible uses to remind Christians of our privilege, responsibility, and accountability as ambassadors for Christ. Even the great apostle Paul feared not winning his "gold medal," the prize of hearing Christ say, "Well done, good and faithful servant." He unashamedly told the Corinthians that he competed for the prize, running the race with all his might, constantly thinking about standing before Christ on that day (1 Cor. 9:24–27).

When I look back at the Jesus Movement revival, I wonder what might have happened if we had read on in Revelation 22:12–13. If we looked forward to Jesus' soon coming, but also, if we had looked forward to the reward He would bring. Would some of us who dropped out of the race early have hung in there a little longer, striving to run another lap? Would those who got tired of all the commitment and training have persevered, knowing that they would face Coach Jesus to give an account for our reasons for missing practice? Would the ones who just gave up in the face of the persecution and hardship of service have finished the race, longing to hear our team Captain's "well done"?

I know it did for Judy and me, many times—the toughest times and darkest days, when following Him seemed foolish or impossible.

And I believe that the doctrine of rewards will make that same difference in the revival I'm asking God to let me be a part of before I die. I believe that the critical mass of the coming revival will be an army of disciples who know why they should stay in the battle. Ranks of men and women who are living for the world to come, for the day when they will hear their King Jesus' "well done."

Do you want to be a part of that multitude? Have you counted the cost of everything? Do you believe that you won't miss any of it? Then tell Him!

> Lord Jesus, I have counted the cost of being Your disciple and I'm telling You that I'm willing to trust You enough to pay the price. I know it will cost me everything, but I believe that I will not miss any of it. I believe that nothing compares to pleasing You and hearing Your "well done" when I stand before You at Your *bema*. That's what I'm living for. Use me to fulfill every remaining work You had in mind for me to complete when You saved me. Make me a part of the coming revival. Please Lord, I pray, in Your precious name, amen.

If you really meant what you just prayed, you're going to have a great opportunity to prove it in the next two chapters. Don't read on if you didn't mean it, because Jesus will ask you to put it all on the line for revival, and for your reward He's bringing with Him.

And He's coming … quickly!

Chapter 12

Our Only Treasure, Our Only Investment

For where your treasure is, there your heart will be also.
—Jesus Christ, Matthew 6:21

Everyone who lives in the real world knows what it means when someone says, "I'm calling you out!"

If we want to know that someone is sincere or can deliver, we challenge their commitment or ability with those four words: "I'm calling you out!" It could be a bold play in a game of cards or a risky move on a chessboard, an athletic team's arrogant claim to superiority or a salesperson's boast of what they're prepared to do, a politician's promise to make everything better or a friend's assurance that they will never let us down. If there's any doubt in our mind that they really mean it, we might say, "I'm calling you out."

Through the first eleven chapters of this book, I hope you joined me in telling God that we want revival. You may be an old Jesus Movement rocker like me who remembers our revival and longs to see it again. You may be a fed-up churchgoer who's tired of going through the meaningless religious motions of sanitized Christianity. Or you may be part of that bright hope for tomorrow—the authentic core of the emerging church—and you want to make sure your generation doesn't mess it up like we did.

For reasons you may or may not understand, the Spirit hasn't let you put this book down. And you have arrived at this page in a conversation with God. Perhaps you're saying that you want to see Christ's church get back on track and that you're willing to do your part. If so, you're agreeing with me when I say to the living God, "Whatever the cost, Lord Jesus. I'm ready. Sign me up. I want to see revival before I die. I want to be part of something *that* big and *that* eternal. Revival—I want it so much I'll do anything."

I believe God is calling us out.

He wants to know if we really mean it, because if we do, He'll work through us in a mighty way. And we must prove our desire and capacity for revival by making two of the hardest decisions a follower of Christ can make. Decisions so difficult you can count on one hand the number of times Christians have made this choice in large numbers. We call those rare times *revival*.

What are those two hard things? Deciding to love Christ more than our money, and to love our brothers and sisters in Christ more than ourselves.

And I don't think He means love in the ways we're used to saying we love Christ or our brothers and sisters in Christ. I think He's calling us to *radical* expressions of love for Christ and His church.

Did I say radical? Sounds like the sixties to me! Except this time we'll be so radical that the world won't be able to ignore what God's doing through us. Not just us—the spiritual revolutionaries of the Jesus Movement getting radical for Christ again—but everyone begging God for revival ... because you can't separate the two—revival and radical love for Christ and His people.

He's calling us out. Can you hear Him? *I'm calling you out. If you really want to see revival, show Me that you love My Son more than you love your money!*

Earnest Money

Nobody watching our Jesus Movement lives had any doubt that we loved Jesus more than our money. We considered it a badge of honor—we lived on nothing and gave what we had away. "Mature" Christians even reprimanded us for our reckless commitment of our resources to Christ.

A troubled young man in our Bakersfield High Young Life Club didn't have enough money to go to camp. I remember our thought process clearly: *This guy isn't a believer yet. He needs Jesus. So, let's pay his way.*

Nobody in our group of leaders even hesitated. Bobby was the only one with a good job, so he contributed the most. But even the ones who didn't know where they would find the money to buy next semester's books at college immediately threw in. Of course we would give any money we had. Who cares about money when there is a soul at stake?

A few days later, when we were driving one of our old beater cars back from that same camp, the guy who owned the car asked, "Anyone have any money left? We're running on empty and we're still 100 miles from home."

We pulled up to the pump of the next gas station and asked for "fifty-eight cents of regular, please." Fifty-eight cents bought a lot more gas forty years ago than it does now, but not that much more. Jim, who had followed Jesus longer than any of us, took the lead. "Okay, boys, we don't have any money because we gave it all away so that kids could hear about Jesus. So now God's just going to have to take care of us. We need a miracle, guys. Let's pray."

And we did. And He did. That old jalopy made it all the way to Bakersfield and deposited each of us to our front door. It felt like a miracle, so we told everyone about it.

"Not so fast, young naive one" was the surprising response of older Christians when we enthusiastically reported our miracle of the immaculate perpetuation of petrol. "You need to understand that there are priorities in life. You may think this is cool, but it's really irresponsible. You probably just had more gas in the tank than the gauge registered. There's no way you drove that far on fifty-eight cents."

I remember absolutely ignoring their advice and feeling more spiritual because *we* put *our* money on the line for Christ. I also remember being pretty ticked off that they brushed aside our miracle.

We felt more spiritual because, according to Jesus' definition, we were. We recognized that commitment to Him had everything to do with our money, and that His commitment to care for us in this way had everything to do with our radical trust in Him.

If I could do it over again, I'd try to find that moment when I stopped listening to my reckless revival heart and started listening to the prudent commentary of people who had already suppressed theirs. I would step back from that moment and shout, "Don't do it, Ed. Don't start believing that your money is yours. It's His! Stay reckless in your giving. He'll take care of you. Don't believe the 'It's all mine' lie."

I'd give away a lot more of my money, and pray a lot more for His provision to care for me. I'd spend a lot less time looking for the credit card with the best interest rate and a lot more time looking for opportunities to drive on empty, begging for miracles.

Turning to God in ways that transfer our trust from our own abilities to take care of our money to His ability to take care of our money involves more than just a prayer. That's why I told you to write that check in chapter 9—so that you could discover some of the excitement of running on empty!

Think of it as *earnest money*. When Judy and I bought our home in

Southern California, it wasn't enough to say to the seller, "Oh, this is the one we love. Don't sell it to anybody else. We promise you that this is what we want." If we wanted the owner to hold that house for us, we had to demonstrate our intentions by writing them a check of good faith: *earnest money*. This told them that we really meant it; we actually wanted that house.

You might deceive yourself and all your Christian friends by saying you really want your life to count for Christ, and that significance in His kingdom is what you want most, but you're not fooling God. He knows that every time the gas gauge falls below a quarter tank, you depend more on yourself than you do on Him. He's looking for some earnest money—your good-faith deposit of your *little* that tells Him you might just be the type of Christian He can trust with His precious *much*. He's beginning to see you as the type of believer He could bless with a miracle, because you're willing to run on empty.

So I'm telling you again: "Write that check." Remember, I'm not calling you out, God is. If you're not able to write the check, underline the next sentence in red: *Warning! Don't read on until you're able to let God know you're serious.*

And then, put a bookmark on this page, and close this book until you're ready to be a part of the coming revival. That will be the day that my story about five reckless and hopelessly broke Jesus Movement guys praying for one more mile on the way home from Young Life Camp makes you wish you were riding with us.

If you were able to trust God enough to give Him your earnest money, you're leaning toward that radical commitment that He needs to know is in your heart before He'll trust you with the true riches of revival.

What's in Your Heart

If you're wondering what your money has to do with what God knows is in your heart, just ask Jesus. In His most famous sermon, He said that the two (your money and your heart) are inseparable.

In Matthew 5—7, Jesus stood before a great multitude, gathered His disciples to Him, and gave them a picture of a new way of life. I'm convinced the Lord addressed the character traits of every citizen in His future kingdom. But I'm also sure that we would all have to admit that the type of person He's describing is also the type of person He wants His followers to be even now.

The question He's asking every one of His followers to answer is, "Where is your heart? Have you given it to Me, or are you still holding onto it?"

There's no need to get too technical when trying to define what Jesus means by "Where is your heart?" All of us have used the phrase "My heart's just not in it" to explain why we couldn't follow through on a rash commitment or a previous plan. What we mean is "You know, I thought I was passionate about this, but I'm not."

How else do you explain doing something as stupid as buying fifty-eight cents of gas one hundred miles from home and asking God to miraculously keep you going? If our hearts weren't in it, we would have called someone to come pick us up or wire the money. What doesn't make sense to the minds of more prudent survivalists makes perfect sense to the heart of revivalists.

The challenge in the Sermon on the Mount is that our heart determines our behavior; it is the compass of our life. We walk the direction our heart points. Jesus' radical message was this: *I'm far more interested in your heart than I am in your performance, because that's where it all begins. I'm looking for men and women whose hearts belong to Me. Those who will follow Me!*

He began by forcing that crowd of people to look beyond what the world sees to what is really true on the inside, from His perspective as the God who knows hearts. The Beatitudes radically change their idea of the sort of people God affirms (Matt. 5:1–12). God is not looking for the rich, happy, and powerful people; He seeks the poor, sad, merciful, peaceful, and persecuted. Those are the ones the Son knows will let their light shine in ways that will glorify His Father (Matt. 5:13–16).

He's talking about a radical new type of follower—one with a transformed heart—and Jesus lets them know that the righteousness they want is deeper than they ever imagined. Jesus demands a threshold of purity and devotion to His Father that is beyond the reach of mere humans (Matt. 5:17–48). Those still clinging to their static definitions of purity and devotion are exposed as hypocrites in all of their religious works of good deeds, prayers, and fasting (Matt. 6:1–17).

His entire message swings from preparing His audience for His main idea to stating it in Matthew 6:24:

> No one can serve two masters; for either he will hate the one and love the other, or else he will be loyal to the one and despise the other.

So who are you serving? That's the pivotal question. Are you serving My Father, or are your loyalties divided?

If all you did is read my words here, you are probably asking, "How can I know if I'm totally devoted to my heavenly Father?" But if you had your Bible open to the Sermon on the Mount, you already know the answer.

The only measure the Son offers to gauge our devotion to the Father is *how we invest our treasure!*

> Do not lay up for yourselves treasures on earth, where moth and rust destroy and where thieves break in and steal; but lay up for yourselves treasures in heaven, where neither moth nor rust destroys and where thieves do not break in and steal. For where your treasure is, there your heart will be also. (Matt. 6:19–21)

We cannot separate our heart from our money, and Jesus knows it. God didn't put this verse in here to give writers like me a neat insight to sell books, or preachers a way to raise money. Jesus said this to tell His people how He knows if their heart is the type of heart that will follow Him. He said this so that you would know exactly what He knows about your heart: Either it's dedicated to Him or it's not.

You don't need to go to a retreat somewhere or sit under a spiritual coach to know where your heart is. You only need to check your bank account. If all your money, or most of it, is being spent on the things of this earth, then your heart isn't very much His, is it? You're just driving around with a full tank and a pocketful of credit cards. If a lot of your money is being invested in the things that move His agenda forward and support His work on earth, if you're the one driving on empty because you gave your gas money to His work, you are investing in heaven and your heart is more fully His.

Jesus said it, not me: *Your heart and your money are inseparable.*

So, you tell me. Do you think Jesus is going to let you be a part of the coming revival you say you want because of what He knows about your heart?

If not, you can change your heart by reinvesting your money. If you want your heart to be a revival heart that wants heaven's agenda, then you need to invest your money in heaven.

Jesus wants your heart for this revival. And the best way I know to make sure that more and more of your heart is His is to make sure that more and more of your money is His.

If you're still thinking that this chapter is a little over the edge and you're saying, "Okay, Ed. Enough already" if telling people to drive on empty praying for a miracle seems too radical to you, Jesus has already diagnosed your problem.

Blurred Vision

Have you ever tried to read or focus your eyes right after the doctor put those drops in to examine your retinas? You can't see clearly, can you? No matter how hard you try, the effect of the drops can't be reversed. You just have to wait until the influence wears off, and then you begin to see more clearly, little by little.

I think this is similar to Jesus' point in the next two verses. If you're unwilling to invest in heaven, you're going to have blurred spiritual vision:

> The lamp of the body is the eye. If therefore your eye is good, your whole body will be full of light. But if your eye is bad, your whole body will be full of darkness. If therefore the light that is in you is darkness, how great is that darkness! (Matt. 6:22–23)

The word translated *bad* in verse 23 makes it clear that this is the type of problem Jesus had in mind: a serious eyesight problem. The Greek word for *evil, poneiros,* can also mean "in poor condition, to be badly off, to be ill." Think of this as a virus of the eye sourced in evil, or drops in your eye from a dropper held by Satan himself, for he is *ho poneiros,* the evil one (Matt. 13:19).

We see the world through our eyes. If our eyes are spiritually healthy, we see the world clearly, as full of light—as God wants us to view it. If our eyes are spiritually sick, we see the world with blurred vision, as dark and cloudy, and confusing—as the devil wants us to view it.

Think of it! When we selfishly invest our treasure here on earth, we're choosing to view the world with an evil eye. If we're not able to see that, the virus of covetous materialism has already begun to infect our eyesight.

If you're a fiftysomething former Jesus Movement radical turned suburban hoarder, perhaps you're objecting with this defense: "Hey, come on, Ed. I have to secure my portfolio. I mean, who's going to take care of me when I'm old? And then there are the kids and the grandkids. I can't just start giving money away irresponsibly. Come on here, I give some, more than most. This seems reckless to me."

"Who's going to take care of you when you're old? What kind of stupid question is that?" Jesus would say. "I'm going to take care of you, your children, and your grandchildren. I take care of everything. Since when did your financial security depend on you? Look again at My words":

> No one can serve two masters; for either he will hate the one and love the other, or else he will be loyal to the one and despise the other. You cannot serve God and mammon [money]. (Matt. 6:24)

If you're a twentysomething wannabe radical, frivolously spending six dollars a day at Starbucks, you might be objecting with this defense: "Dude, you're too old. I'll be lucky if I enjoy even half of my parents' lifestyle. I can barely afford gas in my 1996 Mercury Sable. So I 'go out' a lot and buy a lot of clothes. So what? How else can I enjoy life? Who would begrudge me having a little fun, a little relief from this hopeless world?"

"Who told you that your reason to be here was to have fun?" Jesus would ask, "Your only hope is Me; your only satisfaction is in Me. I'm not calling you to a life of fun; I'm calling you to a life of serving Me! Look again at My words":

> No one can serve two masters; for either he will hate the one and love the other, or else he will be loyal to the one and despise the other. You cannot serve God and mammon [money]. (Matt. 6:24)

Investing your resources in this world is the eye drop that blurs your vision, whether it's a trip to Paris or a cup of Caffè Verona. If you're indulging to satisfy needs only Jesus can meet, you won't get it … until the effect wears off. And the only therapy Jesus offers to recover your eyesight and draw your heart back to Him is to invest in His kingdom.

The same Jesus who said that we *cannot* be His disciple unless we forsake all (Luke 14:33) also said we *cannot* serve His Father until we stop serving our money. But you won't see that until you *start* investing in His Son's work.

Until you and I separate ourselves from our money and unite our heart to Christ by giving our money to Him, we have not forsaken all and we are not serving His Father. We'll miss the very revival for which we're praying. Not because it won't happen, but because we won't *see* it!

When we do begin separating ourselves from our money by giving it to Him, God's Spirit will draw our heart toward Him and clear our vision. We will see things as we've never seen them before. With eyes wide open, we unapologetically pull up to the pump and ask for fifty-eight cents of regular, smile, and drive on claiming Jesus' promises to get us home.

All Your Need

Jon and Karen approached me after church asking me to pray for them. While they transitioned into the new challenges of purchasing their own business, he lost his job because his employer had been hit by hard times.

Before I put my arms around them and asked the Lord to care for them, I said something that caused the young expectant mother to look at me with one of those "Some pastor you are!" looks.

"I'd be happy to pray for you," I said. "But I have to tell you that you don't have a thing to worry about."

I responded to her questioning eyes as soon as we finished the prayer.

"I've known about your husband's sacrificial stewardship for years. Some of the men I've mentored discipled him, and we're all amazed at his faith in giving since his youth. So don't think that I'm insensitive or some type of weirdo who sees into the future. I'm just telling you what I wish I could tell every Christian who's facing money problems or crises: Your worshipful giving guarantees that God will supply your every need in a way that will make it possible for you to keep on giving."

As a student of the Scriptures and a devoted disciple of Christ, she immediately knew the passage I was talking about—Philippians 4:19. She looked into her husband's face with the type of respect every husband longs for, hugged him, and they walked off together with the financial confidence and security known only by those who can claim His promises about money.

If you were standing with me that day and asked me, "What happened to her? How could she walk up to you, the desperate mother-to-be whose husband had just lost his job and walk away the confident wife of a man whom she admired more than ever?" I would answer, "What you just witnessed was God improving the vision of a steward who submitted her finances to the lordship of Christ!"

The promise they claimed is the same promise Paul claimed for his beloved Philippians when they sent him an encouraging financial gift during his first Roman imprisonment:

> Not that I seek the gift, but I seek the fruit that abounds to your account. Indeed I have all and abound. I am full, having received from Epaphroditus the things sent from you, a sweet-smelling aroma, an acceptable sacrifice, well pleasing to God. And my God shall supply all your need according to His riches in glory by Christ Jesus. Now to our God and Father be glory forever and ever. Amen. (Phil. 4:17–20)

Christians who aren't generous givers invariably read this wrong, because they're still looking at the world through their evil, self-centered, sick-eyed prism and thinking with their me-first, investing-in-earth heart. They might say something like, "I gave for awhile, but God didn't take care of me. I have a lot of needs right now that He's just ignoring. In fact, right after I gave a few months ago, my car broke down and my boss cut back my hours. Don't tell me God will meet my needs, because He won't!"

Is that what you're thinking?

The only way to see what Paul promises is to start giving. Only then will the Spirit begin to open your eyes so that you can see the result of bonding your heart to God through heavenly investments.

Here is a guide from the same passage in Philippians:

- Every dollar given to God is an investment in eternity—a deposit into our heavenly account (Phil. 4:17).
- Every dollar given to God is an intimate experience of worship—a sweet-smelling aroma, our acceptable sacrifice, well pleasing to God (Phil. 4:18).
- Every dollar given to God is an insurance policy on earth—securing our lives against financial ruin and underwritten by His unlimited resources (Phil. 4:19).

Revival-hearted believers view the world with the clear vision of a generous and sacrificial steward. They're not giving to get a tax deduction; they're giving to invest in their heavenly bank account. They're not giving so they can brag to their Christian friends; they're giving to express their worship to God. They're not afraid to risk giving large portions of their income to God; they're afraid to risk losing God's promise to underwrite their income.

The more you give, the more apparent this becomes. You begin to look at your giving as your first and most important financial decision every month. You begin to look at the way of a steward as the only safe way home in the dark and dangerous valley of earthly economies. *God will take care of all my needs,* you say to yourself as your needle sits on *E* and you have miles to go.

As you look ahead for the next sign marking God's highway to financial security, you see another sign that causes you to recklessly press down on the accelerator. With your steadily improving spiritual eyesight, you can read the sign for the first time. What it says takes your breath away.

All Your Bounty

The affluent Corinthian Christians stood at the crossroad to revival. Only twelve months ago they enthusiastically committed to give generously to their poverty-stricken Jewish brothers and sisters in Jerusalem and Judea (2 Cor. 8:10). Encouraged by their initial pledge, Paul had used their story to challenge the less fortunate churches of Macedonia to the north to give sacrificially. God moved so powerfully that even in their "great trial of affliction" and "deep poverty," the churches of Macedonia gave "beyond their ability" because they were "freely willing" (2 Cor. 8:1–5).

But the Corinthians weren't faithful in their giving. We don't know the cause of their sudden reluctance to deliver on what they promised to God. Maybe the harvest wasn't as robust as they had anticipated. Maybe they second-guessed their earlier exuberance for giving.

Paul sends Titus with a letter telling them that their wavering faith is an embarrassment to the cause of Christ. "How do I explain your refusal to give generously from your abundance to these Macedonians who have given sacrificially from their poverty?" (2 Cor. 9:1–4). And then, he exhorts them to fulfill their obligation by exposing the reason for their lack of giving: *greed*.

> Therefore I thought it necessary to exhort the brethren to go to you ahead of time, and prepare your generous gift beforehand, which you had previously promised, that it may be ready as a matter of generosity and not as a grudging obligation. (2 Cor. 9:5)

The word translated "grudging obligation" literally means "covetousness, selfishness, or greed." In this sentence, it conveys the idea of having to wring the money out of them, as you would water from a wet towel.

God's calling them out, isn't He?

Where would you put yourself in that equation? Are you more like the Macedonian Christians—barely scraping by in a poverty-stricken economy, driving on *E* in a full-tank world? Or are you more like the Corinthian Christians—rich by any worldwide measurement, driving on full in an empty-tank world, yet never satisfied because of the materialistic culture you live in?

God isn't going to squeeze the money out of your life. He doesn't need your money! But He is going to open your eyes to the wonder of what He could do with your bounty, if you would only commit it all to Him.

> But this I say: He who sows sparingly will also reap sparingly, and he who sows bountifully will also reap bountifully. So let each one give as he purposes in his heart, not grudgingly or of necessity; for God loves a cheerful giver. And God is able to make all grace abound toward you, that you, always having all sufficiency in all things, may have an abundance for every good work. (2 Cor. 9:6–8)

This isn't a book about the mundane expectations of the just-trying-to-get-by Christians filling most of the seats in our churches today. It's a book about the extraordinary faith of revival-hearted disciples. So I'm not going to waste the ink and effort it would take to wring a few more dollars out of a materialistic and covetous heart. I'm not going to write another word about God promising to meet our little needs.

From this point on, all I'm going to focus on is the bounty He promises to every Christian who allows Paul's words to the Corinthians to open their eyes. The principle is stunning: *How you sow your bounty is how you will reap your bounty.*

Never think that Paul was talking about anything other than bounty. This principle is a message to rich Christians like us! We may not feel rich when we look at our neighborhoods, but if we looked at most neighborhoods in this world we would feel rich beyond compare. Compared to them, our tank is always full. If rich Christians like us will sow our resources bountifully, we will reap spiritual bounty.

And what is the bounty? The bounty is the measure of God's grace needed to have *all* the financial sufficiency to do *every* good work for Him we would *ever* desire.

This isn't a promise that God will make me richer so that I can live in a richer neighborhood. This is a promise that God will make me rich enough to invest as much as my heart desires in His work.

God's calling you out! You're standing at the same crossroad of revival the rich Corinthians stood at thousands of years ago. If you will invest your bounty in the revival, in His kingdom, He'll give you even more bounty to invest. The coming revival will follow His law of the harvest: You reap what you sow.

If you're still protesting, "What do you expect from me anyway, Jesus? If I give like that, why I'll only be left with …" Jesus would answer, "With what? Fifty-eight cents?"

Before you say, "This is impossible," think about what God can do with your possible, your fifty-eight cents.

All Your Possible

One of the greatest missionaries Church of the Open Door ever sent out was Cam Townsend, the founder of Wycliffe Bible Translators. Early in his life, God taught Him a lesson about how much *He* could do with *Cam's* little.

On June 23, 1922, a man named Pedro brought a gift to Cam's first partner in ministry in Guatemala, Robby, to thank him for what he had done for him.

Robby told Cam the story: Pedro's wife had had a serious case of gangrene poisoning. A doctor had passed through town and told Pedro that there was no hope for her. She was surely going to die. Seeing how desperately ill she was, Pedro prepared his wife's funeral; he even readied a crypt for her body.

Robby, however, believed that God could heal the woman, and he began to encourage Pedro to pray with him. He visited the woman and sat through the night with her. He sang hymns to her and soaked her infected feet in warm water. By morning, the gangrene receded, and slowly the woman began to recover. Within a week she was well again.

Cam was heartened by the story and said, "If we will do the possible, God will do the impossible." As soon the words came out of his mouth, he knew that this was the only way to view the impossible vision the Lord had put in his heart—to translate the Bible into every language on earth.

God didn't ask Cam and his missionary partners to complete that humanly impossible task. God only asked them to do the absolutely possible tasks His Spirit would point out to them along the way.

God's not asking us to finance the entire revival; that would be impossible! He's asking us to finance the entire part of that revival that is our responsibility: *our possible.*

When you start asking in earnest what is possible, you will be surprised by His answer. It will be a lot more than you expect, and He wants all of it!

Judy and I have been amazed at His definition of our possible. He's told us it's far more than the meager 10 percent we used to consider impossible. He's let us know that even when we dedicate that intimidating portion to His work, He's going to surprise us with other needs included in His definition of our "possible." He even told us that our portfolio is not our own. Our possible includes a significant bit of our retirement, because it's not our nest egg; it's His—and *He* will tell us how much we can keep!

That's God's message to rich people like us. If we want to *take hold* of revival, we have to swallow our pride and suppress our greed so that we can be "rich in good works, ready to give, willing to share, storing up for ourselves a good foundation for the time to come" (1 Tim. 6:18–19).

Let's do it. Let's grab hold of that revival together. Let's ask God what all of our possible is and be willing to share it, investing in the time to come. And then, when He tells us what our part is, let's do it.

Let's blow up our church budgets and blow the minds of our missionaries around the world. Let's go to our accountants and lawyers and restructure our financial plans and portfolios.

Let's write a new and surprising chapter in church history. Instead of being known as the most affluent generation of Christians ever, let's become known as the most generous.

And when we get to heaven and we're asked, "Why did you do it? Why did you give God *all* of your possible?" we will say, "Because we wanted revival more than anything else, and God taught us to love Christ more than our money!"

Chapter 13

Our Only Community, Our Only Care

This is My commandment, that you love
one another as I have loved you.
—Jesus Christ, John 15:12

As hard as it is not to love our money, it's even harder to love Christians. You know the ones I'm talking about, don't you? Those Christians who make you wonder, just for a moment, if grace is really that great of an idea. *Why did You ever save people like this?* Then, when God reminds you that if it weren't for grace you would be sunk, you wonder for far more than a moment if the church is a necessary concept. *Why did You ever plan to get it done with all these losers and weirdos?* Then, when you admit that if God didn't use weirdos and losers He couldn't use you, you look around and ask the real question:

Why did You put me with these specific losers and weirdos? You know I can't stand some of them! This is all wrong. If You expect me to love Your people, then You need to find some better people for me to work with.

In the preface I wrote that I wanted to help you become the type of disciple Jesus uses in a revival. In the months since writing those words, I've realized many times that if I don't make some changes in my life, I won't be the type of disciple Jesus will use in the coming revival.

This chapter is the one that challenges me the most. I'm a rebel at heart and a loner by temperament. Not much of a "mixer," and for sure, not a "joiner." Friends tell me I live with a subterranean dissatisfaction with all things churchy and evangotrendy. *They're right.*

In the past, when I have had opportunities to love Jesus' people more than myself, I find that I am more interested in being heard than listening and preparing to see God heal. I failed to see it as a revival choice.

Now I see it as a revival choice, as God calls me out with one simple sentence from His Son's lips: "This is My commandment, that you love one another as I have loved you" (John 15:12).

And I suspect He's calling you out with me. He's calling us to care more for His Son's community and reputation than we do for our individual comfort and rights. We know that Jesus and His apostles teach the importance of unity in the church. And we know where to find those teachings in our Bible. So why don't we do what God says?

I'm convinced that the problem isn't the interpretation of these passages, but their application. We're more than willing to talk about the importance of unity, and even condemn the church for "not doing what Jesus says" throughout history or in our city. What we're failing to do is condemn ourselves for "not doing what Jesus says" in our relationships and in our churches. We haven't connected the dots between the hard-to-get–along-with Christians in our own lives and these hard-to-live-out texts in our Bibles.

I want to help you connect your life to these words of Jesus and His apostles by showing the way God connected them for me. If I could do it over again, I'd pay a lot more attention to unity. God is asking me to love the Christians who bother me most more than myself. If I could do it over again, I'd pay a lot more attention to the following passages that tell me that true revivalists love Christ's people.

Dine with Me

Let's say you meet someone and you just hit it off. You can't believe how much you have in common. It seems that everything you value, this person values. The things you get excited about, he gets excited about. Those issues that you're most passionate about and what you care for most in life, he seems passionate about as well. Then, after you get to know him better, you discover that he is a believer, with a heart for God. This is important to you, so you decide to move forward with the relationship.

You do a few things together—go to a ball game or a movie, meet for dinner at one of your favorite restaurants—and you feel yourself accepting this friendship and anticipating enthusiastically where it's heading.

After a few weeks or months, he invites you over to his house. You check out his address on MapQuest, stop by the corner bakery to pick up a pie for dessert, and drive to his home. As you pull into the driveway, the thought of this friendship makes you happy.

You walk up to the door of his home, stand outside, and knock. He comes to the door, asks who it is, and you answer, "It's me." He hears your voice, opens the door, and says enthusiastically, "Come in, please. Let's have dinner."

The table is set elegantly, and the smell of one of your favorite dishes fills the air. You sit down; he gives thanks for the meal, looks up, and smiles as you begin with a tremendous salad.

Imagine how you would feel if he then looked you in the eye and said, "You know, there's something I need to tell you about your son. I think he's an idiot. I mean really, how do you tolerate the kid? I can't stand him. I'm sure happy he didn't come with you. And your daughter, why do you let her dress that way? She looks like a slut. She's so boy crazy. I'm never going to let my daughter be her friend. By the way, why do you hang around with those two people at church I always see you with?" He goes on and on talking about your friends and loved ones, telling you what he heard about them, relishing every rumor, and pointing out every fault.

He pauses briefly to tell you, "I made these rolls especially for you. There's nothing I wouldn't do for you. I found out that these are your favorite and I made them from scratch. It's just a small thing. I hope you know that I'm absolutely devoted to you and really want you to come over any time. Just knock on the door and when I hear your voice, I'll let you in and we will dine together. How about tomorrow, same time? Isn't fellowship wonderful!"

I know what I would say. "Wait a minute here. This doesn't make sense. You want to be my friend, you want me to come into your home and dine with you. You say that all I have to do is knock on the door and you will let me in. But you say these hurtful things about people I love, my own family and friends? I don't know your definition of friendship, but it's certainly not one I would use. And as for your understanding of fellowship, you don't have a clue. Of course I'm not coming tomorrow night. Why would I? I don't feel comfortable here, not at all. Unless you change the way you talk about and treat the people I love, I will never feel welcome here! You have broken my heart."

Jesus uses that scene from everyday life to picture His desire to enter the inner life of His church. Speaking to the church at Laodicea, Jesus said, "Behold, I stand at the door and knock. If anyone hears My voice and opens the door, I will come in to him and dine with him, and he with Me" (Rev. 3:20).

How do you think Jesus feels when Christians tell Him, "Oh yeah, come on into our church, but don't stop there. Have a seat in our sanctuary and relax. You're welcome into my home any time. After church, we've saved You a seat around our table. I'm totally dedicated to You; there's nothing I wouldn't do for You. What an honor it is to have You in our home." But He knows that these people are in a big fight with other Christians in the church and the main topic around that table is, "What's wrong with other Christians, and how are we better than them?"

It's no exaggeration to say that the church's lack of love for other Christians and divisive behaviors are the main reasons the presence and power of the Lord Jesus Christ is missing from some of our homes and churches. My understanding of the way Jesus uses the word *abide* is that He simply refuses to dwell *comfortably* and *intimately* in a life, a home, or a church that doesn't abide in His Word by obeying His commands (John 15:1–8; see also 1 John 3:24).

I'm sure that I have run Jesus out of our home and probably out of the churches I've pastored many times in my dealings with the most difficult Christian for me—*the entitled.* You know who I'm talking about, don't you? These are the people my friend Dave Burchett calls the "Spiritual Hall Monitors." They know the way things ought to be: the way they always were. And they know who should be in charge: the people who always have been, usually them.

I call them Brother Blowhard and Sister Wheatcakes, and they just make me nuts! How many times have I sat around a meal with my family, over coffee with a friend, or late into the night with Judy griping about these Christians who want church as it was in the 1940s and only care about their family and their interests, and how I wish they'd just leave, and why does God tolerate their legalism and stiffness? And … oh, I could go on and on.

However, I have failed to notice Jesus Christ standing up from the table with a tear in His eye and quietly slipping out the door.

Then He's gone and I wonder what happened and why I feel so lousy, and why everyone's looking at me like that, and why our church doesn't have better worship, and on and on.

I don't know who your Brother Blowhard and Sister Wheatcakes are, but everyone has people like this in their life and church. They may not be the entitled pillars who make you want to choke a Christian for Christ. Maybe it's people like me, those edgy-always-wanting-change-push-the-envelope dudes who never seem satisfied. Maybe it's the bag-o'-need-my-life-is-sadder-than-anyone-else's-and-I'll-prove-it-to-you-in-about-three-hours lady who wears you out. Or maybe mister big-shot-name-dropping-I-know-all-the-big-important-people-in-this-church guy whose voice makes you wish it were okay to flip people off in church.

The Lord knows who they are, even if you won't admit it. And when you release the evil, divisive energy in your life through words or actions, He just gets up and walks out. Not out of your life forever, because He promised to be with you always, and He never goes back on a promise (Rom. 8:28). But out of your life intimately, and out of your home and your church, for now. And He for sure isn't taking you with Him to revival, because He warned you that He doesn't abide with those who don't obey His directives to His church—especially His foremost commandment.

Jesus' Directive

I don't know which of the disciples made the others crazy, but I'm sure some of them did. When passionate followers of Christ gather to do something significant for Him, they come under satanic pressures and face challenging crises that strain the relationship. We know that the disciples argued over who would be the greatest in Jesus' coming kingdom. If they were anything like us, and they were, that was just the beginning.

For years they backpacked around the country with Jesus, sleeping on the ground, running from the authorities, listening to criticism from their families, and defending against charges of heresy from friends and Jewish leaders. All the while they believed Jesus was the Messiah and tried to figure out what He was talking about. They're tired, scared, and confused—the perfect environment for petty bickering, power posturing, and self-protective behaviors.

Jesus tolerated none of it.

John wrote that Jesus repeated something three times when He gathered them together for the last time: *Love one another.*

Twelve disheartened men sit around a quiet room above the city streets. Jesus tells them things they don't want to hear. They awkwardly look at one another as their Master washes their feet. "If I do not wash you, you have no part with Me" (John 13:8). "You are not all clean" (John 13:11). Depending on their view of Peter, they're either pleased that the Lord is finally putting that loudmouth in his place or wishing that the Lord would listen to him more.

In the next few minutes, Jesus looks at them in a way they have come to know: with a sadness in His eyes that causes them to brace for bad news. But they never anticipated how bad the news would be: Peter, their leader, would deny their Lord, Jesus said, and another from within their own circle would betray Him!

Jesus pauses and Judas runs into the night, though no one notices. Like a dying parent, Jesus begins to tell them good-bye. "I'm going away to a place you cannot follow," He says. And *this* is the moment Jesus chooses to disclose His foremost priority for them, that distinctive quality that will set them apart as His followers.

> A new commandment I give to you, that you love one
> another; as I have loved you, that you also love one another.

By this all will know that you are My disciples, if you have
love for one another. (John 13:34–35)

Two on one side of the room immediately look at one another guiltily.
*Did the Lord hear our jealous words and our sarcastic joke about the "sons of
thunderous ambition"?*

They're not alone. Each disciple feels uneasy about the things he's said
about or to one of the others. Before their discomfort deepens, Peter makes
it all about him again. Jesus rebukes him, saying something about laying
down his life and a rooster crowing in the morning.

Then amazingly, Jesus tells them not to be troubled. *Easy for You to say,*
a few are thinking. *I'm the one left behind with these knuckleheads.*

They struggle to grasp Jesus' sentences. Thomas wants to know where
He's going, Philip asks to see the Father, and the other Judas can't understand how Jesus will show Himself to the disciples, but not to the world.
Where is the other Judas, Judas Iscariot? they wonder. Then Jesus abruptly
gets up and leads them out into the night.

At least Jesus is talking about something they understand now, vines
and branches. He's the vine; they're the branches. If they abide in Him, they
will produce a lot of fruit.

I picture some pushing and shoving as they try to keep up with Jesus.
They all want to be next to Him, to show the Lord they're really one of these
fruit-producing, commandment-keeping disciples.

"Gosh, Peter, do you always have to be right up front?"

"Look at John. I'd like to wipe that smug look off his face. Did you see
him during the Passover meal? Leaning all over Jesus? No wonder Jesus tells
him the best stuff. No one else can get close to the Lord while 'little Johnny'
is around."

Jesus raises His voice in a way that quiets their thoughts and stops the
murmuring. He says it a second time, with an explanation they understand
immediately.

This is My commandment, that you love one another as I
have loved you. (John 15:12)

Even Peter doesn't say anything. James and John stop pushing. In all
the years they have followed Jesus, not once did He try to manipulate
them, compete with them, hurt them, lie to them, or talk about them to
one another. All He ever did was serve them, put them first, encourage
them, tell them the truth, stand with them, laugh with them, and cry
with them.

They stop thinking about who's getting credit or who's sitting next to
Jesus and start thinking about all the hard times they have faced together:

*Peter may be a loudmouth, but he's the most courageous leader in the bunch.
I'm glad Jesus chose him to lead us.*

*I have to admit that I like talking to John too. He always listens. That's
probably why Jesus tells him the things He doesn't want us to forget.*

Jesus lets them know why their group is so special—He chose them
and put them together. They're all on His team. And then with eyes full of
tears, Jesus gathers them together, makes eye contact, and says it again …
the third time.

These things I command you, that you love one another.
(John 15:17)

Hey, come to think of it, these are the guys I'd go to war with. Reading their
thoughts, Jesus tells them that they are indeed going to war—the world
hates them and there is nothing but pain and persecution ahead.

The sobering truth is that the church is at war even today, and every
Christian is a soldier in Christ's army of righteousness. Just because you
don't like to think about it doesn't make it less true. Read Ephesians 6!

I once gathered a few of the most committed young men in our church
to meet one of the most effective missionaries I've ever met. This man and

his wife have planted churches and built communities in some of Africa's most dangerous tribal areas. I asked him, "What is the one lesson you would like to share with the next generation? If you could say anything that you feel they need to hear, this is the time."

He looked at their eager young faces and solemnly said, "The devil is real, boys. I'm concerned that young missionaries coming to the field don't understand that we're in a spiritual battle." And then, as is the African way, he told story after story of his up-close encounters with Satan and his demon hordes.

Whether you know it or not, even if you don't like the idea of war, at this very moment there are thousands of powerful spirit beings in your immediate area. The Bible calls them demons, and they are Satan's troops, attacking the church, your family, even you! They hate you, especially if you're reading this book and thinking about revival. That's why Paul tells you to put on your spiritual armor.

I served my time as a soldier and a leader of soldiers. I learned that the highest priority for any commander is to send his men to war as a unit, as a band of brothers. He knows that if they're not unified, if they can't fight together, they won't survive the battlefield.

If you think of revival and picture huge gatherings of Christians asserting their power over the culture and holding hands while circling the flag and singing praise songs, know this: *That's a fairy tale.*

Revival is war and war is hell. Worse than that, revival is war against hell. The devil and his forces will come against us with murderous rage. You have to know who's on your right and on your left in that trench, and that they are loyal not only to the Commander, but to each of His warriors.

Revival warriors can't be looking over their shoulders, wondering where the friendly fire is coming from. The Lord knows it. That's why He's not taking any petty, rear-echelon, I-gotta-be-comfortable-and-important-and-it's-all-about-me cream puffs with Him.

It's gonna get ugly. It's time to put on the armor, strap on the helmet, shoulder your weapon, and man up. You gotta look Him in the eye and say, "I'm all in and this is my team," or He's going to leave you behind.

And it's not like He hasn't prayed for you.

Jesus' Desire

Stunned, the disciples can only whisper questions to one another as their Master talks about going to His Father and sending them a Helper. *What does He mean we'll never see Him again after "a little while"?* (John 16:17–18). Jesus answers them plainly: "I came from the Father into this world and I'm about to leave this world and go to Him" (see John 16:28).

They can accept that (John 16:29–30), but when the Lord explains what He means by "a little while," they realize that it's much sooner and far worse than they previously thought.

> Indeed the hour is coming, yes, has now come, that you will be scattered, each to his own, and will leave Me alone. And yet I am not alone, because the Father is with Me. These things I have spoken to you, that in Me you may have peace. In the world you will have tribulation; but be of good cheer, I have overcome the world. (John 16:32–33)

As comforting as the last three sentences are to our hearts today when we read them, I doubt the disciples heard those words that night. If I were standing there, I wouldn't have heard anything past "the hour has now come, you will be scattered, each to his own, and will leave Me alone."

The staggered men look at one another, refusing to believe that anything could separate them from the Messiah and one another. Then the awareness sets in. *Jesus is always right, so it must be true. This is it. Tonight we say good-bye. It's over.*

John made sure we feel the drama of the moment. No more teaching, no more explanations, no more questions. Instead, Jesus turns their attention to their only real hope when He turns His eyes to heaven and talks to His Father. His prayer is a conversation between Father and Son, but Jesus makes sure the disciples are listening.

I picture eleven wide-eyed disciples focused and listening for the first time that night.

Burning in their heart since they heard Jesus utter the word *scattered* is the question, *Will we ever see each other again?*

I don't know if I could go on without these guys. Sure, there are times when I feel like Jesus should never have chosen some of us. But we've always had each other. I don't think I could do this alone. Jesus has never asked us to follow Him alone before.

Their gut relaxes a little every time Jesus uses the word "them." "I have given *them* … I pray for *them* … while I was with *them* … the world has hated *them* … keep *them* … sanctify *them* … I have sent *them*" (John 17:6–19). That can only mean that they will be together again someday.

But how will they ever find each other? With the dark expectations Jesus plants in their hearts, it doesn't seem possible. Denial, betrayal, abandonment, hatred, scattering—in just a few minutes they'll be running for their lives in eleven different directions without Him!

Then Jesus says these words:

> I do not pray for these alone, but also for those who will
> believe in Me through their word; that they all may be one,
> as You, Father, are in Me, and I in You; that they also may
> be one in Us, that the world may believe that You sent Me.
> And the glory which You gave Me I have given them, that

they may be one just as We are one: I in them, and You in
Me; that they may be made perfect in one, and that the
world may know that You have sent Me, and have loved
them as You have loved Me. (John 17:20–23)

The church today often reads these words as a challenge rather than
a comfort. This is the surest sign of how far the church today lives from
this truth. We're so satisfied with our disunity that we don't realize Jesus is
teaching us something about diversity and humility. If we're reading these
words in the context of that dark night and the disciples' fear of serving
Christ alone, we know the truth: *Unity is our only comfort zone, our only
care, because the church is our only community.*

Jesus doesn't need unity, we do!

Jesus doesn't ask God to make us one so we'll be happy. Jesus asked His
Father to make us one so we could get the job done!

I can't recall one meeting of leaders or a single gathering during the
exciting days of revival dedicated to "fellowship." Our friendships *in* Christ
flowed from our service *to* Christ. We were missional and didn't know it.
Since then, I've come to believe that those relationships in Christ that are
the most fulfilling personally are also the most purposeful for Him.

Look at those four verses (John 17:20–23) again in your own Bible.
Every time you read the word *one,* underline it.

So how do you feel about Sister Wheatcakes and Brother Blowhard
now? You need them, don't you? Unless you want to walk out onto the
battlefield alone.

Jesus knew that the moment after He finished His prayer, His friends
would step into the fiercest eternal conflict the world would ever know. In
the confusion of combat, He would be killed and His men scattered. The
one thing He wanted them to know before He saw them again three days
later was that His Father would reunite them and make them a part of an
army that the enemy could not stop.

Jesus' Revival

Acts tells the story of their victory. Against all odds, Christ built His church. The movement that turned the world upside down for the Lord Jesus began with about five hundred people led by the same disciples who wondered at Jesus' words in the upper room.

Acts was written to strengthen the faith of a new believer named Theophilus (Acts 1:1) and every Christian through the centuries. Throughout his account, Luke presents Christianity as an irresistible force in the face of great opposition and persecution.

For years I've known that the two structural keys to Acts describe the history of the early church in wondrous ways designed to ignite a longing to be like those first Christians.

The first structural key is the following theme verse, which anticipates a report of dramatic growth:

> But you shall receive power when the Holy Spirit has come
> upon you; and you shall be witnesses to Me in Jerusalem,
> and all Judea and Samaria, and to the end of the earth.
> (Acts 1:8)

The second structural key is the progress reports, which confirm what Acts 1:8 predicted in emphatic and surprising detail. People are added to the church in Jerusalem (Acts 2:47); disciples multiply in that church, including priests (Acts 6:7); churches multiply across Judea and Samaria (Acts 9:31); the Word of God becomes a growing and multiplying force in the world (Acts 12:24); strengthened churches increase in number daily (Acts 16:5); the Word of God grows mightily and prevails in the world (Acts 19:20); and finally, Paul preaches Christ unhindered in the epicenter of world paganism, *Rome* (Acts 28:30–31).

This was the church Jesus had in mind when He promised the disciples that His Father would gather them together again. That's the church I want to be a part of, don't you?

One morning I was studying Acts when I just couldn't take it any longer. I closed my laptop, set aside my notes, and begged God to show me what was missing from the church today. *What is lacking in us?* I asked. Or, *What was so different about them?*

His answer shouldn't have surprised me. The Spirit directed me to read the Acts progress reports in their context. "Look for a report on the unity of the church before the report on the progress of the church," I knew the Spirit was telling me. The correlation amazed me:

Unity Event	Progress Report
Acts 2:44–46: Together, all things in common, with one accord …	Acts 2:47: And the Lord added to the church daily those who were being saved.
6:5–6: Whole multitude pleased as they chose seven to serve …	6:7: Then the word of God spread and the number of disciples multiplied greatly in Jerusalem … including priests!
9:31: After Barnabas stood up for Saul, *"the churches throughout all Judea, Galilee, and Samaria had peace and were edified."*	9:31: And walking in the fear of the Lord and in the comfort of the Holy Spirit, they (churches) were multiplied.
12:5: Peter imprisoned by Herod who had already murdered James, "but constant prayer was offered to God for him by the church." God kills Herod (Acts 12:23).	12:24: But the word of God grew and multiplied.
15:1—16:4: Jerusalem council and the conflict over circumcision and Jewish sensitivities. Paul circumcises Timothy and shares the decrees of Jewish sensitivities with the Gentile Christians.	16:5: So the churches were strengthened in the faith, and increased in number daily.

19:18–19: Ephesian believers repent together of idol worship.	19:20: So the word of the Lord grew mightily and prevailed.
28:15: Roman believers encourage Paul by coming to meet him in spite of great persecution. Some met him 33 miles south of the city (Three Inns), others 44 miles south of the city (Appii Forum).	28:30–31: Then Paul dwelt two whole years in his own rented house, and received all who came to him, preaching the things which concern the Lord Jesus Christ with all confidence, no one forbidding him.

As soon as I saw what the Spirit showed me in God's Word, I quit begging God to let me see this kind of revival, got on my knees, and begged Him to forgive me:

- For resisting my Father's efforts to gather Jesus' disciples.
- For defining myself by what I'm against rather than what I'm for.
- For allowing minor theological differences to divide me from other Christians in my life.
- For caring more about winning biblical arguments than I do about winning souls for Christ.
- For the mean things I've said and thought about other Christians.
- For disobeying Jesus' foremost directive to love one another.
- For not wanting to have to work with Christians I consider "uncool."
- For decades of missed opportunities as I disregarded His concern for unity and the correlated blessings.

These verses clearly show the link between our attitude toward other believers and our chances of seeing revival. If you're not on repentant knees right now begging God to forgive you for your divisive words and actions, something is wrong. If your heart isn't breaking over the ways we have messed up Christ's reputation by our dysfunctional reputation in the world, you're not ready for revival.

Do you believe that the more you *endeavor to keep the unity of the power of the Spirit in the bond of peace* (Eph. 4:3), the more you and your church *shall receive power to be His witnesses* (Acts 1:8)?

Did you know that you can invite Jesus into your church or home, and then break His heart with divisive conversations, attitudes, and behaviors?

Are you convinced that He values love and unity among His followers more than your relational tensions and biblical opinions?

Do you realize that you cannot separate your walk with Christ from your love for other Christians?

Are you ready to admit that you can't walk with Him toward revival without relinquishing your rights for the sake of unity?

If you can answer yes to those questions, and if you're ready to stop fighting other Christians and start fighting the forces of evil, I encourage you to join me in declaring your enlistment in the ranks of His coming revival:

> Lord Jesus, I'm so sorry for the ways I have put myself first. I confess that over and over I have broken Your new commandment to love other Christians. I'm thinking of the specific times I have hurt them and You. I have heard what You said to me about unity and revival. I'm tired of being a part of the problem; I want to be a part of the solution. I relinquish my rights and renounce my loyalty to any system of theology, any religious culture, any institution, any teacher, and any leader that pulls Your devoted disciples apart. My only loyalty is to You, my only community, Your church, and my only care, to love Your people. Sign me up! I want to march forward together in

Your army of Christian soldiers. I want to be a part of that irresistible force—Your church. And I beg You to let me see revival.

They'll Know We're Christians

We sang the words in Young Life clubs, college dorms, and at mountaintop retreats: "They'll know we are Christians by our love." And they did, for about four or five years.

Then we started fighting, and we haven't quit since.

And then, Jesus walked out on our revival, and He hasn't come back.

Sadly, I've noticed the same trend in the emerging church. They're already starting to fight over silly things like their name—who's really an emergent worshipper, and who gets the credit, or which Web site is the most authentic source. They're beginning to divide over how dedicated they are to diversity and ecology, over what matters most to their "movement," or what their impressive leader said about another group's impressive leader.

And if they haven't noticed, Jesus is about to get up and excuse Himself.

He's not interested in their movement any more than He was in ours. He's only interested in the people in the movement—His people—and their impact on the world He loves and died for.

It's time to stop defining ourselves by what we're against and to start talking about what we're for, or we will never see revival.

Here's what I'm for: I'm for what Jesus is for. I'm for grace and faith, for God's Word and God's people, for the hurting and hopeless, for healing and hope, for the church and unity.

I'm for revival.

We could be the first Christians since the Pentecost generation to answer the question, "What would happen if millions of Christians and thousands of Christian communities actually pulled together in love?" We could be a positive answer to the Lord's deepest prayer to the Father. We could leave this earth knowing that we showed them we were Christians by our love for one another!

Our unity could qualify us to receive His revival power. And then, nothing could stop us … *as long as we followed His simple plan.*

Chapter 14

Our Only Plan, Our Only Power

But you shall receive power when the
Holy Spirit has come upon you;
and you shall be witnesses to Me in Jerusalem,
and in all Judea and Samaria,
and to the end of the earth.
—Jesus Christ, Acts 1:8

God created the church to be the greatest force for good on earth. Our job is to reach the world with the life-changing, culture-transforming message and power of His Son, Jesus Christ.

We're failing.

But it's not because we don't have *enough* ideas, studies, and strategies. There are plenty of competing voices telling us how to grow a big church or how to avoid becoming a big church by planting a bunch of little ones, how to focus our efforts on our culture or contextualize the message cross-culturally, how to market Jesus by targeting seekers, how to concentrate our movement or diversify our movement, how to lead our followers and follow our leaders.

We're failing because we have *too many* ideas, studies, and strategies. We're failing because we listen to every voice but Christ's. We've complicated the heck out of His simple plan and forgotten that we can't do this without Him, that His power flows through His plan.

One of the most distinguishing marks of revival is its simplicity, not its complexity. Our revival not only claimed the name of Jesus; we heard His simple command, followed His simple plan, relied on His simple promise of power, and asked Him for greater works.

If I could do it over again, I'd get up every morning picturing myself standing with the disciples outside of Jerusalem, listening to His final instructions: "But you shall receive power when the Holy Spirit has come upon you; and you shall be witnesses to Me in Jerusalem, and in all Judea and Samaria, and to the end of the earth" (Acts 1:8).

I would make sure that I connected His power with His plan, and lived as if it were true. I wouldn't have paid any attention to statistics and consultants telling me where people were "ready to hear." I'd be more afraid of missing His promise of power because I ignored His plan than I'd be afraid of what the sophisticated theorists and strategists thought of me.

In this last chapter, I want to discuss the seven simple truths that guided our revival as we witnessed for Christ. I'm not saying that these are the seven steps to a guaranteed revival. I am saying that as I look back on ours, God put these seven principles in place.

It was simple. And it all began with simple faith.

Faith in Me

The first three words from our Lord I wish we paid more attention to are "faith in Me."

I sat one evening on our patio visiting with a recent seminary graduate whose exciting vision for his upstart urban church stirred my Jesus Movement heart. As a seasoned veteran of church ministry, I've had hundreds of conversations like this, but this man was one of the few who asked me, "What can my generation learn from you 'Jesus Movement guys'?"

A recent study of the Lord's instructions to Paul in Acts 26 had convinced me that my own generation was beginning to neglect the central dynamic of Christianity: *faith in Christ*.

"It's not just your generation that needs this lesson," I told him. "We need it too! For some inexplicable reason, we all seem a little hesitant to talk about faith in Christ. Back then, just about every conversation about God revolved around the need for faith. If I were you, I'd do what I've determined to do. I'm going to talk a lot more about our need for faith in Him and what He can do for us. That's where it all began—not only our revival, but Christianity."

When Paul met the Lord Jesus on the road to Damascus, Jesus told him plainly what he would be doing. Paul would open the eyes of the Jew and the Gentile:

> So I said, "Who are You, Lord?" And He said, "I am Jesus, whom you are persecuting. But rise and stand on your feet; for I have appeared to you for this purpose, to make you a minister and a witness both of the things which you have seen and of the things which I will yet reveal to you. I will deliver you from the Jewish people, as well as from the Gentiles, to whom I now send you, to open their eyes, in order to turn them from darkness to light, and from the

power of Satan to God, that they may receive forgiveness
of sins and an inheritance among those who are sanctified
by faith in Me." (Acts 26:15–18)

This supernatural eye-opening would accomplish two purposes: (1)
turn Jews and Gentiles from darkness to light, and (2) turn them from the
power of Satan to the power of God. When Paul accomplished this purpose
there would be two results: (1) Jews and Gentiles would receive forgiveness
of sins, and (2) they would receive an inheritance among those sanctified
(set apart to God).

However, notice that Paul himself would not be the cause of this eye-
opening. The last four words of Christ's prophecy to Paul leave no doubt
who and what would open the eyes of these men and women: *Christ is the
who and faith in Him is the what!*

I sometimes wonder if evangelicalism's preoccupation with the hereafter
and its neglect of the here and now caused us to falsely conclude that an
emphasis on faith in Christ leads to an emphasis on "going to heaven when
we die." My young pastor friend admitted that he felt a little awkward challenging his people to believe in Jesus, because he didn't want them to think
that all he cared about was their eternal destiny.

It's not an either/or situation, but a both/and. The same Jesus who
stayed up all night caring for the sick and called His followers to defend the
poor and powerless told Paul that *faith in Him* was what the world needed
most. We may be ashamed of the gospel, but Paul wasn't.

The salvation Paul refers to is the full deliverance from the consequences of sin that faith in Christ brings—the transforming power to make
a difference in this world and the world to come. It's important to remind
ourselves that we can't stop there, that it's not only important what faith in
Christ is doing *to* us and *for* us, but also what it should be doing *through*
us and *for* the world. Faith in Christ is also the only way to enter into that
great adventure of partnership with God.

In the Jesus Movement, we never doubted that faith in Jesus was the only eye-opener for blind souls. Our message was simple, "Believe on the Lord Jesus Christ, and you will be saved" (Acts 16:31). For most of us, that was *all* we knew, but it was more than enough to connect our friends to God's grace. It was the message we believed and the message we took to the streets. It was the message that changed our lives: *Christ died for your sins and arose. Believe in Him and He will give you eternal life.*

However, it was the way we shared that message that set us apart from mainstream Christianity. The Spirit's deep work in our hearts moderated the confrontational spirit of our generation when it came to telling someone they needed faith in Christ. Though we believed in hell and that faith in Christ was the one way to avoid it, we rejected turn-or-burn evangelistic models. We wanted to have a conversation about Jesus. The gospel was a story—His story, our story, how we met Him, and the difference He made in our lives.

Church people told us that we needed to talk a lot more about sin and a lot less about grace. We didn't listen, of course, because we knew that the call of grace is far more powerful than the condemnation of sin. Our reasoning was simple: "All I ever heard from Christians was how bad and sinful I was. It didn't attract me to Christ. I came to Christ because I wanted grace; I wanted to live for something. And that's what I'm going to tell others." Sure, we told them they had a sin problem, but we never dwelled on that. Jesus called us to be witnesses to Him and His grace. Grace is at the core of His plan and those who tell of His grace are the ones who experience His power.

If I could do it over again, I'd talk less about theology and church and proofs for God and the Bible, and I'd have a lot more conversations about faith in Christ. I'd listen to people's stories, and then I'd tell mine. I'd make sure that they knew that faith in Him was the only explanation for my story. And then, without apology, I'd invite them to begin a new chapter in their story; a chapter titled, "Everything changed the day I met Jesus." We had no uncertainty about the power of simple faith in Jesus.

You Make Disciples

The second phrase that guided our revolution was Jesus' foremost command to His followers: *Go make disciples!* That night years ago when I met Jesus on the streets of Bakersfield, the same guys who introduced me to Jesus offered to teach me how to walk with Him. Before we said good night, Keith made sure that Bobby would take me through a little book published by Campus Crusade for Christ, *Ten Basic Steps toward Christian Maturity,* and assigned me to work with Bobby at the Bakersfield High School Young Life Club.

The next day, Phil stopped by with a little book by C. S. Lewis called *The Screwtape Letters,* and told me that if I had any questions to call him. Keith told a few of the more mature Young Life leaders about me and they all offered to "get together with me" to talk more about "Jesus and the Bible."

Before I even knew what the word meant, friends began "discipling" me. It was seamless—the same people who told me about my need for faith in Christ told me how to read the Bible, how to pray, how to tell others about Jesus, and gave me a book about the devil and demons that helped me stop seeing that old girlfriend I used to do bad things with in the back of my GTO!

I just thought they were my new friends trying to help me.

Now I know that their help had something to do with their love for me, but it had a lot to do with their love for and obedience to Jesus. They did what Jesus told every Christian to do: *Make disciples of all nations.*

> And Jesus came and spoke to them, saying, "All authority
> has been given to Me in heaven and on earth. Go therefore
> and make disciples of all the nations, baptizing them in the

name of the Father and of the Son and of the Holy Spirit,
teaching them to observe all things that I have commanded
you; and lo, I am with you always, even to the end of the
age." Amen. (Matt. 28:18–20)

We were the ultimate "missional Christians" forty years before it became
a buzz phrase bandied about on Christian Web sites and pasted into every
wanna-be-cool church's values list. We knew that the Great Commission
was our assignment from God, and the job description for every Christian.
They are the Lord Jesus' final words to His doubting disciples assuring them
of His authority from the Father (28:16–17; see also Acts 1:8).

Jesus always chose His words carefully. Jesus wasn't saying, "Bye, hope
it works out for you all while I'm gone." Jesus meant, "Okay, let Me tell you
exactly what I want you to do until I come back!"

Matthew makes sure that we know that the Great Commission is
about making disciples by using only one stand-alone command: "Make
disciples of all the nations." The Greek verb *matheiteusate* is the only
imperative in the Great Commission, meaning: "This is what I want you
to keep on doing, this is what you are about—make disciples of all the
nations, from every people group."

The other verbs, *go, baptizing,* and *teaching,* are not imperatives; they
simply tell us *how* we should make disciples. So the Great Commission
would read something like this to the original Greek-speaking audience:
*Having gone, or as you go, through real life, make disciples of every people group
by baptizing new believers you have shared the grace of God with and then by
teaching believers to fully grasp and fulfill all that I commanded* (all Scripture).

Making disciples requires more than working through a workbook
with someone for six weeks. This is a consuming assignment and the one
closest to the Lord's heart. He's telling us to pour our lives into making
disciples to Him. The word Jesus used in this well-known command, "disciple" *(matheiteis)* can refer to any pupil, student, or adherent to an idea

or teacher, but in the ancient world it usually referred to people who were *devoted* followers of a great teacher or philosopher. This is what we're called to do—to be used by God's Spirit to grow devoted followers (disciples) of the Lord Jesus. Before we get too overwhelmed by the burden of our responsibility, notice that the Lord Jesus closes by assuring disciple-makers that He will be with us to the end (Matt. 28:20b).

Maybe, like most Christians and the majority of ministry leaders, you've neglected Jesus' last instructions to His followers telling us exactly how to be His witnesses: "Pour your life into others so that they become My devoted followers, My disciples." If so, you're probably wondering about the answer to this question: *What would the life of a disciple-maker look like?*

Nowhere does the New Testament offer a comprehensive and sequenced list of what a disciple-maker should do. There's no "First do this, and then do this" from the apostles. The Lord only says, "Be witnesses to Me," and "Make disciples by baptizing and teaching." The rest of the New Testament fills in the blanks with truths we should learn and share in relationship. I would say that making disciples includes any act you do to encourage someone else to walk with Jesus. But I would also add that discipleship has to happen in the context of building redemptive relationships with those same people.

As you read Jesus' simple command to be His witnesses by making disciples, you might remember days when this was what your life was about. Days when one passion burned in your heart: to see God's Spirit work in your life to draw someone you cared for closer to your Savior. Memories like yours transformed my personal service to Christ many years ago. I decided to return to what worked so effectively in my Jesus Movement years. I was going to make disciples. Period! And everything else would be secondary to that, because the Master's plan has not changed and I wanted His power. His is a straightforward plan but a great plan—a startlingly simple insight, a quick study, and a great strategy ... a Great Commission.

So, how long has it been since you poured your life out as a devoted disciple-maker? How long has it been since you filled your living room with people wanting to know more about how to walk with Jesus through life? How long has it been since you told a young believer that you'd be willing to meet with him or her to talk about what faith in Jesus can mean to the rest of his or her life?

If your answer to that question discourages you, that's good. Your exasperated response to all of this may be the same one I hear from worn-out, dispirited church leaders and Christians all the time: *This sounds great in theory, but it doesn't work in the real world. I'm buried with administrative duties, meetings, and dealing with people's problems and emergencies. I have too many responsibilities at church and with my family. How could someone like me possibly find time to make a disciple?*

Let me challenge you with the same contrast I offer them. You're going to see that our objection that we "don't have time to make disciples" in the busyness of a local church or a modern Christian life has to do with our failure to distinguish between Jesus' Great Commission *for* His church and His great promise *to* His church.

I Will Build

The third principle undergirding our revival had more to do with trusting Him to do what He said He would do while we focused on making disciples: *I will build My church.*

Turn in your Bible to another passage in the book of Matthew that preceded the Great Commission—Matthew 16:13–20.

Let me remind you of the context of Christ's words. Jesus left the city of Bethsaida and traveled northward toward Mount Hermon until He came to the region of Ceasarea Philippi, the place He often gathered His disciples for a time away. When they arrived, He questioned the Twelve: "Who do people say the Son of Man is?" When Simon Peter answered correctly, Christ indicated for the first time His intentions to build a church. On the basis of Peter's revelation from God and confession of Christ (Matt. 16:15–17), Jesus told them this: "On this rock [*this rock of revealed truth from Peter's lips*] I will build My church, and the gates of Hades shall not prevail against it" (Matt. 16:18).

Warning His followers that the powers of evil will try to stop Him, the Lord Jesus assures His church that He would give her the *authority* to open doors of deliverance for the peoples of the world. Sounds like the power He would later promise to those who would be His witnesses, doesn't it?

Peter would be the first as he led the church beyond the borders of Jerusalem and Judea, but it didn't stop there. Jesus gave this same privilege to all the disciples in John 20:22–23, and this same authority and responsibility to all believers in Matthew 28:18–20.

It's critical for you and me to distinguish the difference between Jesus' words in Matthew 16 and His words in Matthew 28, or we will never get back on track.

Read the two sentences from Jesus again.

I will build My church (Matt. 16:18).

[You] make disciples of all the nations (Matt. 28:19).

Now, looking at the chart below, place a check under which of the two is:

	Matthew 16:18	Matthew 28:19
A promise *to* the church		
A responsibility *of* the church		
Jesus' job		
Church's job		
His declaration *about* the church		
His directive *to* the church		
God's guarantee		
God's guidance		

If I could do it over again, I would shout, "Hey, we're confusing His command with His promise!" No wonder we're not experiencing His power to make witnesses to Him. We're trying to take responsibility for what Christ has guaranteed (building the church) while ignoring His command (make disciples). And the result is that we're making the single most deadly mistake any organization or member of a team can make: *We're pursuing the wrong purpose!*

If you're honest about your own life and your own church, you know that this is true. If you and I ever want to be a part of another revival, we have to forsake our plans and embrace His. We must start concentrating on doing our part—obeying Jesus' simple command to make disciples, be witnesses to Him, and start trusting Him to do His part—building His church in His way and in His time in spite of the power of evil in this world, to powerfully expand His church to the ends of the earth.

The most rewarding evening of my week is Sunday evening when I meet with twelve guys whose hearts burn for the Lord Jesus. We call it the emerging leaders' discipleship group, and it gives me that critical opportunity to build into the lives of the future leaders of Church of the Open Door. We've been reading a classic on discipleship, *The Master Plan of Evangelism* by Robert Coleman,[9] which encourages all Christians to follow our Master's simple plan to pour our lives into others in the name of Jesus. They are fired up.

"This is what the church needs, Ed. We have to get the word out," a man who leads one of our most dynamic small groups said.

"Where has this been all my life?" asked a recent Christian college graduate who teaches Bible in a Christian high school.

A somewhat older man protested, "I wish this would have been around when I was younger."

You should have seen the look of incredulous dismay on their faces when I asked them to find the copyright date of Coleman's wonderful piece on the Master's plan: 1963! They simply couldn't accept the idea that this book has been around for almost fifty years and is required reading in most Bible schools and seminaries, yet nothing has changed.

I didn't have the heart to tell them that Dietrich Bonhoeffer had warned the church prior to World War II that "Christianity without discipleship is always Christianity without Christ."

How long will it take us to admit or rediscover that our influence in the world will not be determined by the size of our churches but by the number of disciples we send into our neighborhoods, workplaces, schools, and world? How long will it take us to stop measuring our significance by the number of influential people in our church and start evaluating our impact by the number of people around the world we influence for Christ?

If you're wondering why you've never heard this before or where to start in the process of disciple-making, it may not be your fault. It may be the result of the leaders in your church or your organization wrongly defining their own roles. It may be due to the fact that in their desperate pursuit of growth, they overlooked another simple truth that must be in place before revival can occur:

Leaders should know their job description.

Equip the Saints

The fourth truth capturing our attention came from the apostle Paul:

Equip the saints.

Have you ever sat in church wondering where you fit in? Most Christians have felt this way, including the majority of those sitting around you. There's something terribly wrong with this picture of hundreds, perhaps thousands, of God-destined believers sitting passively in a crowd once a week. They come and sit with no idea of what they can do for Christ while looking at a few terribly overworked, highly sought-after leaders standing on a stage trying to accomplish an impossibly long list of things for Christ.

Before you conclude that God must not be very smart to do it this way—expecting a few star players to come up with a game plan, run all the plays, cook all the hot dogs, serve all the drinks, clean up the stadium after the game, and maintain all the facilities until the next game—turn with me to another foundational passage, Ephesians 4:7–16.

Paul identifies Jesus as the exalted Christ of Psalm 68 who sets His people free and gives gifts to His people (Eph. 4:7–11). This dramatic fulfillment of prophecy is the basis for God's simple plan to supply leaders for the church. The apostles, prophets, evangelists, pastors, and teachers whom Christ appointed (Eph. 4:11) to lead the church are charged with the distinct purpose of *equipping the saints* (Eph. 4:12–16).

How could God be more clear? Read it yourself and notice the underlined "fors" in verse 12:

> And He Himself gave some to be apostles, some prophets, some evangelists, and some pastors and teachers, for the equipping of the saints for the work of ministry, for the edifying [building up] of the body of Christ. (Eph. 4:11–12)

Christ's simple plan is to build His church by giving especially gifted leaders to His people (saints) to equip *them* to do the work of the ministry (make disciples of all nations)!

And look at the powerful results—what happens when we follow His simple plan. The church becomes doctrinally mature and functionally stable (Eph. 4:13–16)—a discerning, displaying, and dynamic presentation of Christ to the world.

We've allowed this sick, codependent dance between ego-driven leaders and passively irresponsible followers to define our approach to doing Christ's work. We've built a culture of superstars onstage ranting at the bench-sitters in the crowd. It's no wonder everyday believers aren't making disciples! Nobody's teaching them to do ministry; nobody's equipping them to serve Christ.

Those of us who have lived through revival know this is true. Our Jesus Movement leaders knew their job description. It wasn't a coincidence that men and women like Ted and Jo Stone and Keith Osborn were the ones who guided us toward revival. God chose them because He knew they would equip us and release us to *our* ministry rather than capture us and use us for *theirs*.

When you and I stand up to the rock-star mentality of the church today and demand that our leaders serve Christ by simply equipping us, His people, for disciple-making, we will begin to turn the corner toward revival.

That's what this chapter is all about—*the seven simple truths from God's Word that will turn His people toward revival*—a simple plan that invites God's power. There's only one source for those revolutionary truths: the Word of God.

Preach the Word

Paul's exhortation to Timothy to "preach the Word" was the fifth simple commitment characterizing our movement.

When the Church of the Open Door began offering both a traditional service for those whose worship language was hymns or praise songs with piano and organ, and a contemporary service for those who preferred more modern expressions of worship with guitars and drums, I made a big mistake. I assumed that the younger generations weren't interested in some of the deeper truths I had discovered in my studies; I dropped a lot of the "technical" and explanatory stuff when I taught the contemporary audience. I kind of summarized the in-depth teaching I offered to the more traditional crowd.

Tom Townsend, our hip worship leader, challenged me with these words, "You're underestimating my generation. We want the Bible as much as anyone else. We love it when you offer insights from the Greek and Hebrew text and explain some of these difficult passages. We want you to preach the Word."

I should have known better. The Jesus Movement was the hippest revival in church history and we couldn't get enough of God's Word. We listened to radio preachers like J. Vernon McGee, devoured books by great Bible teachers like Ray Stedman and Hal Lindsey, flocked to seminars and conferences featuring dynamic preachers like Howard Hendricks, Chuck Smith, and Josh McDowell. The truth of God's Word guided our revival.

Many books and articles these days talk about the futility of preaching the Word, or the futility of the practice of preaching itself. They claim to have statistical and experiential insights into the postmodern mind. But no one who is actually hanging around with postmodern Christians would say that God's people have outlived their need for His Word.

Nothing convinced me of this more than the responses from readers of the original manuscript of this book. People my age warned me against having too much content and too many biblical references. "The postmodern mind," they told me, "doesn't learn that way."

But actual postmodern readers said no. Surprisingly, they considered the heavy scriptural emphasis one of the strong points of the manuscript. Bethany, a twentysomething recent graduate of a prestigious Christian undergrad program, wrote, "The strength of the book is that it teaches from the Bible and restates the things that God and Jesus already told us but that we want to contextualize into our own lives. I loved reading passage after passage that began with the Bible and led to Ed's conclusions about how we live. In a lot of cases, I found myself being awed that I had never read the verses with their true meaning."

It seems the Bible and its propositional truths aren't as dated as the "experts" told us. If I was from the postmodern generation, I'd be a little ticked off that people so easily wrote me off as a self-absorbed, ADD air-head who couldn't read sentences anymore and could only learn about Jesus through cleverly disguised entertainment.

As a Bible student, I want to ask, "Whatever happened to the Holy Spirit? Don't you think He can reach their hearts with Scripture?"

I attended maybe the most content-oriented seminary in the history of the church, Dallas Theological Seminary. Most of the faculty and gradu-ates I know would fully admit that we were a part of an unbalanced focus on the accurate interpretation of the Word that often ignored the need to experience the reality of Christ. Many of us praise God for the emerging church's hunger for a community that lives out the propositional truths of Scripture. We love that the center of the Spirit's movement among the younger generation is in their need to sense God's presence and to see God's work.

But there's an unhealthy edge to the emerging church movement that has overreacted to the exacting teaching of yesterday and the influence of postmodernism. Dr. Dan Wallace, one of the most influential New Testament scholars of our day and a fellow Jesus Movement radical, said in his courageous address at a Dallas Seminary chapel over ten years ago:

> The Scriptures are increasingly becoming marginalized in our thinking. It's as if we have decided that exegesis must be a bad thing because we know too many good exegetes who are spiritual casualties. But the antidote is not to take back our minds and give God only our hearts! We know God through his Word. If we marginalize the Word, we marginalize God.[10]

That thought, *If we marginalize the Word, we marginalize God,* isn't original to Dan Wallace. He's simply paraphrasing someone Dan would enthusiastically say understands the New Testament far better—Paul!

Paul's final letter to his friend and confidant Timothy should impress this truth on every generation of Christians, especially its leaders. Two-thirds of his last known communication to his devoted partner in ministry has to do with the teaching of the Word of God. His solemn charge to Timothy at the end sums up his passionate plea to leaders in the church of Jesus Christ:

> I charge you therefore before God and the Lord Jesus Christ, who will judge the living and the dead at His appearing and His kingdom: Preach the word! Be ready in season and out of season. Convince, rebuke, exhort, with all longsuffering and teaching. For the time will come when they will not endure sound doctrine, but according to their own desires, because they have itching ears, they will heap up for themselves teachers; and they will turn their ears away from the truth, and be turned aside to fables. (2 Tim. 4:1–4)

My warning to every Christian leader reading this book is simple: Don't decide for God that an entire generation will not endure sound doctrine. And don't decide for an entire generation of new and excited believers that they are "just not capable of hearing the Word of God."

How arrogant and presumptuous can we be? How can we try to do the Spirit's job of illuminating God's revelation?

We should do everything possible to preach the Word with creativity and relevance to reach our audiences. There is no excuse for boring people with the Word of God. But it is His Word that we must preach: God's words contained in the sixty-six books of the Bible ... all of them.

I believe that the emerging generation of Christians desires the same reality we sought. And it's not about spiky-haired pastors with goatees regurgitating the latest trendy, YouTube-downloaded message any more today than it was about huarache-sandaled student-leaders parroting the words of high-powered conference speakers like Josh McDowell and Hal Lindsey in my day. And it's not about candles and icons now any more than it was about rock music and long hair then.

The gospel and making disciples is about God and knowing Him. It's about mentors who know the truth of God's Word and preach it into lives open to His power. It's about coming alongside each other for a lifetime. It's about preaching the Word, even when you can't see immediate fruit or harvest potential, in season and out of season. It's about God's Spirit using God's Word to convince, rebuke, and exhort. It's about under-shepherds teaching with the long-suffering style and commitment—compassionate, other-centered instruction—of the Chief Shepherd.

Preaching the Word has always been an integral part of His simple plan and a requirement for experiencing His power. Preaching the Word is an indispensable part of any revival. And if we want to be part of one, it must be an indispensable part of our lives.

As God's people begin to understand His Word, something wonderful begins to grow in their hearts—an expectation of His comfort and power.

You Shall Receive Power

The sixth distinctive was our firm grasp of the Lord's promise to give us power through His Spirit.

Luke portrays the connection between knowing God's Word and expecting God's power in Acts 1:12–26, when the leaders of the church gathered in an upper room in Jerusalem. For ten days they did exactly what Christ told them to do—they begged the Father (Acts 1:12–14) to give them the Holy Spirit (Luke 11:13), expecting Him to do exactly what He promised—asking His Holy Spirit to empower them to be His witnesses (Acts 1:8).

They interrupted their prayer to make the only provision they knew to make for Jesus' coming kingdom. Peter led them to replace Judas with Matthias so there would be twelve disciples to sit on twelve thrones in the messianic kingdom judging the twelve tribes, just as Jesus had said (Acts 1:15–26; Matt. 19:28; Luke 22:30). Peter felt it necessary to replace Judas and turned to the Scriptures for guidance. He validated his leadership with the messianic psalms he now understood applied to Jesus Christ (Ps. 69:25; 109:8).

I'll leave it to other theologians to debate whether this was the right decision, but the point is that they turned to the words of Christ and the words of the Old Testament for guidance. And when they thought they found it, they obeyed.

Think of how difficult it must have been for them to follow Jesus' orders. In Acts 1:4, He commanded them not to leave Jerusalem, and in verse 8, He told them to go into all the world. They didn't ask how this could be; they just did what He told them to do and expected Him to keep His promise to give them power.

They didn't complain or question, "This doesn't make sense, 'stay here and go there.' This isn't logical. The Lord needs to be absolutely clear and consistent from my perspective if He wants to start this church right!"

This is a picture of the type of people God uses to start revivals: expectantly obedient Christians willing to follow God's Word and anticipate His power. What would have happened if they had responded the way you and I sometimes do when it seems the Lord is giving us contradictory commands?

Before we Jesus Movement converts learned enough about the Holy Spirit to fight over what the New Testament says about Him, we gathered in rooms, begging God for His power and promising Him we would do what He says. We didn't know a lot, but the little we did know, we tried to do. We even made some debatable decisions, like the one Peter made when he led the other apostles to appoint Matthias.

We committed ourselves to obedience and expected God to work. We weren't afraid of the Holy Spirit; we just wanted to be Christ's witnesses.

We weren't afraid to boldly obey what we thought the Bible taught; we just wanted to make sure we pleased Christ … even when we didn't fully understand.

What is the Lord telling you to do right now that you do not fully understand? When was the last time you asked Him outright to send His Spirit's power into your life so that you could be His witness?

It's a simple promise: "You shall receive power." But I believe that the only ones who can claim the promise are those who demonstrate their willingness to obey His guidance and those who ask.

Speaking of asking …

Ask in My Name

The seventh component of the Master's simple plan that we embraced in our revival is Jesus' promise to answer any prayer offered "in His name." When most Christians think of prayers "in Jesus' name" they probably don't think of revival, but I believe that's exactly what Jesus had in mind when He gathered His disciples in the upper room:

> Most assuredly, I say to you, he who believes in Me, the works that I do he will do also; and greater works than these he will do, because I go to My Father. And whatever you ask in My name, that I will do, that the Father may be glorified in the Son. If you ask anything in My name, I will do it. (John 14:12–14)

Just a few simple observations tell us that praying in Jesus' name can't be some magical formula that forces Jesus to say yes. Notice that the "whatever" of verse 13 refers to the greater works Jesus tells His followers they will do because He goes to the Father. All you have to do is reread this chapter to realize that the greater works Jesus is talking about are the coming works of

His church—that world-changing body He will build as He empowers His people and gives them leaders who will equip them to make disciples of all nations.

When we ask the Father to let us do these greater works that glorify Him in His Son, we are asking Him to do what Jesus told us He would. Therefore, we are asking it in His name.

One of my duties as the lowly first lieutenant adjutant to our battalion commander, a lieutenant colonel, was to authorize requests "in his name." He didn't have time to sign all the paperwork addressed to him, so he gave me authority to sign for him. My signature read, *For the Commander, Ed Underwood, First Lieutenant.* Before I got too carried away with that authority, my lieutenant colonel made me memorize his large book of policies and procedures. Then he said with a sternness I will never forget, "Ed, be sure you know that it's something I would sign off on before you use my name."

This is what Jesus says to His followers: "Make sure you know it's something I would sign off on before you use My name before My Father!"

If you've read my first book, *When God Breaks Your Heart,* you know that I encourage Christians to pray bold and dangerous prayers for themselves. I offer evidence from Luke's record of Jesus' teaching on prayer, which shows that every believer should feel free to ask God for what they want—the specific and daring requests a cherished child would make of his or her Father.

But I don't believe this is what Jesus is talking about in the upper room with His disciples. Rather than encouraging believers to ask His Father to meet their personal needs, He's challenging the disciples to ask His Father to do the "greater works" (NKJV) or "greater things" (NIV) that His death, resurrection, and ascension make possible: the work of the church that glorifies the Father in the Son, making disciples of all nations. When we ask for that, and when we ask "in His name," we're asking for something He would endorse, for our commander.

"In Jesus' name" is so much more than a silly add-on that somehow makes our prayer acceptable to God and the Christian community. There's nothing magical about the phrase. The Father would never say yes to a prayer just because someone asked in Jesus' name. But He always says yes to a petition His Son would endorse. And His Son told us exactly which prayers He always endorses—requests to do the greater works of the church.

Can we really know in advance if God is going to answer our prayers to do greater works in Jesus' name? Jesus, our Advocate who has His Father's ear, said, "If you ask anything in My name, I will do it" (John 14:14). We *can* know for sure that God will let us be a part of Jesus' greater works of the church age. But we must ask!

It is one of the surest signs that revival is coming when Christians are spending more time on their knees begging for revival than they are in staff meetings, planning sessions, and strategy conferences trying to figure out how to make revival happen.

If the fear of one more disappointment causes you to hesitate before you bow down at God's throne of grace, you're not alone. I'm standing there with you, telling God that I just don't have the energy to take another run at revival if it's not going to happen. There's no use denying what I'm really thinking: The possibility of seeing these seven simple truths lived out in the church today on the scale it would require to see revival in my lifetime seems remote.

Fortunately, the Lord isn't asking us to make this happen on a large scale. He's just asking us to cling to these seven truths as we follow Him, one step at a time.

Climbing Revival Mountain

It was after midnight when we finally pulled to a stop at the end of the road. We had watched the fire rip through the high country for over an hour as we drove next to the Kings River.

Our crew truck passed others looking up as the flames devoured acres of ponderosa pine and manzanita brush several thousand feet up the steep canyon wall. Some onlookers seemed afraid, but all were impressed with the power of the blaze and the glow that lit up the night sky.

One huge difference set our thoughts of the fire apart from the onlookers. They were wondering if this fire would interrupt their vacation plans camping in the Sequoia National Forest. We were calculating how difficult it was going to be to walk to the fire's edge.

They were tourists, but we were the Fulton Hotshots—one of a handful of elite firefighting crews from Southern California. The hotter the fire, the more dangerous the terrain, the more sure we were that we would join the other hotshot crews of the West on the fire line.

Bill, our grizzled superintendent, could see and feel our discouragement and fear in the way we unloaded the truck. There wasn't the usual hustle and small talk. It was a long way up that mountain, and we were beat. That morning they told us we would get our first day off in three weeks. But then this fire started and they changed their minds. Instead, we loaded up and drove for four hours.

To make matters worse, we knew that the helicopters wouldn't be flying for another five or six hours. We would have to haul ourselves up the face of Kings Canyon with our food, saws, fire shelters, tools, and water.

And this was a ferocious timber fire burning through the crowns of hundred-foot trees. *A fireman's worst nightmare.*

"Gentlemen," Bill said, looking at us, "you know how we're going to get up that mountain?"

Nobody said a word.

(Danger does that to you. You just shut up and listen.)

"Here's what we're going to do." Bill slung his Swedish brush hook over his shoulder, picked up his shovel, and said, "We're going to put one foot in front of the other. Follow me." And he started up the trail.

And that's what we did. We put one foot in front of the other, climbed that mountain, and put that fire out.

Bill didn't ask us to take responsibility for the whole thing—the mountain, the fire, the logistics, or the strategy. That was his problem. He simply asked us to take a few more steps and follow him.

I don't know what intimidates you when you look up at this mountain called revival Jesus is asking us to climb. What I do know is that our hesitation shows that we've forgotten that the Lord Jesus isn't asking *us* to find the way up the mountain.

He's just asking us to embrace these seven simple truths, take a few more steps, and follow Him. Instead of putting out the fire, He's calling us to set it ablaze … but it all starts with the fire in our own hearts.

What If?

If you sense God leading you to make the radical changes that will keep your revival heart on track, I urge you to think in terms of what *you* must do rather than what *others* should do. The question here is not, "What if the church embraced these seven simple revival truths?" but "What if I let them guide me toward revival?"

- What if you dedicated one hour of your life to preparing your story of what faith in Jesus means to you?
- What if you practiced that three-part story—my life before Jesus, when I believed in Jesus, and my life after Jesus—so that you could share it in about five minutes?
- What if you asked God to let you tell this story to just one person this week? And then another, and another, and another.

- What if, after a few months of this, you noticed that there were three or four people in your life that had just met Jesus, and they began asking you to tell them more about Him?

You make disciples—the church must take responsibility for its role in revival to make disciples of all nations.

- What if you told these people you would love to meet with them for breakfast or dinner once a week, or if two or three of them agreed to come over to your house or meet in a conference or break room at work or school weekly?
- What if you asked them to tell their own story about Jesus so that they could get to know one another better?
- What if you asked them how you could pray for them, and if they knew anyone who needed Jesus?
- What if they said yes, and you showed them how to tell their friends about Jesus?
- What if their friends believed in Jesus and suddenly you were hosting a "minichurch" in your home or at your workplace or school?

I will build—the church must trust Him to do His part, build the church, as we do our part and make disciples.

- What if you opened the book of Ephesians or the gospel of John and read a chapter a week with these same people?
- What if the brokenness in their lives pulled your heart to devote your life to them because you loved them?
- What if they became some of your closest friends because you opened your life up to them and talked about the difference Jesus made in all of you?

- What if the changes in their lives caused their husbands and wives, children and parents, coworkers and friends to ask what happened?
- What if you began to sense it was time for them to start their own groups but you didn't know how to do that?
- What if they started asking you questions about the Bible and Jesus that you couldn't answer?

Equip the saints—the leaders of the church must follow their job description to equip the saints to make disciples of all nations.

- What if you went to your church or found a church, and asked the leaders if they could help you with this, and they said they were too busy, so you just left that church and asked God to show you one where the shepherds knew their job description?
- What if you found a church that said they would equip you, but when your friends showed up they shamed you so much that you decided to keep looking for a church that God would use to release your spiritual gifts into the lives of these people?
- What if you finally found a church where the pastors and leaders were more about you and what you were doing for Christ than they were about themselves and what they were doing for Christ? What if these same shepherds cared more for the people you brought with you than they did about their religious reputation?
- What if this community of faith was such a safe place that the friends you introduced to Jesus grew to the point that they didn't need you anymore and walked with Christ toward their own destiny in Him?

Preach the Word—the church must keep teaching the content of the Word of God in the context of redemptive relationships.

- What if the leaders of this church taught you the Scriptures in such a way that you and your friends began to get to know Christ as a good friend?
- What if, as you grew in your interaction with God's Word, you opened up your life to Christ in ways that released His power in wondrous and marvelous ways?
- What if your understanding of the Bible gave you a confidence in life you never imagined was possible?
- What if God's Spirit used Christ's Word to transform your friendships, your marriage, and your family?
- What if you began to believe that what you read about the early church could actually happen again … to you?
- What if this belief became a passion for revival that made you know that you would never be satisfied with anything less?

You shall receive power—the church must live expectantly, trusting God's Spirit to empower leaders and saints to make disciples of all nations.

- What if the demands of pouring your life into others for Christ moved you to beg for the supernatural power of the Holy Spirit?
- What if the heartbreaks and disappointments of making disciples moved you to beg the Comforter to strengthen and encourage you?
- What if your growing awareness of God's willingness to give you power from above caused you to live on the reckless edge of radical trust?

- What if the power of God in your life as you walked that reckless edge caused your friends and family to worry and talk about you as you dedicated more and more of your time, money, energy, and talent to the cause of Christ?
- What if what God did through your life was so satisfying, you didn't care what they thought?

Ask in My name—the church must beg God for the greater works of the church age—making disciples of all nations—asking in faith as she claims Jesus' promise to do it.

- What if the joy of being used by the Lord Jesus to change lives so captured your heart that it began to eclipse all former dreams and purposes for living?
- What if the anticipation of hearing the Lord Jesus' "well done" when you stand before Him began to overwhelm all former incentives and desires?
- What if the Lord's promise to underwrite any petition to His Father to do greater works in His name began to replace your former prayers for personal happiness and fulfillment?
- What if the possibility that if you begged the Lord Jesus to let you see revival He might just grant it became the preoccupying obsession of your life?

What if you noticed other believers living with the same passion for revival, and when you gathered together in Jesus' name you discovered the most stimulating and rewarding friendships of your life?

What if you found out that what God did in your group He had also done for others, and these groups began to cluster in churches and communities where the revival fires burned?

What if you suddenly look up and realize that what you are seeing the

Lord do around you hadn't happened in America for forty years … not since the Jesus Movement?

What if at that moment in your life, you smile and think to yourself, *This is what Ed wrote about in his book. This is it. This is revival!*

Could It Be?

I'm sixty. I don't feel old, but I know I'm probably older than a lot of you reading these words.

My greatest fear in writing this book is that it would read like some old guy talking about himself. Old people should talk about life rather than talking about themselves. When we're talking about ourselves, we're clinging to this world. When we're talking about life, we're blessing this world.

But unless you're about my age, you missed the 1960s and the revival we lived. A lot of church people and church history scholars try to tell our story, but we're the only ones who can tell it from an insider's perspective.

We're the only ones who know what it feels like to lose the momentum, to get sidetracked. I believe God is asking us tell our story in a way that will call millions of His sidetracked people back to revival.

Could it be that God wants His people to come out of hiding? To show the world who they are and how His grace changes things?

Could it be that He doesn't really care about the stuff the church is so hung up on? All the stuff you don't care about anymore either?

Could it be that some of His favorite words are some of your favorites? Words such as radical, risk, and faith? That He dislikes words like sameness, safety, and control as much as you do?

Could it be that Christianity is really as simple as you thought it was when you first believed? That you really did become a new creation with a new agenda and new power the moment you believed?

Could it be that if enough people just did what Jesus said—make disciples—He would build His church, and the gates of hell would be powerless? That if you concentrated on the one thing He promised you couldn't mess up, He would clean up the mess we have made?

Could it be that God never meant for His people to be so predictable and powerless? That what discourages you most about the church today wasn't His idea in the first place?

Could it be that He has one more wonderful surprise for history before His Son returns? That His people are going to turn the world upside down for Christ one more time?

Could it be that all that is standing between you and that revival is getting back on track? To start living as if what His Son says about life is really true?

I think it could be so. I can see it. Can you?

I wrote this book to help you see it. The rest is up to the only One who can really get us back on track, the only One who can keep us on track, the only One who can lead us to true revival.

His name is Jesus, and I want to be a part of His Movement.

An Invitation

There's no secret to revival. God isn't hiding anything. All the information you need is there, in His Word. Neither is He withholding revival from any of His people; it's always there for the taking. We must be the ones to decide whether we're willing to pay the price.

I hope this book convinced you that you can be part of a coming revival.

As I've shared my passion to see revival again with Christians around the world, they've asked me how they could connect with like-minded believers from every generation who resonate with the message of this book. If that describes you and this book encouraged you to ask God to let you see revival in your lifetime, I would love to hear your story and help you in any way I can.

I invite you to visit me online at www.EdUnderwood.com or www.JesusMovementBlog.com to find others around the world who are begging God for revival as they tell Him they're willing to pay the price. As you navigate through our Web site and links, you'll meet a lot of my Jesus Movement friends and some modern-day revivalists. We've also provided some resources and events to encourage you in your journey to revival.

I look forward to hearing from you.

Notes

1. Bob Deffinbaugh, "Greed: The Affliction of the Affluent (Luke 12:13–21)," Bible.org, http://bible.org/seriespage/greed-affliction-affluent-luke-1213-21.
2. Bob Deffinbaugh, "A Disciple's Perspective on Possessions (Luke 12:22–34)," Bible.org, http://bible.org/seriespage/disciples-perspective-possessions-luke-1222-34.
3. Philip Yancey, *What's So Amazing About Grace?* (Grand Rapids, MI: Zondervan, 2002), 41.
4. C. S. Lewis, "Williams and the Arthuriad," *Taliessin through Logres, the Region of the Summer Stars, and Arthurian Torso* (1948): 340, quoted in Wayne Martindale and Jerry Root, eds., *The Quotable Lewis* (Wheaton, IL: Tyndale, 1989), 272.
5. Fritz Rienecker, *A Linguistic Key to the Greek New Testament*, edited by Cleon Rogers (Grand Rapids, MI: Zondervan, 1982), 588.

6. C. S. Lewis, *The Weight of Glory* (New York: HarperOne, 2001), 109.

7. William J. Gaither and Gloria Gaither, lyrics, "The King Is Coming," *The King Is Coming* © 1970 William J. Gaither Inc.

8. Ralph Carmichael, lyrics, "He's Everything to Me" © 1964 Bud John Songs Inc.

9. Robert Coleman, *The Master Plan of Evangelism* (Grand Rapids, MI: Baker Publishing Group, 1963).

10. Daniel Wallace, "Crisis of the Word or A Message to Pastors and Would-Be Pastors (2 Timothy 2:15)" (speech originally given at Dallas Seminary, Dallas, TX, March 11, 1997). Also printed at Bible.org, http://bible.org/article/crisis-word-or-message-pastors-and-would-be-pastors-2-timothy-215.

CHOOSE HOPE
in the Midst of
Faith-Shattering Circumstances

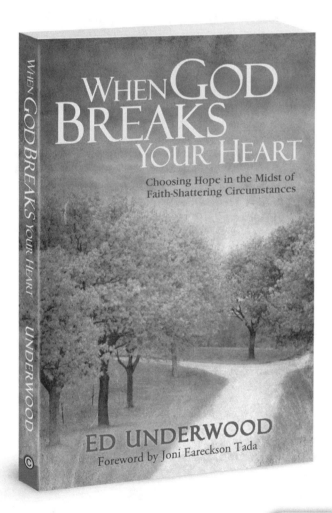